WEALTH, POVERTY AND ENDURING INEQUALITY
Let's Talk Wealtherty

Sarah Kerr

First published in Great Britain in 2024 by

Policy Press, an imprint of
Bristol University Press
University of Bristol
1–9 Old Park Hill
Bristol
BS2 8BB
UK
t: +44 (0)117 374 6645
e: bup-info@bristol.ac.uk

Details of international sales and distribution partners are available at policy.bristoluniversitypress.co.uk

© Bristol University Press 2024

British Library Cataloguing in Publication Data
A catalogue record for this book is available from the British Library

ISBN 978-1-4473-7055-0 hardcover
ISBN 978-1-4473-7056-7 paperback
ISBN 978-1-4473-7057-4 ePub
ISBN 978-1-4473-7058-1 ePdf

The right of Sarah Kerr to be identified as author of this work has been asserted by her in accordance with the Copyright, Designs and Patents Act 1988.

All rights reserved: no part of this publication may be reproduced, stored in a retrieval system, or transmitted in any form or by any means, electronic, mechanical, photocopying, recording, or otherwise without the prior permission of Bristol University Press.

Every reasonable effort has been made to obtain permission to reproduce copyrighted material. If, however, anyone knows of an oversight, please contact the publisher.

The statements and opinions contained within this publication are solely those of the author and not of the University of Bristol or Bristol University Press. The University of Bristol and Bristol University Press disclaim responsibility for any injury to persons or property resulting from any material published in this publication.

Bristol University Press and Policy Press work to counter discrimination on
grounds of gender, race, disability, age and sexuality.

Cover design: Nicky Borowiec
Front cover image: OlegDoroshin/AdobeStock

For Mum and Dad

Contents

List of figures, tables and boxes — vi
Note on the author — viii
Acknowledgements — ix
Preface — xi
How to read this book — xiii

PART I What have we become?
1 Why wealtherty and why now? — 3
2 The state of wealth and the state and wealth — 27

PART II How have we become what we are?
3 Knowing: how the state came to know richer and poorer people differently — 49
4 Governing: how the state came to govern richer and poorer people differently — 70
5 Being: how ways of thinking and governing enabled different forms of self for richer and poorer people — 95

PART III What sustains the problem?
6 Producing knowledge: think tanks, policy networks — 113
7 Shaping behaviours: space and the visual as tools of government — 134
8 Shaping selves: wealth and identity — 155

PART IV In conclusion
9 Ways out — 175

Notes — 191
Bibliography — 194
Index — 232

List of figures, tables and boxes

Figures
0.1	'The law locks up the man or woman who steals the goose from off the common'	xi
1.1	Governmental dispositions and sanctioned responses	12
1.2	Hasegawa Tōhaku (16th century Azuchi-Momoyama period) Shōrin-zu byōbu (pine forest)	21
1.3	A tree drawn to illustrate negative space	22
4.1	Universal Credit Claimant Commitment form (sample excerpt)	77
4.2	'Marylebone Workhouse Dining Hall'	79
4.3	Free School Meals holiday pack, January 2021	82
4.4	Section of a drawing for the machine that produces nothing	85
5.1	An image of page 2 from the HMRC 2017	109
7.1	The Jobcentre Plus sign	136
7.2	An image of a Jobcentre Plus screened private interview room	139
7.3	Jobcentre Plus office zones	141
7.4	Jobcentre Plus welcome poster	142
7.5	Salvatora Rea looks out at the communal play area and garden his children are not allowed to use	145
7.6	Dougie Wallace, *Harrodsburg* (2012)	147
7.7	Daniel Mayrit (2012) – still from *You Haven't Seen Their Faces*	148
7.8	Still from *Eleven Privatised Public Assets*	149
7.9	Richard J. Geisenberger (standing), Delaware's Chief Deputy Secretary of State	150
7.10	Still from Richard Billingham's *Ray's a Laugh* (2014) showing Richard's mother Liz	151
7.11	Reproduction of a graph from the World Inequality Report (2018) showing the slide of capital from public into private hands	152

Tables
3.1	Dispositions of ignorance and scrutiny across the domains of knowing, governing and being in two contexts (historical and contemporary)	51
4.1	Inhabitants of the Southwell Union Workhouses in April 1837	80
5.1	Ways of being under governmental dispositions of scrutiny and ignorance	101
5.2	Four ways of describing the relationships between people with low or no wealth and people with high levels of wealth	107
6.1	Career map of CSJ interlockers	122

6.2	Standard Industrial Classification (SIC) codes of companies in which directors of left-leaning and right-leaning think tanks held contemporaneous directorships between 2000 and 2005	127
6.3	Standard Industrial Classification (SIC) codes of companies in which directors of left-leaning and right-leaning think tanks held contemporaneous directorships between 2015 and 2020	128
6.4	Summary of agnotological mechanisms in three sectors	130
8.1	Epistemic dynamics	172
8.2	Relational inequalities	172

Boxes

6.1	Iain Duncan Smith select biography	118
6.2	Stephen Brien select biography	119
6.3	Philippa Stroud select biography	120

Note on the author

Sarah Kerr is a Research Fellow at LSE International Inequalities Institute. Her research interests are in the broad area of justice making.

Acknowledgements

Thank you to Nottinghamshire Archives and The National Archives digital team for support with sources during the COVID-19 pandemic and for helping to secure permissions for the archival material used in this book. I only got to use a very small amount of the material I reviewed – many other punishment books, letters and architectural drawings did not make the cut, but certainly fed into my thinking about punitivism that infuses a lot of the writing here. Thanks are also due to the Economic and Social Science Research Council (ESRC) for the doctoral funding that enabled the research on which much of this book is based. I very literally could not have done the research without the funding.

Thank you to the team at Nottingham's Bromley House Library, which was my home for much of the work on this book. They have the most amazing collection of local historical material, and their staff are helpful and knowledgeable. It is a treasure of a local resource. Thanks to Louisa Britain for permission to reproduce her free school meals image, and to artists Lewis Bush, Dougie Wallace, Paolo Woods and Gabriele Galimberti, Richard Billingham and Daniel Mayrit for letting me use their images. I also want to thank Consultants in Design for the use of their Jobcentre images in Chapter 7 and at the same time affirm that the views expressed in this book are my own. I paid for most permissions myself. Some of these artists let me use their images for free. So I want to say thank you, but also to acknowledge quite how much unpaid creative labour went into this book. To my PhD supervisor, Professor Stephen Ball, a heartfelt thank you for your patience, encouragement and calm. I lost three close members of my family in an 18-month period during my PhD, while also watching my lovely mum disappear into the fog of Alzheimer's dementia. Stephen's support felt like an act of kindness and solidarity and humanity, a recognition that sometimes just getting through the day is enough. To my LSE International Inequalities Institute (III) colleagues – especially Mike Savage, Liza Ryan and Michael Vaughan – thank you for the support and welcome. III is a unique, collegiate and dynamic environment and I am privileged to have the opportunity to work there.

The final acknowledgements I want to make are personal and I want to make them in recognition of the fact that for some writers, the journey is longer and more arduous than for others, and sometimes individuals along the way exert an influence that stays with you for life, but which you only fully appreciate at a distance. It takes a village … So a big thank you to Adrian Smith for being the best primary school teacher; to Phil Baker, who not only told me about university in a way that my parents couldn't, but also believed that I should go, and helped me to get there. To Professor Margaret Reynolds and Tom Davis and Deidre Burton who recognised the culture shock I experienced on my arrival at the University of Birmingham in the early 90s and helped me get through to the end, with a mixture of intellectual stimulation and empathy: Thank you. Finally, to family. I am from an Irish immigrant family. Being aware of the hardships and injustices they endured is the fire that drives me. But the kinship and culture they nurtured, the music and songs and laughter we share – like immigrant families and communities the world over – is also my guiding light. To my fantastic sons Peter and James and their dad, Ben, to my sister Katy and her partner Gary, whose support has been emotional and also practical (looking after Peter and James to allow me space and time to write), and to my extended family past and present, Winnie and Peter, Annie and Horace, Eileen and Tommy, Joe, Mari, Tess, Rob, and the cousins, Helen, Marie, Anna, Bridie and Jack. And finally, to my partner Joe, for helping me through it all in every conceivable way – from data support, to emotional support and financial support. I'm lucky to have the warmth and love of this family at my back. Sláinte.

Preface

Figure 0.1: 'The law locks up the man or woman who steals the goose from off the common, but leaves the greater villain loose, who steals the common from off the goose' (from a 17th-century folk poem)

Every day as I have walked into town to the library to write this book, I pass this sign. It hangs on the fence of a local community garden on the Forest, a public park to the north of the city. The Forest was created by the 1845 Nottingham Inclosure Act, which marked the abolition of common grazing rights to the land, but also gave it to the town forever, with limitations as to what could be done to it (a very detailed local history of the act is available in Bromley House Library in Nottingham, written by local historian June Perry). The image sums up nicely what I'm talking about in this book: the ways of thinking and acting that enable wealth inequality, and the ways in which this inequality manifests in very different ways of treating people in law, in the media and in public discourse. Today, in 2024, Nottingham is the poorest city in the UK, the council has declared itself effectively bankrupt, and there are tents hidden among the bushes on the Forest, where people who are homeless shelter. Meanwhile, just over a mile away, the gated enclave of 'The Park' houses the city's rich. This is a city, like others the country over, in which the social effects of incredible wealth hyper-concentration are played out in plain sight.

This book is about finding ways to talk about wealth, poverty and enduring inequality that ignite a spark about the villainy of stealing the common off the goose, and the inequities of the institutions and practices of state that enable it.

Sarah Kerr
January 2024

How to read this book

This book is written for academics *and* for people who are interested in wealth, poverty and inequality, but who aren't academics. It has a lot of academic references, which link to the Bibliography at the back. If you are an academic or another kind of researcher, you might wish to follow these up. But the book should also stand as it is, without the need to do so. It is normative (wants to change things) as much as sociological (interested in how and why things exist like they do) and there's little point wanting to change things, but then only talking to people who already know what you're talking about.

There are different pathways through the book. You could just read Part I (Chapters 1 and 2). Chapter 1 comprises a summary manifesto and an introduction to wealtherty and to the whole book, while Chapter 2 provides an introduction to wealth and the state. You could then jump straight to Chapter 9, which unpacks the manifesto and offers a summary of the book and a conclusion. This is the 'short read'.

You could just read Part II (Chapters 3, 4 and 5). This part is mostly historical. It seeks to answer the following question: 'How have we become what we are?' Or you could just read Part III (Chapters 6, 7 and 8). This part is mostly contemporary. It seeks to answer the following question: 'What sustains the problem?'

The chapters divide into natural pairs, too. Chapter 3 looks at the emergence of specific ways of knowing about the poor and the rich in the late 18th century, while Chapter 6 looks at producing knowledge about the poor and the rich in our now-time; Chapter 4 looks at techniques of government (including hunger, restrictions on mobility, confinement and management of time) in the workhouse regime of the early 19th century, while Chapter 7 looks at (spatial and visual) techniques of government in the 2000s. Chapter 5 looks at identity making for poorer and richer people in both time periods, while Chapter 8 explores how contemporary policy-making manages these processes of identity making (and relatedly power building) very differently for richer and poorer people.

If you are an academic, you might find this book annoying: I am an interdisciplinarian and I sometimes skate over, rather than dive deep into, sets of literature that you hold dear and about which you know lots more than I do. You might say things like 'how can she talk about economics and not mention X?' or 'that feels like a superficial engagement with Y'. You are right. This is one of the pitfalls of interdisciplinarity, and I look forward to you telling me where and how I'm getting it wrong.

PART I

What have we become?

A wealtherty manifesto

Wealtherty is presented in this book as a means of disrupting a poverty paradigm that has run its course and which, I suggest, in light of what is now known about the scale and effects of wealth inequality, is no longer fit for purpose. Foucault described words as fireworks which should ignite and then disappear (Wade 2019). My aim is to spark other conversations and invite engagement with and challenge to the concept of wealtherty rather than to police or defend it. It is undoubtedly imperfect. But in the light of the urgent social and environmental context in which we find ourselves, we need to shift the debate into a frame that can ignite social and political will, and build pressure for change. The wealtherty manifesto summarised here prefaces the rest of the book, in which I will explain in more detail what wealtherty is, how it operates and how it is made to endure. This will allow me to elaborate on and sketch out the foundations for this manifesto position and start to build a case to support it. The manifesto is described in full in Chapter 9.

1. Stop talking about poverty

The 'social' of social change – with its deepening poverty and destitution – is increasingly shaped and harmed by the ownership and owners of wealth. Talking about poverty keeps us 'looking down'. We need to look up and centre wealth in new narratives of social change.

2. Make extreme wealth into a social problem

Having 'too much' wealth is not morally justifiable when people are struggling to eat or to heat their homes. We are unlikely to be able to reduce or alleviate poverty unless we can problematise extreme wealth.

3. Describe the 'encompassing welfare universe': we are 'all in it together'!

The prevailing narrative about welfare hides the fact that over a life course, we *all* make asks of the collective wealth of the state. This includes the already wealthy, who benefit from fiscal welfare in the form of enabling legislation and forms of tax relief. To bring perception into line with this reality, we need to describe our encompassing welfare universe.

4. Describe the pathways to wealtherty

The book will make the case that we live in a state of wealtherty. We can only tackle wealtherty if we understand how it was made in the first place. This process necessarily involves writing new histories.

5. Change the focus of research funding: it needs to look up and back

Lack of new knowledge about poverty is not what is preventing political engagement with poverty reduction. The UK government has spent over £752 million on poverty-related research since 2006 and less than £28 million on economic and wealth inequality work in the same period. It might be easier to mobilise political will and ignite public passion with a more comprehensive understanding of wealth (what it is, who owns it, what it does and why this matters).

6. Hear from the harm causers and not just the harmed

The voices of the very wealthy are well heard in the making of economic and fiscal policy via tax advisors and lobbyists. They are less well heard in social policy-making contexts, even though wealth is increasingly recognised as cause of social harm. Let's make more room to hear from rich people as 'harm causers' in social policy-making contexts.

7. Measure what needs to be measured, not just what can be counted

Problematic wealth (surplus wealth and excessive wealth) matters because it causes social and environmental harm. Its impact at an individual and community level is less well understood, in part because it is harder to 'count'. What should we be counting in order to understand the social effects of extreme wealth?

8. Reframe, rename, do better social science: let's talk wealtherty

Wealtherty is a new frame for the state we are in that places the critical analysis of wealth at the heart of social policy debates. It creates new space in which to think. Let's stop talking about poverty and talk about wealtherty if we want to tackle inequality.

1

Why wealtherty and why now?

> What thoughtful rich people call the problem of poverty, thoughtful poor people call with equal justice the problem of riches
>
> R.H. Tawney, 1931

The problem of riches is not a new one: wealth concentration has characterised many types of societies, both feudal and early capitalist, and debate about a proper (efficient, moral and effective) balance between the better and worse off has occupied economists, politicians and social justice campaigners for as long. The particular problem of riches we have in the first half of our 21st century *is* new. The *things* of wealth have changed and the context in which these things exist has shifted. Our problem of riches may not be Tawney's, but a problem of riches it nonetheless remains. In the UK and across many rich nations, wealth hyperconcentrates as poverty deepens. Since 2020, the richest five men in the world have doubled their fortunes while five billion people globally have become poorer (Riddell et al 2024); in the UK, a country with 171 billionaires, 22 per cent or 14.4 million people were living in poverty in 2021 (JRF 2024). The top 10 per cent of the UK population hold 57 per cent of the total wealth stocks, while the bottom 50 per cent share less than 5 per cent of the total between them and around a quarter of the population has no wealth at all and instead is managing debts (Savage 2024). These stark distributional differences ramify and renew inequalities of sex and race: men have on average £92,762 more wealth than women (a gap of 35 per cent) and 90 per cent more pension wealth (Women's Budget Group 2023); Black African and Bangladeshi households have ten times less wealth than White British people (Khan 2020); and the Irish in England are 30–50 per cent poorer than the English (Cummins 2022). In addition, the unchecked decadent consumption patterns of the wealthiest risk causing environmental disaster (Chancel 2020). The operation of wealth and the actions of the rich are harming poorer people and the planet. It is a question of such deep and rapidly escalating injustice, that existing descriptive and analytical paradigms seem insufficient to the task of articulating the problem and working towards meaningful solutions.

This is in part because existing descriptive and analytical paradigms tend to centre poverty and the poor, and we struggle to make wealth and the rich a social problem in the same way (Rowlingson and Connor 2011).[1] Prevailing descriptive and analytical frames contribute to the exculpation of wealth and the rich from its/their enduring role in the production of inequality and, ultimately, of poverty. This leaves solutions being proposed, like redistributive wealth tax, struggling to gain or maintain political and social traction (Prabhakar 2023). And even when the public perceives inequality to be too high – 72 per cent of the public thought so in a recent poll (Hirneis 2023) – this concern does not straightforwardly catalyse public pressure for redistribution (Hebden et al 2020), and sometimes it entrenches the system-justifying beliefs (meritocracy and equality of opportunity) that maintain this highly unequal status quo (Trump 2018; Kerr and Vaughan 2024b).

In 2021 I wrote an article for the *Sociological Review* magazine (Kerr 2021) in which I asked whether talking about poverty increasingly mitigates against us doing anything useful about it. I asked: 'What if producing new and increasingly granular knowledge about it (its causes, its effects, its genesis) causes more harm than good?' This question was prompted by the fact that we expend incredible amounts of effort and resource trying to 'solve' poverty: since 2006, UK Research and Innovation (UKRI), the body which brings together the seven research councils, has spent more than £752 million on projects on poverty (compared to nearly £24.5 million on projects on economic inequality and under £3 million on projects specifically on wealth inequality);[2] Google Scholar holds records of 6,680 articles with the phrase 'poverty in the UK', 1,050 articles with the phrase 'wealth in the UK' and only 162 with the phrase 'wealth inequality in the UK' in the same period.[3] There are 5,784 charities registered in England and Wales focusing exclusively on the prevention or relief of *UK-based* poverty alone, with a combined annual expenditure in excess of £8.1 billion.[4]

This incredible investment of human and financial resource into variously knowing more about or acting to mitigate the effects of poverty does not translate into decisive change: 14.5 million people in the UK were living in poverty pre-pandemic, and 2024 figures show that we have almost returned to this figure (JRF 2020a, 2024). Furthermore, extreme poverty, or 'destitution', defined as a lack of access to essentials (shelter, food, heating, lighting, clothing and footwear, and basic toiletries) and extremely low or no income, was 'rapidly growing in scale and intensity', rising by 35 per cent between 2017 and 2019 (JRF 2020b: 2). By 2024, the percentage of people in poverty who are in very deep poverty now makes up the largest group: 6 million people – four out of ten of those in poverty – are living in deep poverty (JRF 2024). Within these figures, already vulnerable populations – those experiencing homelessness, drug and alcohol addiction, domestic violence, those who migrated to the UK and those living in care – are significantly overrepresented (Edmiston 2022). So while a 'politics of poverty reduction' has served historically to 'raise living standards and capacities', it is arguably ill-matched to the scale and nature of contemporary inequality (Savage 2021, p 319) and to the nature of the barriers preventing change. Ultimately, and most importantly for the focus of this book, a poverty lens lacks 'analytical traction in recognising and seeking redress of the pulling away at the top' (Savage 2021, p 319).

In social policy sociology, decades of the dominance of descriptive and explanatory anti-poverty research evident in journal content and conference programmes has gone hand in hand with a marked increase in inequality, and the sidelining of work on feasible strategies of change (DiPrete and Fox-Williams 2021, p 4). Research into aspects of the sociology of wealth, although beginning to flourish (as I will show shortly), is nascent in comparison to that on the sociology of poverty and has been an inconsistent focus of scholarship. An enduring poverty frame in the media, academia, social campaigning and policy has, over the long term, maintained the gaze down towards poverty and the poor long after it should have been looking up towards wealth and the rich. Meanwhile, data on wealth accumulation and distribution has until recently either not been available or has been (and continues to be) patchy and unreliable. Distributional data still misses an estimated 8–10 per cent of total wealth (WIL 2022; Advani and Tarrant 2022). If we were to try and deduce the contemporary social problematic from the policies and proposals of the main political parties rather than their rhetoric, we could resolutely say that wealth as a social problem does not enjoy political salience. Labour Chancellor Rachel Reeves' 2023 dismissal of a wealth tax on the grounds that it is unnecessary for Labour's economic plans is indicative of the immaturity of the political debate in this area. Her comments in effect shuttered out a growing body of research detailing the richer, broader social meanings and functions of wealth which strongly indicate that addressing extreme wealth might (should?) have an economic and social justice aim as much as a revenue-raising one (Crerar 2023; Savage 2024).

The aim of this book is to place the critical analysis of wealth at the heart of social policy debates. I adopt a problem-questioning rather than problem-solving approach on the basis that we, the public, are 'governed, not through policies, but through problematisations – how "problems" are constituted' (Bacchi 2013, pp 22–23). I start to explore what happens if we shift descriptive and analytic focus to the state of wealth and being wealthy – not just the distribution of financial resources, but also their conversion into other forms of power, their impact on the environment, the histories they carry with them and the unequal relationships they reproduce. And then I think about what might happen if we reorient the discipline of social policy and policy sociology towards this new focus. If we need to articulate 'more effective narratives for social change' (Scott Paul 2017), then surely, given the increasingly defining role of wealth and the rich in shaping the lives of most of us on the planet and the life of the planet itself, these narratives should centre the harm-causes/causers rather than the harmed? My contention in this book is that we should talk about wealtherty, not poverty if we want to tackle inequality.

Definitions of 'wealth' and 'wealtherty'

Before I introduce my definition of 'wealtherty', I want to first make it clear what I mean by 'wealth' and which parts/type of wealth it is the aim of this book to problematise. 'Wealth' per se is not what I am problematising here, but rather – in line with Robeyns – *'the effects of the situation of extreme wealth on society'* (Robeyns 2019, p 258, emphasis added). This is what is behind my definition of 'wealtherty'. I'm making the case in this book that *some forms* of wealth and *some wealth practices* are a social problem. They shape the lives of individuals, societies and the planet. My references to *surplus* wealth in this book derive from Robeyns' work on limitarianism, and her description of a level of wealth over and above what one needs for a fully flourishing life (Robeyns 2019, p 252). I am less interested in what that figure may be or whether the public recognises and values such a figure (the focus of Robeyns et al [2021] for the Netherlands and, in a similar way, Davis et al [2020] for the UK) and more interested in the idea of surplus wealth being an amount which, in certain conditions, becomes politically, environmentally and socially unsustainable. I use extreme wealth and surplus wealth interchangeably in this book, unless I am talking about a particular facet of Robeyns' specific use of surplus, in which case I will make that clear. Throughout this book, when I say 'surplus' or 'extreme' wealth, I am typically denoting a conceptual 'amount of wealth that enables a departure from the normal life of citizens' in a particular context (Scott 1994, p 17) rather than a concrete amount. Robeyns' contention is that given mounting social and environmental crises, 'we can no longer afford to work with theories and normative frameworks that do not enable us to say that at some point one is having, taking, or consuming too much' (Robeyns 2019, p 264). Her articulation of nonintrinsic limitarianism sees riches as 'morally objectionable to a world *where certain intrinsically important values are not secured and where limitarianism is instrumentally valuable to securing those ultimate ends*' (Robeyns 2017b, p 5, emphasis added). These values might include the right not to live in poverty. Robeyns also explores the risks posed to democratic processes by the bleed between financial and other forms of capital (political and media). Again, this bleed is a feature of several chapters in my book.

I am marrying these ideas of surplus wealth with the detailed work done recently by Beckert (2023) in order to understand what privileges are enabled by different levels of wealth and the context in which wealth inequality is more or less relevant to individual wellbeing. I'm going to introduce this in some detail here as I will return to it at several points in my book. Beckert notes that in German, the term for wealth is 'Vermögen', which means 'to be able to accomplish something' (Beckert 2023, p 4). He suggests that wealth 'enlarges the capacity for action, allowing its owners to do things they would otherwise be unable to do' (2023, p 5), including: (1) achieving security – this is the capacity that *ordinary* wealth [Hecht et al 2022], which I will come to shortly, makes available to those people who hold it (they are able to insure against negative shocks and develop long-term orientations); (2) accessing opportunities (to start a new enterprise, buy education or citizenship); (3) gaining income through asset-based income and asset appreciation rather than through labour; (4) securing benefits (through bequests) that can be passed between generations; (5) having enhanced social status; and (6) achieving personal, economic and political power. These capacities are more or less concentrated in different parts of the wealth spectrum: those with little wealth may have access to none; those with some wealth might have access to the first capacity (security); those with extreme wealth have access to all of them. The relevance of wealth ownership is also impacted by local regulatory, institutional and cultural contexts: where public investment and welfare provision are high, wealth inequality may be less harmful because 'security needs are satisfied and opportunities are provided by public means and because the use of wealth finds cultural and legal restriction' (Beckert 2023, p 18). Where public investment and welfare are low, the converse will be true. And in these contexts, when a small number of people can use wealth to secure all of Beckert's six capacities, surplus wealth ownership opens up the opportunity to harm others – by wielding undue self-interested political influence, by shaping media discourse in ways that cause harm and by passing on extreme wealth to children in a way which passes inequalities between generations. Put simply, holding a lot of wealth 'enables its owners to do things they otherwise could not do' (Beckert 2023, p 4), and some of these things are harmful to people and planet.

Surplus or extreme wealth can be distinguished from more quotidian forms of wealth that Hecht et al (2022) have defined as 'ordinary' wealth. Ordinary wealth is 'associated with the reasonable prospects of living "the good life", and allows widely shared personal aspirations relating to planning for the future and cementing and expressing familial bonds' (Hecht et al 2022, p 8). It enables people to '[take] responsibility for the self and family, which become particularly salient in times of retrenchment of collective social provision and which represent 'private insurance against risk' (2022, p 1). Extreme wealth is also distinguished from forms of 'collective' wealth ownership (collective wealth comprises assets made and shared by communities) achieved either through renationalisation or through localised communal ownership of resources like the sovereign funds and other assets owned in common explored in Byrne (2024). And it is distinguished from the many nonpecuniary forms of wealth (life, health and love) explored by moral economists and embodied in the ideas of Ruskin ('There is no wealth but life' (Ruskin 2010 [1862]), and in contemporary work on prosperity. Citizen juries working for the Institute for Public Policy Research (IPPR) Environmental Justice Commission, for example, developed a combined wellbeing framework that sought to account for 'what really matters to most people in society' beyond gross domestic product (GDP) (Dibb et al 2021). The outcome demonstrated that '[c]reating a more prosperous society ... will ... have to mean more than just economic growth ... we must broaden our definition of prosperity to take into account of all of a "good life". When asked what a good life meant to them, participants in citizens' juries cited 'fundamental goods like health, security, connection to others, access to nature and feeling in control of their own lives' (Dibb et al 2021, p 11).

Support for ordinary wealth is high among the public in the UK (Davis et al 2020; Hebden et al 2020) who also 'distinguish it conceptually from wealth acquisition that is seen as strategic, or associated with 'corruption and erosion of public values' (Hecht et al 2022). The resonance between this contemporary work and the moral economy of Ruskin writing in the 1860s is stark. Ruskin believed that not all wealth was equally socially valuable – its social value depended on its processes of accumulation and the 'moral sign' attached to it (May 2010): 'That which seems to be wealth may in verity be only the gilded index of far reaching ruin' (Ruskin 2010 [1862], p 51). Wealth as an outcome of good work was to be contrasted with 'illth', connoting wealth created for no useful purpose or that causes 'various devastation and trouble' (Ruskin 2010 [1862], p 14). When I talk about excess or surplus wealth in this book, I am also drawing on this idea of 'illth' on the basis that the processes of accumulation as much as the amounts itself are a defining part of the social harm that it does.

I use this distinction (between ordinary and surplus/extreme wealth) heuristically for the purposes of this book. There is undoubtedly further work to be done to better quantify or clarify precise distinctions between the two, which I do not claim or aim to do here. As such, when I speak about 'the rich', I am not referring to a decile necessarily, but more broadly to the group of people whose assets enable them to access restricted capabilities (Burchardt and Hick 2017). And when I refer to 'the poor' in this context of wealtherty, I am referring to those with insufficient assets to achieve security.

There are 'technical' definitions of wealth, which usually comprise a list of assets – for example, 'all private pension assets, financial assets, other business assets, physical assets, and property assets net of formal and informal financial liabilities' (Advani et al 2021). These data are useful in terms of telling us how much wealth there is, who owns it, and what specifically they own. But as Advani et al also note, the definition of wealth will 'depend[s] on the purpose for which it is being used' (2021, p 403). The purpose for which I am using a definition of wealth here is to establish extreme private wealth as a social and social policy problematic. So while I am interested in how much there is, who owns it and, specifically, what it is that they own (I will unpack this in Chapter 2), I am mostly interested in the *social effects* of these patterns of distribution – in short, in how they shape the lives of individuals, societies and the planet.

I'm now ready to introduce my working definition of wealtherty:[5]

1. The *active enablement of hyperconcentration of prosperity* in the abundance of possessions or riches, with a stark polarisation between the richest and the poorest and with distributions and processes of accumulation renewing older social relations (of class, empire and patriarchy). This is about the legal codes and the 'effective' institutional strategies that enable hyperconcentration (Pistor 2019; Cobham 2020).
2. The *perpetuation of social and policy divisions* based on this distinction (fiscal and social policy, claimants and customers) and related polarised and polarising cultural/media identities (winners and losers, value creators and scroungers, us and them). Differential governmental 'orientations' towards these groups of scrutiny (demands for full disclosure) and ignorance (acceptance of secrecy). This is about governing richer and poorer populations *differently*.
3. Concomitant *unequal access to political power and influence*. Richer people are able to access a restricted set of activities or 'capabilities' (for example, buying media, setting media agendas, and donating to and lobbying political parties) which allow their voices and interests to predominate. This poses risks to the democratic process, and social and environmental justice. This is about dominating political discourse and steering it to reflect the needs of the rich.
4. *Active gatekeeping of epistemic and epistemological resources* (for example, who gets to know, what kind of knowledge, who is an expert, what constitutes expertise and evidence, and what are the 'things' of poverty, inequality and wealth that shape prevailing understandings) leading to the 'capture' of the research and nongovernmental organisation (NGO) agenda and the enshrining of a relative authority of knowers, knowing and knowledge. This is about gatekeeping who gets to know and what constitutes knowledge such that the ascendency of the wealthy cannot rationally be questioned within the terms of debate which the wealthy themselves have set.

Wealtherty exists when the dynamic between these elements is self-sustaining and has made itself invisible – a form of wealth privilege. This makes it unlikely that beneficiaries of the system will be motivated to enact change.

The experiment attempted in this book is not about replacing poverty. But it is about displacing it. This process of reorienting around a new term acknowledges not only that we might be looking in the wrong place for solutions to poverty and disadvantage, but, more fundamentally, that we might be looking at the wrong 'thing' altogether (after Ball and Collet-Sabé 2021). The debate about whether to focus resources on 'the water in the bath' rather than 'switching the tap off' has a long history. I'm not suggesting that we can or should ignore the material needs of people living in poverty in order to solely focus on structural questions relating to why they are suffering in the first place. I am simply saying that the urgency of the situation means that we need to do more of the latter, and more of that should focus on institutional causes/causers of harm. In her 2021 essay 'Decolonising critical theory? Epistemological justice, progress, reparations', postcolonial sociologist Gurminder Bhambra made the case for epistemological justice as necessary for social justice on the basis that it is unlikely that the latter will be achieved if we fail to challenge 'the categories of critique and their associated normative claims' (Bhambra 2021c, p 74). In my context, this means that it is not sufficient to continue to explore poverty and inequality and simply 'add wealth'. This leaves intact the nature of the understandings that had previously excluded it, or rendered it socially and politically unproblematised (Bhambra 2021c, p 82), a point also well made by Federici (2000). In short, the very terms in which these conversations have been framed have shaped the outcome, and in the interests of social and environmental justice more broadly, we must urgently 'unmake' our existing ways of knowing (Bhambra 2016, p 337). We need to actively consider how we write about things, what we write about and what we don't write about, and what we distance from questions of contemporary justice making by confining to the past, or to history (Bhambra 2021c, p 83). As Bhambra argues, only 'through acknowledging the histories that produced them and the historiographies that have obscured them' can we address 'the injustices that disfigure the world that we share in common' (Bhambra 2021c, p 85).

In this book, I make the case for wealtherty as an alternative description of the state we are in. The shift of focus upwards seeks to turn the conceptualisation of the social problem on its head by making the case that we are living in a state of wealtherty, with specific social, cultural, economic and political characteristics, including (but not limited to) poverty and inequality. It aims to accelerate the shift of sociological scholarship, public debate and social action upwards towards wealth. My approach very explicitly borrows from the work of Mills (2008) and others writing about white ignorance: Mills explicitly suggests that the ignorance lens can usefully be applied to all forms of elite studies (Mills 2008, p 240). The concept of wealtherty seeks to bridge the gap between poverty and wealth, and the fiscal and social policy disciplines. It goes beyond questions about the distribution of economic resources to account for what Robeyns calls the 'Power of Material Resources' (Robeyns 2017b) – that is, the ways in which these material resources are converted into other forms of power. It is a way to describe: (i) the hysteretic effects (the temporal ripples in our now from the past) of empire, patriarchy and capitalism; and (ii) the social symbolic ramifications of distributional inequalities in wealth (how media frames reflect *and reproduce* inequality and harm). And it is a way to think about how and why these matter, and how we might use this frame to spark connections between new problem articulations and new, more radical solutions. The contemporary inequalities brought into focus by the concept of wealtherty embody the operations of the neoliberal Centaur State described by French sociologist Loïc Wacquant, which practises 'liberalism at the top of the class structure and punitive paternalism at the bottom' (2012a, p 66). Where Wacquant's primary analytic focus is on the work of the Centaur State to 'mould, classify and control the populations deemed deviant, dependent, and dangerous' at the tail (Wacquant 2008, p 27), my focus shifts upwards, to ask what liberalism at the top actually looks like. In explicitly looking 'both ways', I seek to flesh out how the institutions, histories and cultural practices of our neoliberal state define and defend its liberal head, as well as its paternalist tail. I find, for example, that the rich and the poor in the UK are subject to radically divergent legislative and administrative approaches on the part of the state – the behaviours of the poor are relentlessly scrutinised and punished, while those of the rich are ignored or enabled.

Dispositions of government

The state of wealtherty has a long history which I start to tell in this book. It is a history of parallel governmental dispositions towards richer and poorer people, dispositions of, respectively, ignorance and scrutiny: ignorance as the dominant governmental disposition of the state towards the rich, and secrecy as the expected or sanctioned behaviour in response. Scrutiny as the dominant governmental disposition of the state towards the poor, and disclosure as the expected or sanctioned response. Over the long term, these dispositions manifest in specific pieces of legislation – for example, Universal Credit is a policy that demands disclosure, and 'Cooperative Compliance' – an approach to the government of the rich and their wealth – de facto sanctions degrees of secrecy or withholding. The four facets of wealtherty that make up the preceding definition are enabled by the operation of these contrastive dispositions towards richer and poorer people, which entrench norms of behaviour (for a government and a governed subject) and articulate them to specific ways of knowing, ways of governing and ways of being (see Figure 1.1). This history of *wealtherty* allows us to reveal some of the

Figure 1.1: Governmental dispositions and sanctioned responses

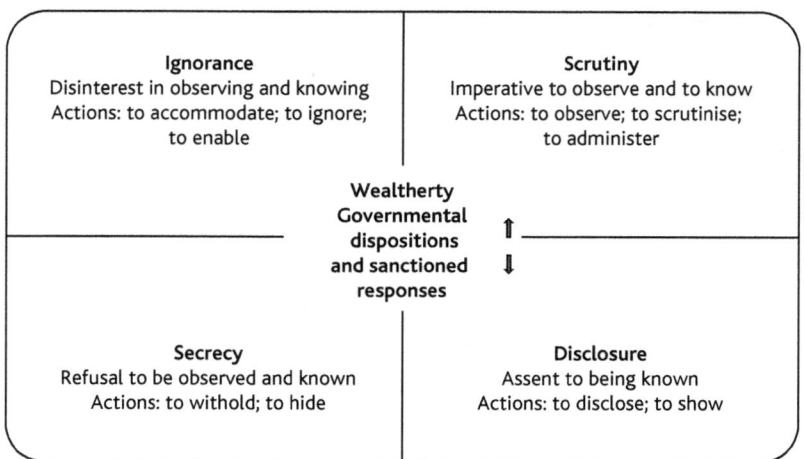

deep-rooted social, cultural, political and discursive norms enabling wealth's operation as power and to understand how it endures.

A convergence of scholarly focus

Although political economists have written persistently about the 'real, supposed, or desirable differences in wealth between the poor and the rich' since the time of Plato (Piketty 2021, p 4), it is also the case that the absence (or the maintaining beyond the scope of scientific inquiry) of data on incomes and wealth undermines the validity of resultant economic and social histories (Piketty 2021, p 5). Since the turn of the century, and especially since the financial sector failure of 2008, scholarship across diverse disciplines has been beginning the process of problematising wealth and the rich as social problems and clearing space for new questions. This has been enabled in part by the new availability of data on wealth and assets (primarily, on a global scale, the World Inequality Lab [WIL, since 2018] and in the context of the UK, the Office for National Statistics [ONS] Wealth and Assets Survey [WAS, since 2006]). Analyses based on this new data have more starkly revealed that the distribution and operation of wealth, more so than income, has an increasingly defining role in terms of wellbeing and life outcomes. In part, this is simply because there is significantly more of it: between 1991 and 2022, net household wealth in the UK almost doubled relative to GDP from about three and a half times as large to seven times as large (Bourquin et al 2022). So although relative wealth inequality has remained more or less stable in the same period, and the global trend is towards rather than away from inequality, the increased amount of wealth is stretching out the distance between different parts of the wealth distribution – people feel they are further apart from their richer or poorer neighbours. Because the stretching out of gaps between groups is largely an effect of inheritance (or 'luck'), it becomes difficult for those not born into wealthy families to 'counter the historical weight of past wealth accumulation' of those who are (Savage 2021), shattering hopes for social mobility and undermining the idea of meritocracy.

It is not just the amount that matters; the contemporary composition of wealth across the spectrum matters too. This is what I alluded to in the opening paragraph when I said that the 'things' of wealth have changed: if they have any wealth at all, poorer people tend to own physical assets (a car or a TV); increasingly, rich people hold their wealth in often complex financial ones. This is true in the UK, and globally, where the disadvantaged classes [the poorest 50 per cent] have very little in savings; the middle classes (the next 40 per cent) centre their assets on housing; the wealthy classes (the richest 10 per cent) 'distribute their assets between housing, business assets and financial assets; the dominant classes concentrate on ownership of the means of production (business assets and especially stocks and shares)' (Piketty 2021, p 39). Because the rate of return on the financial assets is more than the growth rate in the economy as a whole (Piketty's R>G [Piketty 2014]), the stock of wealth at the top grows faster than workers' incomes, which ultimately leads to an 'endless inegalitarian spiral' (Piketty 2014, p 572): quite simply, wealth begets wealth. This inegalitarian spiral is further accelerated by a tax system which favour[s] people who earn their income from capital over those that earn it from work (Nanda and Parkes 2019) and by the way in which legal code more generally (laws of property, contracts, trusts and so on) transform assets into capital and generate and protect private wealth as it transitions between generations (Pistor 2019). Pistor notes that while the wealthy often make the case that their fortune arises from special skills, hard work or personal sacrifice, 'without legal coding most of these fortunes would have been short-lived. Accumulating wealth over long stretches of time requires additional fortification that only a code backed by the coercive powers of a state can offer' (2019, p 4). Most specifically for this book, the attributes that this legal code 'attaches' to different assets include 'durability' and 'universality' (alongside 'priority' and 'convertibility'), which serve to extend capital in time and space. They, rather than individual hard work and ingenuity, are the key enablers of the duration of wealth and fortunes within families.

Beyond economics, there has been a wider shift in the focus of scholarly work since the turn of the century, which, with increasing intensity and regularity, has been arguing that if we are to make progress towards a socially and environmentally sustainable future, we urgently need to 'turn the telescope' to see the rich and wealth as a social problem. In the field of policy sociology, Orton and Rowlingson (2007) argued that the failure to expand the lens upwards towards the rich served to shore up the ontological stability of the poor as the authors of their own misfortune and the righteous focus of social policy. Ridge and Wright (2008) argued that 'poverty and inequality cannot be understood or adequately addressed without an equally clear critical understanding of richness and wealth and its role in society'. They began to craft new definitions of 'states of being' at each end of the wealth spectrum – for example, poverty as 'a severe and damaging exclusion from economic and social resources', while at the other end, 'wealth and richness buy economic, social and political power and advantage in abundance' (Ridge and Wright 2008, pp 1–5). Several articles played with 'reversing' tools and approaches previously applied to the poor: Rowlingson and Connor (2011, p 438), for example, sought to 'extend and test the application of the notion of desert [historically a means of differentiating deserving poorer populations from undeserving ones] to the problem of riches'. They also started finding ways to articulate the 'things' of wealth: fiscal welfare (Rowlingson and Connor 2011, but building on Titmuss 1955), and distinctions between the rich and the richest, for example (Rowlingson and McKay 2011). They attributed the then lack of work in this area to the fact that 'poverty [is] seen as a social problem whereas wealth is generally not' (Rowlingson and Connor 2011, p 438), and increasingly made calls for establishing wealth as a problem in its own right, distinct from poverty and requiring a discrete response. New definitions of the 'stuff' of inequality have been produced. Scott (an outlier in 1994) for example, described the Wealthy Line; Beaverstock et al (2010) proposed distinctions in amounts and lifestyles between the rich and the super-rich.

Data on previously hidden wealth made public through a series of leaks (Panama 2016, Paradise 2017, Pandora 2021) and the systematisation of resultant data by the International Consortium of Investigative Journalists (ICIJ), along with the new longitudinal data produced and analysed first in Piketty's 2014 *Capital in the 21st Century* and then in the work of the World Inequality Lab (WIL 2018), ignited a spark in political economic scholarship. A flurry of work looking at wealth distribution and concentration, inequality, and the cultural, social and political processes that enable it proliferated in the 2010s both in academia and in the world of 'professional' economists in think tanks and civil society organisations (Shaxson 2012, 2018; Urry 2014; Atkinson 2015; Harrington 2016; Bullough 2018, 2022; Deneault 2018; Giridharadras 2019; Atkinson 2021; Cobham 2020).

Sociological work has increasingly asked us to look not only up, but also back, to understand the enduring nature of wealth and the 'weight of the past' it drags with it into the present (Savage 2021; Bhambra 2021a, 2021b), and to recognise that there is no such thing as 'benign inequality' (Desmond and Wilmers 2019). The great fortunes which persist and consolidate today often derive from moments of primary accumulation: colonial exploitation and/or the sequestration of women's labour that began during the transition from feudalism to capitalism (Federici 2000; Mies 2014). Because it accrues over time, contemporary economic, racialised and gendered patterns of distribution carry with them and renew historical power relations of class, empire and patriarchy (Khan 2020; Waitkus and Minkus 2021; Bourquin et al 2022; Koram 2022; Bessière and Gollac 2023): they are not the unblemished outcome of application, ingenuity and entrepreneurship, but are instead empire's 'afterlife' (Koram 2022, p 16) and patriarchy's renewal. Sociologists have also explored the persistence of myths such as meritocracy (Littler 2018; Mijs and Savage 2020; Sandel 2020), with framing literature revealing the defining role that 'system-justifying beliefs' have on preventing perception of high levels of inequality translating into political pressure to act (Kerr and Vaughan 2024b). Work on public opinion and preference formation has deepened our understanding of how opinions about equality are made and challenged, and empirical work has gauged the public appetite for different forms of predistribution and redistribution (Davis et al 2020; Hebden et al 2020a, 2020b; Robeyns et al 2020; Summers et al 2022; Waitkus and Wallaschek 2022). Economists and sociologists have designed new wealth tax systems, and have sought to communicate their modest financial effects on the fortunes of the very richest, and the significant gains for the public purse (Advani et al 2020).

Significant new work on stigma – stigma and the portrayal of poverty (Skeggs 2014; de Benedictus et al 2017); stigma and social welfare (Spicker 1984; Taylor-Gooby 2013; Tyler 2015); the history of stigma (Tyler 2020); and the historical roots of racialised stigma (Virdee 2018; Hickman and Ryan 2020) – has revealed regressive social and cultural norms operating to shore up prejudice and injustice. Work on framing has helped us understand how specific problems, causalities or solutions gain media and/or political salience (McGovern et al 2020; Lierse et al 2022), and new ways of thinking about framing equality and justice (for example, as 'fairness': Janbur and Snell 2019; Fairness Foundation 2023) have sought to generate a broader and more effective consensus for change. Elite studies scholarship has furthered understandings of elite group membership and forms of cultural and social distinction (Friedman and Reeves 2020). It has described the reproduction of gendered relationships in elite families (Glucksberg 2016; Hecht 2017; Bessière and Gollac 2023), and it has explored how their use of philanthropy (Sklair 2018; Sklair and Glucksberg 2021) and impact investing (Sklair 2023) helps to secure intergenerational continuity of dynastic wealth.

Engagement from moral economics, demographics and moral philosophy on the ethics of wealth hyperconcentration has married economic, environmental and moral analyses of wealth inequality to critique the idea of its assumed social value (Sayer 2015; Robeyns 2019; Robeyns 2024), to establish its impact on health outcomes (Dorling 2015) and to reveal stark geographical divides (Dorling 2023). Indirectly, work on epistemic justice and its relevance to power relationships within policy-making contexts has made space for thinking about how communicative practices reproduce power relationships, diminish or enhance credibility, and enable or restrict political agency (Fricker 2007, 2013; Medina 2011, 2013; Simpson 2017; Wicker 2022; Kerr 2023). Relatedly, in the area of authority, expertise and expert studies, writers have laid bare the ways in which definitions of expertise render unequal access to democratic and scholarly debate, or have explored the value of participatory policy making in enabling the voices of those with experience of living in poverty to be heard (Blencowe 2013; Blencowe et al 2013; May et al 2016; Hardos 2018; Meriluoto 2018; Bochel and Berthier 2020; Smith-Merry 2020; Stewart et al 2020). Other areas which hitherto have not typically made wealth accumulation a central concern, like art theory and practice, also experienced an upsurge of interest in the early decades of the 21st century (Smith 2016; Greenfield 2017; Bush 2019): Galimberti and Woods (2015), for example, explored visually the distributional trends revealed in the WIL data (for example, the slide of capital from public to private hands illustrated in Figure 7.12).

Historical and postcolonial sociology has explored ways of using the past to unsettle complacent narratives about the legitimacy of wealth inequality in the present (Bhambra and Holmswood 2018; Tyler 2020; Bhambra 2021a, 2021b; Savage 2021; Koram 2022) and has made explicit the ways in which intergenerational asset transfer reproduces colonial forces and radically undermines claims to meritocracy or desert (Pfeffer and Killewald 2017; Advani et al 2020; Advani et al 2022; Koram 2022; Pellicer and Ranchhod, 2023; Savage 2023). Historical policy sociologists have also asked whether the lived experience of wealth needs more explicit space to be heard in social policy-making contexts (Kerr 2023).

Methodological innovation and analysis has allowed us to question the ongoing legitimacy of the poverty frame (Wolff et al 2015) or to think of multidimensional ways of understanding the relationship between wealth inequality and wellbeing in rich societies (Burchardt and Hick 2018). Ecosocial and postproductivist policy sociology scholarship has sought to shift the focus away from economic growth and towards democratic debates about the meaning of wellbeing and quality of life (Gough et al 2008; Hickel and Kallis 2020; Bonvin and Laruffa 2022). Conceptual innovation has characterised this shift in thinking, as new models seek to forge new problematisations: Raworth's doughnut visualised a shift away from the idea of endless growth and towards a 'safe and just space for humanity to thrive', situated between an 'ecological ceiling' and a 'social foundation' (Raworth 2017; see also Plunkett 2023 on *un*equality).

This work demonstrates a tremendous convergence of focus, a shared sense that a broader and deeper understanding of wealth and power is necessary if we are to understand how to move towards a more socially and environmentally sustainable way of life. It is very evidently, in Foucault's terms, a problematisation, a situation in which government becomes a problem (Dean 2010, p 38) or, in Kuhn's terms, a challenge to 'normal science' (Kuhn 2012). Given this convergence, my call to displace poverty as the structuring idea of social policy and social change narratives seems less extreme. We are, it seems, already doing so! However, the relevance of some of the literatures briefly introduced earlier (for example, philosophy, art history and expertise studies) is currently underarticulated to the area of wealth inequality studies, and some (intentionally or not) defaults to a poverty problematic. My aim here is to give this multidisciplinary work, which currently does not necessarily recognise kinship, a coherence by pulling a descriptive umbrella ('wealtherty') over the top. I aim to make a robust argument in favour of a new paradigm, a challenge to the prevailing 'cognitive and theoretical assumptions about the world which limit [not only] the policy alternatives that policymakers would consider' (Campbell, cited in Clark et al 2020, p 9), but which also constrains the very ways in which we might imagine a more sustainable future.

A new frame

Frames shape how we talk about a problem, linking a diagnosis to treatment. They apportion responsibility and blame (McGovern et al 2020). They are the means through which the media and politicians (more broadly, those who have the capability to influence how issues are conceptualised and communicated to the public) 'guide audiences how to think about [inequality] and thus release or build political pressure' (McGovern et al 2020, p 7). But they are much more than this. Questions of framing are not peripheral to wider questions of social justice. Frames are gatekeepers between ingroups and outgroups, between the past and the present (insulating, as Bhambra (2021c) argued, contemporary renewals of past acts of expropriation and violence from contemporary scrutiny by defining them as 'merely historical'), and between the tractable and the intractable. The reasons why the 'problem of wealth' fails to ignite social unrest is in part an outcome of a very successful and enduring counterframe which operates to legitimise private wealth variously: (i) as an outcome of hard work; (ii) as (ergo) deserved; and (iii) as necessary for the economic growth that will ultimately benefit everyone. This prevailing wealth-legitimising frame is untroubled by lack of substantiation or outright contestation in academic literature (for example, Littler 2018; Mijs and Savage 2020; Sandel 2020; Lierse et al 2022). But it is equally untroubled by public or political pressure for change. Several recent articles in the area of preference formation note the rise of tolerance for inequality that accompanies a rise in inequality itself – Trump's (2018) so-called 'adjustment hypothesis', for example, suggests that 'when income inequality increases, people adjust their perceptions of what constitutes legitimate levels of income inequality upward. As a result, the public can become aware of increased inequality without exhibiting increased opposition to it' (2018, p 930). The endurance of this frame is further aided by a lack of high-level political sponsorship, which would be necessary to catapult the problematic of wealth onto the social policy agenda (McGovern et al 2020). And it is an outcome of how the media operates in a way that is 'legitimising rather than problematising' about the wealthy and wealth inequalities (Lierse et al 2022, p 373). This is achieved in part through communicating about the economy in an overly financialised way, far removed from most people's lived experience of it (Kerr and Vaughan 2024b). Finally, Desmond (2023) observes, quite simply, that poverty (as defined and sustained through social policy, but also through the research and charity spend described in the opening pages) is an outcome of the political settlement as is: richer people benefit from poverty and are in positions of power and influence. All these factors together produce a drag on the conversion of concern about high economic inequality into political preference for redistribution. The result? The absorption of wealth inequality by the 'existing policy repertoire for dealing with poverty' (McGovern et al 2020, p 14), low support for higher or more progressive taxation and redistribution, and lack of political engagement with more radical structural changes to the way we live our lives and respect our planet.

Approach

If we are to 'unmake' this frame, then we need to know how the things of our now were made in the first place. To do this, Parts II and III of this book present a *genealogy of wealtherty*. A genealogy starts with the identification of an area of contemporary shared social concern (in our case, wealtherty) and then looks to the past to identify moments of its emergence. It involves 'reserialising' history (Walter, cited in Tyler 2020, p 21) or talking about the past differently (and about different aspects of the past) to shed new light on our now-time. I am approaching the writing of this genealogy through an *analytics of government* (Dean 2010), using the term 'government' here in Foucault's sense to mean the 'conduct of conduct' rather than the more statist 'the actions of *a* government'. This is key to the understanding in this book. Government is consistently used in this way. It describes attempts 'to shape with some degree of deliberation aspects of our behaviour according to particular sets of norms and for a variety of ends' (Dean 2010, p 18). These attempts to shape behaviour are manifest in ideas and the means of coming to know about individuals and groups (Chapter 3), and in ideas made material (Chapter 4), which in my broadly institutionalist context refers to policies and policy-making mechanisms, but also extends to the symbolic and semiotic work undertaken in practices of communication (media and otherwise). Processes of government concern these practices and institutions alongside 'practices of the self' (the focus of Chapters 5 and 8) in a way which connects 'questions of government, politics and administration to the space of bodies, lives, selves and persons' (Dean 2010, p 20) (see Chapter 5). An analytics of government enables questions about what conditions (political, economic, cultural and regulatory) make certain ways of thinking and acting intelligible and others not.

I will be looking at richer and poorer populations in the same frame. For example, in the 1790s, political discourse in England was dominated by concurrent debates about how to deal with the poor (the Poor Law debates) and how to secure revenue from the rich to pay for war (the Income Tax debates). These debates are rarely brought onto the same canvas historiographically (there are exceptions – Horwell's brilliant 2018 thesis being a relatively recent example) because they deal with two populations traditionally considered socially and legislatively distinct. The concept of wealtherty demands that they be thought together – that they appear on the same canvas.

A genealogy allows us to look anew at things that we perceive as 'natural' in our now (for example, that 'social' policy is about poor people and poverty, and not rich people and wealth) and to recast them as outcomes of choices and actions in the past and in our present: they were made in the past, and we *choose* to reproduce them through our current practices and institutions. In Foucault's words, it allows us to understand:

> how that-which-is has not always been; for instance, that the things which seem most evident to us are always formed in the confluence of encounters and chances, during the course of a precarious and fragile history. What reason perceives as its necessity … can perfectly well be shown to have a history, *and … since these things have been made, they can be unmade, as long as we know how it was that they were made.* (Foucault 1988, p 37, emphasis added)

The knowledge produced through a genealogy is 'not made for understanding, it is made for "cutting"' (Foucault 1984, pp 97–98). What this means is it is made for breaking down ideas that have hardened into truths through what he calls the 'long baking process of history (Foucault 1984, p 79) to 'unfold[ing] a space in which it is once more possible to think' (Foucault

1970, p 342). In the context of our current problem of *wealtherty*, we need to 'look up' towards the rich *and 'back'* to find moments of its emergence, to better recognise its current repertoires and to find ways to challenge them. Other writers have written about the process of genealogy and, relatedly, 'critical history' (Dean 1994; Tamboukou 1999; Garland 2014), and I don't intend to unpack the method in more detail than necessary here, other than to foreground two specific techniques.[6] The first is 'reversal', which refers quite simply to looking at things 'the wrong way round'. Examples might be Rowlingson and Connor's engagement with the idea of the 'undeserving rich' rather than the undeserving poor (2011) or the work on the idea of fiscal rather than social welfare, and on corporate welfare (Orton and Rowlingson 2007; Farnsworth 2013 [after Titmuss 1955]). Wealtherty in and of itself is such a form of reversal through a displacing of poverty. The second is the nature and role of historical sources. 'Reserialising' the past demands a focus 'on 'grey', quiet spaces, to seek events 'in the most unpromising places, in *what we tend to feel is without history*' (Foucault 1984, p 76, emphasis added), or sources whose contemporary relevance was not understood in the past. The aim is to recuperate what he calls this 'profusion of lost events' (Foucault 1984, p 81) into new perspectives on our now. The approach might also legitimately seek to reveal or articulate what is *not* there. As Trouillot (2015) suggests, in making narratives from the past, inference and interpretation increase as the quality or volume of material traces decreases. This is sometimes a question of physical attrition, but sometimes it is a result of material traces never having been retained due to perceptions of their lack of worth and value (so-called 'structural apathy' [Tuana 2008]). In the context of *wealtherty*, this means looking at moments in which the specific governmental dispositions I introduced earlier (scrutiny and ignorance) are manifest in ways of thinking and acting. Because of the process of starting now and then using the past to shed light on a contemporary problem, genealogy as a method eschews the chronological approach of 'traditional' histories. Instead, it 'bends time' to illustrate a 'resonance' between the past and the present, 'zipping back and forth' between then and now to link a contemporary event or phenomenon with a 'scene' from the past (Koram 2022, p 18).

In terms of sources, I am making a particular case for images. On a practical level, this involves including a series of photographs as part of my problematisation (see Figures 7.7–7.11). Each engages with the idea of wealtherty and the parallel trajectories of scrutiny and ignorance that I am developing throughout this book (see Figure 1.1). I will look at them in detail in Chapter 7. The sensibility to visual culture also extends to offering some conceptual tools from visual theory and culture that can help to unsettle the past – namely, the idea of *Ma*. *Ma* is a Japanese word which means something like the 'interval which gives shape to the whole' (Matsumoto

Figure 1.2: Hasegawa Tōhaku (16th century Azuchi-Momoyama period) Shōrin-zu byōbu (pine forest).

Source: Image reproduced with permission from Tokyo National Museum. Created using information on ColBase: Integrated Collections Database of the National Institutes for Cultural Heritage, Japan at https://colbase.nich.go.jp/collection_items/tnm/A-10471

2020) or, alternatively, space/time (Genosko 2005, p 157). It is conceived of not as a static gap, but as 'the distance that exists between objects as well as between time'. *Ma* 'reminds us that what isn't there provides the ability for everyone's story to co-exist' (Matsumoto 2020, emphasis added). It is a way of giving importance to pauses and empty spaces (Murakami 2016, p 22). It is distinct from the idea of 'negative space', in that the latter 'does not ascribe value to the white space' (Genosko 2005, p 157). Figures 1.2 and 1.3 illustrate the difference.

Ruskin's explanation and illustration of the white interstices are spaces between, but they have no value to Ruskin other than to establish the positive forms on the page, and to regulate them: are they in the right relation to one another? This is the idea of negative space, and it is certainly useful conceptually in and of itself in relation to the constitutive role played by wealth in producing the poor and poverty as policy objects while itself remaining obscured. However, as a way of looking at relationships between things, *Ma* gives equal value to that which is visualised and that which isn't: *Senu tokoro ga omoshiroki* is an expression the Japanese use to describe Noh theatre, for example. It means what the actor does not do is interesting (Matsumoto 2020), and I will return to this idea throughout this book. This process of rematerialisation, of scrutinising the role of the seen and the unseen, the present and the past can bring the rich and certain forms of wealth into a new (for them) landscape of dividing practices ('undeserving rich', surplus wealth and fiscal welfare). It repoliticises the landscape. In bringing space and time together, *Ma* is conceptually richer than the flatter idea of negative space. Genosko notes that: 'In traditional Japanese culture

Figure 1.3: A tree drawn to illustrate negative space.[7]

Source: Ruskin (1991, p 30). Image reproduced and used with permission from Bloomsbury Publishing.

space is not neutral and has never been so. [It is] a continuous flow, alive with interactions and ruled by a precise sense of timing and pacing' (Genosko 2005, p 157). The space between the trees in Figure 1.2 is constitutive in this different way. Without wishing to overtheorise the Tōhaku image, the trees on the left might be considered to visualise Savage's understanding of duration (via Bergson [Savage 2021, pp 97–98]). The ghost figures behind the tree at the front suggest not only perspective (spatial complexity) but also duration (temporal complexity). They embody spacetime. In establishing duration as a means of describing the active force of the past in the present, something that I will return to several times in this book, Savage uses James' critique of the 'specious present', and his assertion that 'the unit of composition of our time is a duration, with a bow and a stern' (Savage 2021, pp 97–98). Duration is conceived as a force that presses onward, exerting its influence in the present. Savage concludes that:

> Focusing on wealth accumulation does not simply mean bringing a relatively neglected dimension into the analysis of inequality – though it certainly means that too [Ruskin's negative space]! It involves a deep-rooted concern to understand capital as the weight of history, which brings with it a much stronger awareness of the power of time and direction than is found in much of social science [*Ma*'s spacetime]. (Savage 2021, pp 97–98)

How does this relate to wealtherty and to the dispositions of scrutiny and ignorance, and how am I going to use the idea of *Ma* to shape how I talk about these ideas in this book? The main answer is that wealtherty is about being simultaneously interested in what the actor does and does not do. If the state is scrutinising the poor, why is it not scrutinising the rich and, indeed, what is its disposition towards the rich if not scrutiny? If the state allows the rich a sphere of financial privacy, what is its disposition towards the poor in this regard? In every moment we examine, we should imagine it as a unit of duration; action that takes place on the same canvas. *Ma* encourages us to think things together. Its aim is to 'grab the audience and pull them in to the empty spaces' (Murakami 2016, p 22). Murakami talks about 'putting in ma' (2016, p 22) – this is what I want to do here. Also, in being temporally ambiguous, it affords a way of not insulating from the demands of contemporary justice making, actions that took place in the past on the basis that these actions endure. If we are seeing in the present things we recognise from the past (and many sociologists and historians agree that we are – see Ball 2012; Bailey and Ball 2016; Ball 2016; Thane 2019; Tyler 2020; Bhambra 2021a, 2021b; Koram 2022), or if we recognise not only renewals of past forms of government but also their 'ratcheting' (Bailey and Ball 2016), then we need to write about the things we see in ways which acknowledge that these are new engagements with *enduring* relationships of power (my 'dispositions' outlined in Figure 1.1 and explored from different perspectives in Tables 2.1, 5.1 and 5.2) or, in Savage's terms, a manifestation of the active force of the past in the present.

The second genealogical source I want to mention is bodies. Bodies are a key historical source. It is very difficult to write about the history of the rich and the poor without being confronted with bodies: categorised, segregated, displaced, placeless, settled, incarcerated, immobilised, rendered landless, bored, lashed, whipped, branded, enchained, enslaved, marginalised, starved, 'farmed', raped, dissected, hidden, augmented, pampered or coveted. It is also difficult not to see the very different ways in which male and female bodies are governed within the same disciplinary mechanisms (for example, the different punishment regimes for women and men in the workhouse; the different outcomes for women who claim Universal Credit; the lower wealth holdings that women have; the lower wealth holdings that rich women have in relation to rich men [Bessière and Gollac 2023]). Foucault suggests that if we want to understand power, we should be 'looking at its extremities, at its outer limits at the point where it becomes capillary' (Foucault 1984, p 27). This shift leads to a preoccupation with 'the bodies that are constituted as subjects by power-effects' (Foucault 1984, p 29); indeed, Foucault argues that genealogy is situated 'within the articulation of the body and history' (Garland 2014, p 372). The body, suggests Foucault, is the 'inscribed surface of events', and it is the task of genealogy to expose this 'body totally imprinted by history' (Foucault 1984, p 83). Women's bodies were, and continue to be, privileged sites for the bodily inscription of the power/knowledge dynamic (Federici 2000; Skeggs 2005; Tyler 2015). The body – its sex, its inscription and marking, its setting apart, its hunger and privation, and its sexualisation and objectification – are a necessary focus of both the contemporary and historical parts of this book. I recognise here, too, the obvious parallels with other forms of classification (for example, 'race' and socioeconomic class) and I reflect on these differences throughout the book. Although sex would easily have warranted its own chapter, I took the decision to embed it on the basis that it is not a question of Wealtherty + sexed difference. The two are integrally bound up, and making this explicit challenges the problematic historiographical norms, drawn attention to by Federici (2000), which can otherwise undermine traditional historiography. This book is about wealth, but it is also about history and about writing history, and about how to account for the past in how we write about, think about and ultimately act on and in the present.

There is, of course, a case for not decentring poverty, and this is well made in Wolff et al's (2015) review of the philosophical literature on poverty, where the authors explored the challenge posed to the utility of income and wealth-derived definitions of poverty by the Capabilities Approach (CA – I will address this in more detail in Chapters 2 and 8). They ultimately make the case for retaining prevailing (income-based) definitions of poverty on the basis that a shift towards understanding poverty as a capability deprivation 'risks disconnecting it from a century of empirical research', makes it too hard to count, and is difficult to translate into a policy response (Wolff et al 2015, p 3). But my case here is that perhaps it is less a case of the risk of disconnecting poverty scholarship from a century of empirical research and more the necessity of plugging it into a century (and more) of 'lost events' (Foucault 1984, p 81) to which it is integrally and intimately connected.

Throughout this book, I will seek to add detail to my initial brief conceptualisation of wealtherty. I will undertake my own reserialising of history, tracing trajectories of scrutiny and ignorance as parallel governmental dispositions towards those with and without wealth. I will think about how these dispositions materialise in historical and contemporary policy, public and media discourse. It produces a kind of 'semantic' history, allowing me to trace *meaning continuity*, looking at how the state governs the rich and the poor at past times of significant public policy change – specifically the New Poor Law of 1834 and Pitt's first Income Tax Bill of 1799 – and how this relationship shows up in our now. I think about them in terms of this longer continuum, as renewals of older historical forces. I look at how these dispositions manifest in contemporary society and policy making in 'Centaur' orientations towards richer and poorer people. I recognise the *entanglement* of the economic with the social, cultural and political *over time*, and seek to highlight in this book what historical sociology adds to a debate previously dominated by political economy, in its focus on the ripples in our now-time of past events or relations. The leading economist of inequality Sir Tony Atkinson suggested in 2015 that:

> the eradication of poverty in rich countries requires us to think more ambitiously, beyond the strategies employed to date. We have to view our societies as a whole and to recognise that there are important interconnections: economics tends to assume away or downplay any interdependency between the economic fortunes of individuals (or households). (Atkinson 2015, p 25)

The historical sociological approach embodied in genealogical method enables the 'diffuse theoretical response' advocated by Atkinson.

The structure of the book

Borrowing Tamboukou's (1999) helpfully clear guidance on how to write a genealogy, the book is structured around three questions: 'What have we become?', which is the focus of Part I of the book (the current chapter and Chapter 2); 'How have we become what we are?', which is the focus of Part II (Chapters 3, 4 and 5); and 'What sustains the problem?', which is the focus of Part III (Chapters 6, 7 and 8). The book concludes with Part IV (Chapter 9).

Part II explores forms of government and governmentality of the rich and the poor. Its aim is to reveal the emergence of wealtherty in forms of knowing (Chapter 3), acting (Chapter 4) and being (Chapter 5). I am looking at government (as the conduct of conduct) in the build-up to and key moments in the workhouse movement, and the build up to and key moments in the debate on the first income tax, and then in contemporary policy making in the first two decades of the 21st century. The historical moments broadly coincide (1790s–1830s) and they allow me to make the case that political and social norms shaping the ways of governing richer and poorer people gain a new focus at this time, and reveal stark polarities and orientations. Chapter 3 looks at how ways of coming to know (censuses, mapping and political numbers), and knowledge about the rich and the poor have evolved over time. It considers the ways in which we historically decided and agreed upon who fell into each group and how the idea of 'crisis' functioned as a management tool. Chapter 4 looks at techniques of government for richer and poorer people. This includes hunger, space, mobility and work as ways of 'conducting conduct' in contemporary policy making and in the past. I include a consideration of the visual field of inequality produced in the workhouse – through the segregation between groups of poor people (specifically men and women), and between the inmates and staff, and the staff and the governors. Chapter 5 looks at ways of self-making and subjectivation, and the identities available to richer and poorer people over time through their engagement with the institutions of the state.

In Part III I move on to exploring how the problem of *wealtherty* is sustained in our now-time. Its aim is to reveal the active force of wealtherty in our now and some of its means of production and reproduction. Chapter 6 looks at the capture of knowledge-making processes by economic elites, exemplifying Robeyns' 'bleed' between financial and political power and the ability to convert 'the power of capitalists into a feasibility constraint for democratic policy making' (Robeyns 2017b, p 8). I use the Centre for Social Justice (CSJ) as a case study. The CSJ made a decisive intervention in 2006/2007 to effect a shift in degree if not in type in the Conservative Party's approach to the management of the poor through welfare policy, providing the ideological rationale for the ratcheting of punitivism, along with a blueprint for its implementation (Universal Credit). A secondary effect of this work to promote a low welfare budget social justice agenda exculpated corporations and the wealthy from any responsibility for poverty. Chapter 7 thinks about the contemporary use of space and the visual field as a form of government. It considers the visual identity and the physical spaces of wealth and poverty, and the ways in which bodies are managed in space through the design of buildings (Jobcentre Plus offices or zoned flats with 'poor doors'). I introduce some work by critical photographers who are challenging the narrow visual field of wealth that currently characterises media and campaigning discourse (Vaughan and Kerr forthcoming). Chapter 8 looks at the ways in which wealtherty is sustained through the operation of wealthed privilege. Using the idea of epistemic injustice (Fricker 2007) to decode power relationships between richer people and the state, and poorer people and the state, I look at how wealtherty is legitimated through unequal participation in communicative practices in Her Majesty's Revenue and Customs (HMRC) Wealthy Unit's Wealth External Forum (WEF) and the Work and Pensions 2018 Committee Inquiry into Universal Credit Roll Out and Childcare (WPC 2018a, 2018b). Finally, in Chapter 9 I return to and flesh out the manifesto I summarised at the start of the book. I present it as a set of ideas to help us find a 'way out' of the state we are in.

2

The state of wealth and the state and wealth

This chapter begins with two stories – that of Madiyar Ablyazov (a Tier 1 'golden' visa recipient) and 'Ms J' (an anonymous testifier at the 2019 Work and Pensions Committee Inquiry into Universal Credit and Survival Sex). Madiyar Ablyazov was born in Kazakhstan in 1992 to kleptocrat Mukhtar Ablyazov, who was found guilty in 2012 of 'committing fraud on an epic scale' through embezzling £7.25 billion+ from the bank he once chaired (Bland 2018, pp 1–2). In 2002, at the age of ten, Madiyar was sent by his father to live with family in London in one his father's four London properties in order to access private education there. At the same time that charges of 'huge and systematic fraud' were being levelled and ultimately upheld against him in Kazakhstan, Mukhtar Ablyazov decided to buy a Tier 1 – or 'golden' – visa for Madiyar. The golden visa scheme, which was in place between 2008 (converting from the 'residency through investment's scheme set up in 1994) and 2022, in effect sold residency for money: for a £2 million investment in UK bonds or shares through a bank, applicants became eligible for indefinite leave to remain, and full citizenship after five years. For £5 million, they could settle after three years, and for £10 million, they could settle after just two years (Pegg 2017). In order to qualify, one simply needed money. Between 2007 and 2015, no checks were made on the origin of money flowing into the UK through this scheme. Observers contend that the up to £3 billion that came into the UK under this scheme in this so-called 'blind faith' period potentially implicates the UK government in laundering money for politically exposed people (PEPs) and other so-called high-net-worth individuals (HNWIs). The 'Russia Report', which was published in 2020 by the parliamentary Intelligence and Security Committee, warned that 'the exploitation of the UK's investor visa scheme' was 'the key to London's appeal' for Russian oligarchs and their money (Geoghegan 2024). The behaviours of the rich were not scrutinised: no money laundering checks were undertaken and recipients did not need a UK bank account. Mukhtar Ablyazov was able to deploy his extreme wealth to achieve some of the high-value benefits captured in Beckert's *capacities* (2023, p 5) for his son: security; opportunities (in this case the purchase of education and citizenship); and social status. These were delivered through deploying the last of Beckert's capacities: the exercise of personal, economic and political power.

At the point that Madiyar Ablyazov was admitted (2009), his father was known by the UK government to be corrupt. In September 2013, Madiyar received indefinite leave to remain in the UK, despite his father having had £3 billion in judgments passed against him in the British courts and having fled the country after being found to have acted with 'cynicism, opportunism, and deviousness' and to be guilty of 'lying under cross-examination' (Bland 2018., p 3). This case is not anomalous. Coverage in early March 2018 in the UK press describes the purchase by Russian oligarch Oleg Deripaska (alleged conduit between Putin's team and the 2016 Trump campaign) of Cypriot citizenship (Farolfi et al 2018). In June 2018, fellow Russian oligarch and owner of Chelsea football club Roman Abramovich had his UK visa status queried, but in order to get around residency issues, secured Israeli citizenship, which allowed him to remain in London. Money (dirty or clean) buys wealthy individuals citizenship, and with it seamless, frictionless and transnational mobility. This exemplifies the ways in which rich people 'enjoy special benefits and advantages of a private sort' (Scott 1994, p 152). Citizenship brings with it few of the responsibilities imposed on citizens at the other end of the wealth spectrum, to which I will now turn.

Just as Madiyar Ablyazov represents a departure from the normal lifestyle of the citizen (Scott 1994) at the top of the wealth scale, the witnesses providing testimony to the Work and Pensions Committee Inquiry into Universal Credit Roll Out and Survival Sex in 2018–2019 (WPC 2019a, 2019b) represent a 'departure from the normal lifestyle of the citizen at the other end. Survival sex is 'when people – overwhelmingly, but not exclusively, women – have to turn to sex work to meet their basic survival needs, including money, food and shelter' (WPC 2019c, p 3). As part of the inquiry, written evidence was provided by NGOs working with women who had felt pressured into exchanging sex for money or goods specifically as a result of their transfer from Jobseekers Allowance to Universal Credit. A welfare rights advisor for a housing association in London provided testimony from three of her clients. Most of the testimonies showed that the mandatory waiting period that came into force with Universal Credit – the minimum five-week period between making a claim and a person receiving money – drove women already struggling to make ends meet into measures they felt were degrading and desperate (WPC 2019c, p 52). One NGO attested to that fact that the waiting period can be 'a catastrophe for those *without savings and a support system, such as family* willing or able to provide a temporary loan or emergency accommodation' (WPC 2019b, UCX0014, emphasis added). Claimants of Universal Credit have less than £16,000 in savings and most have much less. These women had none. They continue: 'Those on low income and/or zero-hour contracts prior to claiming Universal Credit or other benefits, these claimants may have no savings, or may already be in debt' (WPC 2019b, UCX0014). Here is Ms J, who I have quoted at length. There were multiple, very similar, stories like this shared with the Committee:

> So, I had no money for almost two months, and when I got paid it was wrong. Well I couldn't hold out any longer, I had to pay the gas and electric, and I was behind with the Council Tax, and that's with the benefit covering some of it. I paid them all to get them off my back, and that was it. Skint. Foodbank vouchers for another month, and they don't like giving them out either. "You must manage your money better" I felt like screaming WHAT MONEY? HOW DO YOU MANAGE WHEN YOU HAVENT GOT ANY!
>
> 'I just couldn't see a way out. I turned to shoplifting to feed the kids. I was bricking it [frightened] as I'd never done it before, and kept thinking they'd put the kids in care. Anyway, I got caught in the [named local corner shop] and I broke down. The manager said if I gave him [oral sex] he'd let me off. What could I do? ... Anyway, he said afterwards that if I did the same next week he'd let me have forty quids' worth of stock [forty pounds]. It seemed like a fortune ... in the end, I held out for two weeks. I got my Credit money, and again it was short, and again it was gone on bills before I'd even thought of food. So, I left the baby with next door and went down to the shop. I felt ashamed.
>
> It's been like that for months now. He knows I can't get through the month, I know I can't get through the month. I try everything I can to cut back to the bone on spending. I just want one month when I don't have to do this. Just one month when I can hold my head high. (WPC 2019a, p 52)

Women already not engaging with statutory services, often with no ID or bank account and no permanent address, attested to finding the process of claiming more dehumanising than sex work (WPC 2019b, UCX0010). The same witness also says that in her interactions with the Department for Work and Pensions (DWP), she felt like she was 'treated like a criminal for daring to ask for my legal right to financial support' (WPC 2019b, UCX0010). Ms J had no access to ordinary wealth to allow her to achieve housing security or to make active choices about work. Her access to the attributes of 'a good life', whether defined in Ruskin's 19th-century moral economist terms (Ruskin 2010 [1862]), or the IPPR's 21st-century 'prosperity' terms (Dibb et al 2021), was curtailed absolutely.

The cases of Madiyar Ablyazov and the witnesses cited earlier represent the intersection of individuals at different points of the wealth spectrum, with the rules and institutions of the state. The contrast between them highlights the differences between the state's disciplinary and wider government endeavours towards differently wealthed individuals.[1] They show what a person can do or be in the more or less propitious environment furnished for them through the regulatory and policy environment of the state. The women have no savings, no security, no family or friends and no wider network with resources on which to draw, which leaves them unable to achieve basic security. Further, they are effectively criminalised at a systemic level: Professor Philip Alston, the then UN Special Rapporteur on extreme poverty and human rights, noted that in the very mechanisms of the *digital by default* system: 'The presumption of innocence is turned on its head when everyone applying for a benefit is screened for potential wrongdoing in a system of total surveillance' (Alston 2018, p 11). Madiyar's citizenship, housing and elite education was secured by his father's (dirty) money, not Madiyar's hard work. As Sayer (2015) states, the economy is not merely a machine that sometimes breaks down, but is a 'complex set of relationships between people' (Sayer 2015, p 9). What does the set of relationships between Madiyar and the state, and Ms J and the state tell us about the relationships between people which make up our economy?

In this largely descriptive chapter I aim to do three substantive things. First, in the section headed 'The state of wealth', I will elaborate on the details provided in Chapter 1 in terms of how much wealth there is and who owns it, and I will identify some key trends relevant to building the concept of wealtherty. This is a sketch, not a fully drawn picture, and I refer readers who are interested in the detail to the excellent literature on trends and distributions.[2] In the section headed 'The state and wealth', I will then consider wealth and the wealthy as a focus of government (conduct of conduct). Finally, I will introduce the idea of capability inequality in order to link pecuniary definitions of wealth to phenomenological ones (that is, to start to think about how we describe and analyse the relationship between the statistical distributions and the lived experience of wealth inequality).

The state of wealth

The World Inequality Lab's 2022 report shows that the share of the bottom 50 per cent in total global *wealth* is 2 per cent and the share of the top 10 per cent is 76 per cent. The report warns that 'since wealth is a major source of future economic gains, and increasingly, of power and influence, this presages further increases in inequality' (WIR 2022, p 3): of the total global increment in wealth between 1995 and 2021, the top 1 per cent captured 38 per cent of it, and the bottom 50 per cent only captured 2 per cent (WIR 2022, p 3). In the UK, wealth inequality is high but *relatively stable*. The data for the UK reveal a decline in the wealth share of the top 10 per cent between the early 1900s when they held above 90 per cent of the total, and 1980.

Since then, 'the declining trend has been reversed' (WIR 2022, p 224). In the 2022 report, the bottom 50 per cent was revealed to own 4.6 per cent of household wealth and the top 10 per cent 57.1 per cent of it. The top 1 per cent *alone* holds 21.3 per cent of national wealth. Data from the UK Wealth and Assets Survey[3] show that total household wealth in Great Britain rose significantly between 2008 and 2020 from £10.4 trillion to £14.6 trillion, but these wealth gains 'accrued mostly to families *that already held financial assets*' (Advani et al 2020b, p 398, based on WAS data for 2016–2018, emphasis added). So although wealth inequality has remained stable over the past 14 years as measured by the Gini coefficient, the rapid growth of overall wealth has stretched the gaps between deciles which are now almost impossible to recuperate through high income, as I suggested in Chapter 1. As a result, the distribution *feels* more unequal, more unjust and more unfair. This trend is mirrored in income inequality figures, too, where Hills notes that: 'The apparent "stability" in income inequality, at least, over the period is … something of a mirage: the nature and depth of economic inequalities have changed markedly for some groups even if overall levels remained relatively stable' (Hills 2017). This message is also evidenced in the latest poverty figures from the Joseph Rowntree Foundation (JRF) (2024), which observes similar 'high but stable' levels of poverty, allied with a deepening of this poverty and empirical evidence of increasing uptake of emergency-type destitution provision (for example, foodbanks). This highlights the need for a phenomenological approach to wealth, poverty and inequality in order to better understand the lived experience in each case, and the reasons why an experiential worsening might not be reflected in economistic measurements like the Gini coefficient (Savage 2021; Hecht et al 2022).

Richer and poorer people hold different kinds of wealth. Median household net wealth in the UK increased by 20 per cent between July 2008 and March 2020 (after adjusting for inflation), and currently stands at £302,500. The wealth of the richest 1 per cent is more than £3.6 million. The wealth of the least wealthy 10 per cent is £15,400 or less. At least half of this latter group only hold physical wealth (with a mean value of £8,000). Almost half held more financial debt than they did financial assets. Physical wealth is the main wealth component for the bottom 30 per cent. For deciles 4–7, property wealth is the largest component. For those at the top, pension wealth is the largest component. For most households, net financial wealth is the smallest component of total wealth, but at the top, it is far more prominent. Similarly, in terms of capital gains: 'More than half (52.2%) of all taxable gains in 2020 went to just 5,000 people, who received an average of over £6.8m per person in gains' (Summers 2024). Beckett (2023) suggests that these different types of holdings enable different functionings: financial wealth enables you to opt out of the labour market, for example, and to live off the interest from investments and savings in a way that physical wealth doesn't, while, as the example of Ms J shows, holding *no* wealth means you are unable to achieve even basic security.

Wealth is unevenly spread between regions. For example, capital gains are 'strongly concentrated in southern England, with more gains in the parliamentary constituency of Kensington *than in all of Wales*. One neighbourhood of Kensington, comprising just 6,400 people, had more gains than three major cities combined: Liverpool, Manchester and Newcastle' (Summers 2022, emphasis added). Overall median wealth in the Southeast is £504,300 (an increase of 43 per cent since 2006); the median in the Northeast is £168,5000 (Summers 2024, p 3). The difference in median individual wealth between the Southeast (£263,000) and Northeast (£79,000) more than doubled between July 2010–June 2012 and April 2018–March 2020 (ONS 2022a). Coupled with high regional differences in income inequality (the average household income in Richmond upon Thames was £42,000 per year in 2021, while in Nottingham it was £13,000 per year) and health inequality (in Richmond, someone can expect to live 70 years without a major illness, while in Nottingham, this figure is 56 years [Thomas et al 2022, p 14]), low wealth holdings in lower-income households further reduces and regionally patterns the ability to withstand economic hardship and crisis (energy price rises, escalating private rents, cost of living increases and low wages).

Wealth is unevenly spread between groups. Men hold 40 per cent more wealth than women on average (Advani and Tarrant 2022). For men, the main source of wealth is private pension (an *individual* source of wealth), while for women, over 50 per cent of their wealth comes from property and physical wealth (which is typically shared with other household members). Men have an average private pension wealth of £83,879 more than women – a gap of 90 per cent (Women's Budget Group 2023). White British households have £10 for every £1 of wealth that a Black African or Bangladeshi household has (Khan 2020 – however, the racial wealth divide is nuanced, with Indian households' holdings being more similar to White households); 11 per cent of individuals in the Indian ethnic group and around 15 per cent of White British and Pakistani ethnic groups are in net debt, compared to 31 per cent, 38 per cent and 44 per cent of people in the Black Caribbean, Bangladeshi and Black African groups respectively (Karagiannaki 2023, p 4). It starts to become clearer why, even when economic inequality as a national measure is high but *stable*, there is a sense of injustice: inequality as experienced by individuals within the same macroeconomic context is patterned by enduring systematic prejudice.

The state and wealth

I want to preface this section by drawing attention to two recent sociological problematisations. The first is Bhambra's problematisation of the definition of the nation state. She describes the British state in the 18th century as 'an imperial state with a national project at its heart. The imperial state was constituted, in part, through "relations of extraction" while the national project comes into being through "relations of redistribution", or welfare' (Bhambra 2021a, p 6): the NHS that we hold dear and to which UK citizens enjoy free access, for example, was funded by taxation derived from colonies whose inhabitants didn't enjoy and often continue not to enjoy these health privileges. She argues that this asymmetry continues to shape issues of distribution and welfare: the asymmetrical state which extracts from some populations and distributes to others is manifestly at work in the ways in which wealth is accumulated and distributed, producing the uneven (regional, racialised, gendered and classed) geography of wealth described previously. It constitutes what Koram calls the contemporary 'aftermath' of empire (Koram 2022, p 18), and analysis like that by Mies (2014) and Federici (2000) might see as the contemporary repertoires of patriarchy. Savage (2021) also engages with a problematising of the state in the context of wealth inequality, drawing attention to its declining organisational and economic power compared to the new emergent imperial blocs, and questioning its continued use as a unit of analysis and comparison. So where data tracks (ordinalises, ranks) nations, wealth effects are experienced across a range of additional/alternative unitary scales (personal, visceral and imperial). Comparative quantitative national data miss many of these effects. When I talk about the state in this book, I would like readers to keep this problematisation in mind.

Second, and relatedly, the relevance of wealth inequality in contexts of higher or lower collective wealth resources and provisions changes in response to the institutional context and the regulatory environment (Beckert 2023). Even high levels of wealth inequality can be considered 'acceptable and less controversial in a society that is more collectively oriented' because in these contexts, security is provided through public means (social welfare, education and healthcare, for example). This has the effect of making existing wealth inequalities less harmful to individual life chances (Beckert 2023, p 18). Where Beckert explored this phenomenon between two states (the US and Germany) with similar wealth inequality profiles, the same tendency is also suggested by the wealth inequality data for the UK that I looked at in the section entitled 'The state of wealth': the relevance of wealth inequality inflects differently between regions, men and women, and racial and ethnic groups.

What do we know about wealth and the wealthy (and specifically what and how the state knows about it/them). We count what matters ... and what we can see. The state has evolved sophisticated tools (administrative, statistical and technical) for understanding the population and for arriving at problem articulations that shape legislative and policy agendas. It stands to reason that if it *doesn't* know about groups or dynamics or accumulations within the population, then this is likely to be, in part at least, a result of apathy rather than simply a lack of capability. As Bacchi (2013) suggests, when trying to deduce what the state thinks is problematic (and therefore in need of change) we should start from the premise that this will be revealed in its proposals and policies and by 'what is left unproblematic'. It is notable, then, that notwithstanding the forensic level of detail known about the lives of the poor from the early 19th century onwards, we still know relatively little about the lives of the rich and their assets. Further, the UK state only started to 'count' private wealth in a comprehensive way in 2006 through the Office for National Statistics (ONS) Wealth and Assets Survey (WAS) (ONS WAS); at a global level, the World Inequality Lab produced its first report in 2018; Piketty's 2013 'data assemblage' *Capital* blazed trails. This is all staggeringly recent. So although there are long-run forms of administrative data (for example, capital gains tax records), the specific and aggregate measurement of private household wealth is a recent form of government (as the conduct of conduct) in the UK and elsewhere: the state has not considered that it needs to know about private wealth. The second key point here is that this new data and resultant analyses of the data are hampered by methodological challenges (for example, the low reliability of survey data), by under-reporting referenced earlier (Advani and Summers 2022, p 5) and by active attempts to conceal (legally and illegally). The effect is that total wealth tends to be underestimated within official data.

I now want to consider the government of wealth by the state. The political right tends to avoid taxing wealth if it can, and wealth inequality and wealth taxation struggle to gain salience as a policy issue on the left too (Fastenrath et al 2022). This has led to a failure to fairly tax wealth. This means that while wealth has grown significantly (as demonstrated at the start of this chapter), we don't generate more revenue from it; taxation has not kept pace with this rapid rate of growth. There is still no single wealth tax in the UK and no prospect of one anytime soon (Crerar 2023). Existing taxes on specific forms of wealth in the UK (council tax, capital gains, stamp duty and inheritance tax) provide 'very little revenue ... compared with income tax, national insurance contributions and VAT' (Rowlingson 2023, p 166). The lack of political salience for wealth inequality is in equal parts puzzling and frustrating: If we don't know how much wealth there is at the top (as the data above attest is the case), then how can we know that its scale alone is *not* a social and political problem? If we don't know how much successive governments spend providing tax relief to the already wealthy (Baker and Murphy 2020; Sinfield 2023), then how can we know who is (fiscally) welfare dependent and who isn't? And how can we know whether redistribution is morally or politically desirable or feasible? If taxes 'define the inequalities we accept and those that we collectively seek to redress' (Martin et al 2009, p 1), then we seem to be saying that wealth inequality – in its stark regional, racialised and gendered form – is one of the inequalities that we accept. It is not one that we 'collectively seek to redress'.

One of the effects of this failure to tackle the state of wealth can be seen in the slide of public wealth (the sum of all financial and nonfinancial assets net of debts held by governments) into private hands. Public wealth has declined dramatically, dropping from 60 per cent of national income in 1970 to *minus 106 per cent* of national income in 2020 in the UK (WIR 2022, p 14 and Figure 33). The effect is that nations have become richer, but governments have become poorer, with obvious impacts on the measures that states can take to address inequality (WIR 2022, p 15). Important work on measuring how states with lower GDP achieve better results than states with higher GDP in terms of the progressive fulfilment of a range of social and economic rights is interesting in this regard (for example, Fukuda-Parr et al 2009). Nevertheless, the sliding of public wealth into private hands is one of the defining macroeconomic trends identified consistently in the WIL data since 2018. It gives practical legitimacy to the claims that states have little to spend on public services, while also making it clear that this is an effect of a political choice.

The final point I want to make in this section on the state and wealth is that wealth 'absorbs past inequalities', *but current policies keep them in place*. I'm going to illustrate this here by going into more detail about gender and then race/empire. It has already been noted earlier that men hold more wealth than women: women own approximately 40 per cent of the UK's wealth. Only 58 per cent of women have a private pension in the UK compared to 68 per cent of men, and men's pension pots are larger (due in most part to the sex pay gap) by a factor of five (Palmer 2020, p 3); women also have lower levels of savings. In being disproportionately weighted to benefit people with large incomes and larger amounts of wealth, the tax system disproportionately benefits men. The Women's Budget Group notes that '80 per cent of those gaining from Chancellor Kwarteng's removal of the top 45 per cent rate of income tax, from April 2023, would have been men, had it not been scrapped' (Himmelweit 2023, p 184, fn 2). These sex-based inequality-enhancing policies are design features of the system, not bugs within it: Himmelweit cites analyses provided for the then Shadow Equalities Minister by the House of Commons (HoC) library, which showed that 'by 2020 women would have paid for 86% of the net changes since 2010; while benefit cuts and freezes impacted particularly on women, simultaneous tax cuts, which were substantial despite austerity, went disproportionately to men' (Himmelweit 2023, p 186). Within these inequalities, further injustices are nested: in the poorest third of households, 'Asian women were projected to lose on average 19%, black women 14% and white women just over 10% of their income due to changes in taxes and benefits in the ten years to 2020'

(Women's Budget Group and Runnymede Trust, 2017, cited in Himmelweit 2023, p 189). Meanwhile, David Cameron called Gender Equality Impact Assessments 'bureaucratic nonsense' in 2012 (Himmelweit 2023, p 185). Married women only gained independent taxation status in 1990; up to that point, married couples were taxed jointly, with the woman's income added to that of her husband and 'taxed as if it was his, with all the tax allowances given to him' (Himmelweit 2023, p 182). Joint taxation disincentivised women from working, thereby cementing traditional gender roles. Crucially for the wider point I'm making in this book related to the link between wealth and certain privileged capabilities like privacy (which I will return to at length shortly), before 1990, married women 'were denied the right to keep their financial affairs private from their husband, while no such disclosure was required from the husband' (Himmelweit 2023, p 182). Anywhere where privacy is afforded differentially, inequality will flourish. Economic inequality is not neutral in its effects; it reinforces regressive (gender, and other group) norms which have material and mutually reinforcing *economic* effects.

These gendered effects are not unique to the UK. Bessière and Gollac (2023) use data from the French Wealth Survey to show that the gender wealth gap is widening in favour of men in France: from 9 per cent in 1998 to 16 per cent in 2015. Men own more capital than women regardless of the form (housing, land, financial or professional assets) (Bessière and Gollac 2023, p 9), and the agency of women in relation to household finances is highly correlated to how wealthy families are: in poor families, 'money problems are women's problems', whereas in wealthy families, 'looking after capital is a man's prerogative (Bessière and Gollac 2023, p 4). Importantly, they observe the role of the legal profession in helping to reproduce class and gender inequalities, which 'emerge in families' but are then 'legitimised and formalised by the professionals charged with supporting heirs, separating people, and implementing the law' (Bessière and Gollac 2023, p xiii).

The ways of counting and coming to know (which I will address in Chapter 3) as much as the distributions themselves are implicated in sustaining these sex-based inequalities. The World Inequality Lab, for example, describes how for 'most statistics presented here, we split income and wealth equally across married couples' (WIR 2022, p 26). In a footnote, it notes that: 'Naturally, not all couples share economic resources equally but data on intra-family resource sharing is scarce' (WIR 2022, p 51, fn 5). Reasons for the scarceness of data are rarely benign, as I suggested earlier, and most often reflect prevailing political assessments of what (and who) matters. As such, as long as these data gaps continue, they demonstrate what (and who) *continues* not to matter. Regardless of what these contemporary data gaps tell us about *past* governmental priorities, the absence of data disaggregated by sex is problematic from an analysis perspective: as Bennett (2021) suggests, the idea of the 'unitary couple' implicit in UK policy and baked into the original administrative records I will explore in Chapters 3 and 4 cannot fail to conceal the far from unitary reality for most individuals living in couples. And it hides often significant imbalances of capital (economic and epistemic). For the ONS, data are collected from individuals 'but then presented at the level of the household', notwithstanding the fact that '[f]or individuals within couples, legal ownership might differ from control and perceived ownership' (Palmer 2020, p 3). Bessière and Gollac also note that methods make it hard to assess and understand the gender wealth gap because '[a]ssets accumulated by men or women in the same household tend to be conflated by data-collection methods' (Bessière and Gollac 2023, p 9). These data collection methods shape the material shape reality of women's economic and social lives.

Old legal codes, then, produce new inequality, which is also evident in the context of race and empire. The identity of 'domicile' was a feature of Pitt's 1798 income tax, which I will look at in more detail in Part II of this book. It was put in place to protect income generated in colonial territories from tax in the UK (unless the income was remitted to the UK). Although the scope was reduced in 1906 by Lloyd George, it remained in place and, as the work by Savage (2023) and Koram (2022) shows, is routinely used by the wealthy as a means of reducing their domestic tax responsibility to the extent. Non-doms are entitled to claim special tax treatment, including not paying tax on their investments by locating them offshore. Non-doms in the UK receive 'at least £10 billion offshore income and capital gains each year, which they are not required to report to HMRC or pay tax on in the UK' (Summers 2022). So although an innovation of the late 18th-century 'heyday of empire', it continues to 'actively shape inequality in the 21st century' (Advani et al 2022, p 35). This is a current policy. It holds historic inequalities in place.[4]

Things that matter but which can't be counted

In the final section of this chapter, I want to return to Madiyar and Ms J via the Capabilities Approach. The preceding sections on the state of wealth and the state and wealth showed that people in the same economic context tend to have different experiences of inequality based on variables such as region, race and sex. Burchardt and Hick (2017) refer to inequalities in terms of what a person is able to do and be as 'capability inequalities'. Wealth has corollary effects on security of housing, food, education and wellbeing, for example. The data described briefly earlier in this chapter are useful in informing us about inequality in terms of money or asset ownership. They tell us that people have more or less. They show – with increasing levels of nuance and accuracy – what the specific dimensions of wealth are and what the *degree* of inequality is. They tell us which groups and which regions own more or less.

The observations in the second section of this chapter show us that the state's role in governing wealth and the wealthy can cause historical inequalities to endure. The Capabilities Approach (CA) offers a rationale for why this inequality *matters* and how it is experienced by different people. It allows us to understand 'difference in kind not just degree' (Burchardt and Hick 2017, p 8). Although traditionally used in so-called 'development contexts', increasingly scholars are exploring its utility for understanding capability inequalities in rich nations by, for example, focusing on the 'capability ceiling' as opposed to a capability threshold – the idea being that there might justifiably be 'limitations on the choice to pursue certain individual actions ... when those actions can have or significantly contribute to the effect of undermining another person's minimum threshold of capability provision and protection' (Holland, cited in Robeyns 2017b, p 4). I am going to introduce two features of the CA approach relevant to the government of *wealtherty*: (i) the idea of doings and beings and multidimensional ends; and (ii) capabilities that the rich have that can cause harm to others and, in particular, those capabilities that inhibit democratic process.

Economic capital secures other forms of capital (including cultural and political capital) which are not available to those without it. In her 2011 explication of the CA, Nussbaum begins with the extended story of Vasanti, a 'small woman in her early 30s who lives in Ahmedabad' (Nussbaum 2011, pp 3–14). We follow Vasanti's story across various dimensions of her life – nutrition, property and inheritance, family, work, marriage, domestic violence, education and finance – arriving at a highly complex, multifaceted understanding of a person, like others the world over, 'struggling for lives that are worthy of their human dignity' (Nussbaum 2011, p 1). The story is used to illustrate the inadequacy of national economic growth indicators (such as GDP) to account for the complexity of the lives people lead, and the very different experiences of lives led *within the same economic contexts*. The story allows us to see that in trying to understand the experiences of marginalised groups, it is useful to know not just what economic resources they have, but also what they are able to do and be: what constrains or enables their flourishing. Vasanti's story reveals forms of experience and knowledge that are neither recoverable nor inscribable through statistics and, in particular, it makes visible what *else* we need to know about a person in order to understand why unequal distribution of *economic* resource matters (and why it matters differently for different people). It counters what theorists call 'resourcist' approaches to inequality by shifting from questions about what people *have* to what they can *do and be* (Burchardt and Hick 2017, p 12). Its questions are about 'quality of life and basic justice' (Nussbaum 2011, p 20), and this shift from a focus on means (how much a person has) to a focus on ends (what a person can do) necessarily generates complexity: ends are inherently multidimensional – health outcomes, educational attainment, political participation and so on. It also demands different metrics. In framing Vasanti's story, Nussbaum asks 'what theoretical approach could direct attention to the most significant features of Vasanti's situation, promote an adequate analysis of it, and make pertinent recommendations for action?' (Nussbaum 2011, p 3). Nussbaum articulates what she considers to be the ten basic capabilities – those necessary to a life worthy of human dignity. She identifies these as: life; bodily health; bodily integrity; senses, imagination and thought; emotions; practical reason; affiliation; other species; play; and control over one's environment (Nussbaum 2011, p 35). These basic capabilities are a useful way for us to think about the constitutive elements required for a fully human life and how we might better recognise them.

The second area in which CA provides a useful perspective on the knowledge needed to understand the operation of *wealtherty* is in understanding how wealth can be translated into political power, or how wealth secures access to the specific and restricted capability of political influence. This can take the form variously of buying votes, gatekeeping, influencing opinion and the 'workings of money as an independent political power' (Robeyns 2017b, p 7). This 'spillover' (Walzer 1983 in Robeyns 2018, p 256) 'turns the power of capitalists into a feasibility constraint for democratic policy making' (Robeyns 2018, p 256). Simply put, those with economic resource can buy other forms of capital that those without these economic resources cannot. Shifting the focus to *ends* can reveal important functions of privilege or advantage in the availability of a wider set of *socially transformational* capabilities (for example, ownership of media) that are the preserve of specific groups of people who own wealth and that can cause harm to others. In so doing, the capability lens 'offer[s] the basis for an analysis of power that goes beyond purely economic means' (Burchardt and Hick 2017, p 3). The CA can reveal inequalities *in kind* that help us to understand '*concentrations of advantage* … across dimensions as an aspect of inequality' (Burchardt and Hick 2017, p 9, emphasis added). It can show us how the exercise of freedoms at the top can inhibit the exercise of freedoms at the bottom. This focus on *capabilities that harm other people* is particularly important for the case I am making in this book about the state of *wealtherty*.

One particular group of capabilities that causes harm to others – those of secrecy and privacy – are of particular interest. They have the amplification effects on *power* that Pistor's legal code does on *capital itself*. The right to privacy around financial affairs is a function of the 'code of capital' (Pistor 2019; however, see also historical work like Beckett 1985; and O'Brien 1988) and is prohibited to those without wealth, who are instead subject to intrusive levels of scrutiny and surveillance (Alston 2018 and Figure 1.1). Warren and Laslett (1977) note that both secrecy and privacy 'involve reduced observability and an increased potential to deny access to others' (p 44). The facilitation of (or tolerance of) secrecy and privacy for the rich 'has allowed them to "step out of"' the laws and expectations of the countries in which they operate, and to live a life which constitutes a deviation from the norm (Dean and Melrose 1998). Secrecy is about hiding. In contemporary tax discourse it equates with evasion and is illegal. Privacy is about being unobserved. In contemporary tax discourse this equates to avoidance and is legal through various forms of more or less *aggressive tax planning* (ATP). The role and objective of the new cadre of professionalised wealth managers described by Harrington is to hide wealth and ensure that it is not counted, to make it private or secret and to ensure that it does not fall under 'the depredations of "confiscatory" states' (Harrington 2016, p 12). Pistor concurs that 'shielding assets from taxes is one of the most sought-after coding strategies that asset holders covet' (2019, p 3). Whole technologies of government – Family Offices – have proliferated to ensure the intergenerational stability of wealth dynasties in part by often legal but definitely socioethically problematic wealth hiding or secrecy (Glucksberg and Burrows 2016). At a macroeconomic level, Koram notes that part of the aftermath of empire resides in the legal reinforcement of the private realm: the legal codes and economic structures 'put in place to facilitate the imperial system of wealth transfer … still drive our world' (Koram 2022, p 18). This private realm 'operates away from the cameras, a world of property and contracts, of debt and capital' (Koram 2022, p 18). In the context of wealtherty, privacy works to undermine democracy. It matters that some people can operate privately and others can't. It is important that so much energy goes into producing legal code to enable this privacy for rich people and companies. It matters on at least two fronts. First of all, it means we don't know how much wealth the richest people have, so we can't accurately assess the scale of inequality; we can't legitimately know enough to understand the potential revenue that could be achieved through specific new forms of taxation: the privacy around wealth shields the rich from the scrutiny ruthlessly imposed on the resources of poorer people. Second, the legitimation of secrecy and privacy is a manifestation of 'ignorance' as a governmental disposition towards wealth and, contrasted with the relentless scrutiny of the resources and behaviours of the poor, is evidence of unjust 'centaur' orientations.

Introduction to Parts II and III

Parts II and III of this book use what I am calling 'sites of analysis'. This refers to four policy moments or mechanisms that I focus on to make the case for wealtherty and to illustrate the operation of the governmental dispositions of scrutiny and ignorance that I sketched out in Chapter 1 (Figure 1.1) and which I will now introduce in more detail.

The governmental disposition of scrutiny is based on an overwhelming interest in behaviour across all domains of life: housing; eating; wearing clothes; reproducing; cleaning; and reproduction. Everything is to be considered a site of government. The historical site of analysis that I use to explore the how the disposition of scrutiny operates is the workhouse system (Driver 2004) and the wider Poor Law Amendment Act of 1834 (NPL). The NPL was the first national system of poor law administration. Parishes – historically the unit of management of the poor – were reconfigured into groups, or 'unions'. Each union was to have a workhouse with elected Boards of Guardians and paid official roles (Master, Matron, Cook and Schoolmaster). The system was overseen by a central board of three Poor Law Commissioners (PLCs) based in London and was supported by an inspectorate of Assistant Commissioners. The NPL had two key components: (1) the complete abolition of so-called outdoor relief or 'out-relief' (relief delivered outside the workhouse); and (2) the pursuit of deterrence, which operated through the 'workhouse test' and the principle of less eligibility. The workhouse test was the process whereby an individual's need for relief was 'tested' by making it impossible to secure other than through the deliberately harsh conditions within the workhouse. The principle of less eligibility (first conceived by Bentham more than 40 years earlier) ensured that conditions within the house were 'less eligible' than those of the lowest labourer outside the house. The idea was to make the experience of the house and its regime so 'irksome' that all but the genuinely needy would choose work. Producing irksome conditions became a key task of workhouse staff. Although workhouses were not an innovation of the 1834 Act – they had been built and used as 'houses of correction' in the period of the Old Poor Law (1601–1834) – their formal recoding as a mechanism of deterrence was. The impact of the Act was immediate and financially, at least, hugely successful: poor rates fell to from historic highs and expenditure stabilised. However, the changes to outdoor relief, and the all-encompassing use of the labour test caused devastation to thousands, particularly women, over the course of the 1800s (Englander 1998). The volume and emotional intensity of letters to the PLC (TNA Source A, MH12) bemoaning their fate is testament to the fact that the poor themselves, either through a diminution of the value of their out-relief or through the sense that they were being forced into the house, disliked the law immensely and were acutely aware that it was a harshening of their government.

Alston (2018) found parallels between the workhouse system and Universal Credit, which is the contemporary site of analysis of the disposition of scrutiny. In setting out its programme in 2010, the Coalition government established its approach to jobs and welfare in the following terms: 'The Government believes that we need to encourage responsibility and fairness in the welfare system. That means providing help for those who cannot work, training and targeted support for those looking for work, but sanctions for those who turn down reasonable offers of work or training.'

(HM Government 2010). This was in effect a restatement of the workhouse test and the principle of less eligibility from the 1834 Poor Law Reform Act, and became embodied in the Welfare Reform Act 2012. In April 2013, as part of the implementation of this Act, Universal Credit replaced six existing payments for working-age people (Income Support, Income-Based Jobseeker's Allowance, Income-Related Employment Support Allowance, Housing Benefit, Child Tax Credit and Working Tax Credit) with the linked aims of 'simplifying the system of working age benefits; making work pay; increasing take-up and reducing fraud and error' (DWP, 2010). Universal Credit has a wealth threshold which makes it accessible to those with £16,000 or less in savings. The policy was designed to make the new benefit operate more like work, with payments being made monthly in one combined amount to a nominated 'head of household'. Compliance was to be encouraged through a series of tough sanctions up to and including a full three-year cessation of the combined benefit, through a process of 'ubiquitous conditionality' (Millar and Bennett 2017; Wright and Dwyer 2020, p 333). For the first time, those in work (part-time and/or low pay), the partners of claimants, and those with a range of disabilities were drawn into a harsh conditionality regime, alongside the unemployed. Wright (2016) notes that Universal Credit marked a shift in intensity, not principle: the endorsement of all the mainstream political parties for welfare conditionality meant that Universal Credit received little opposition up to the start of the implementation period (Dwyer 2018; Wright and Dwyer 2020). Universal Credit aimed to encourage people on benefits to start paid work, and those in work to 'progress' through increasing their hours or by making sure work pays more; to make it easier for people to manage the move into work; to simplify the system, making it easier for people to understand, and easier and cheaper for the government to administer; to reduce the number of people who in work but still living in poverty; and to reduce fraud and error.

An analysis by the National Audit Office in 2018 was unable to say whether any savings had been made, and it noted that the DWP had failed to undertake impact evaluations to model the potential negative impact on vulnerable subgroups of claimants. Research by third-sector groups and think tanks (cited in Alston [2018] and submitted as sources to the 2018 Work and Pensions Committee Inquiry into Universal Credit Roll-out [WPC 2018a]) reveal a direct link between the design and implementation of Universal Credit and increases in hardship up to and including destitution (increased foodbank use, an increase in survival sex, and an increase in homelessness and suicide). The 2018 House of Commons Committee of Public Accounts Report into Universal Credit found that the policy was causing 'unacceptable hardship and difficulties for many of the claimants it was designed to help' (PAC 2018, p 3 and pp 12–13). An inquiry into its roll-out in 2018–2019 found that it disproportionately impacted negatively on women – a fact brought into relief through witness testimonies in the Inquiry into Universal Credit and Childcare (WPC 2018a, 2018c), and Universal Credit and Survival Sex (WPC 2019a, 2019b).

The governmental disposition of ignorance is based on a lack of interest, or a more active facilitation of secrecy and active ignorance about inconvenient or illegal behaviours. I am using ignorance here in the sense intended by agnotologists (Proctor and Schiebinger 2008) – to denote forms of not knowing that allow, in my context, certain behaviours of capital and people to remain in the shade. Those subject to it are afforded a realm of privacy and are enabled (actively or passively) to be secretive about their financial affairs and their consumption behaviours. The historical site of analysis for the disposition of ignorance is the 1798/1799 Income Tax Act. At the height of the abolitionist debates around the Poor Law, Prime Minister William Pitt the Younger was attempting to enact the first piece of direct income tax legislation in order to raise money for the French wars in the face of strong opposition. There was widespread resistance from potential taxpayers to being observed and known: such a tax would be 'An inquisition into every man's private circumstances … would be a source of such continual and endless vexation as no people could support' (Adam Smith, cited in Cousins 2018, p 160). Landed and commercial interests thought a tax on income 'constituted unwarranted official intrusion into the private affairs of its contributors' (Cousins 2018, p 162).

The Act ultimately failed to generate the income anticipated by Pitt, a failure attributed in part to a 'mutually beneficial relationship' between 'business and the political class' (businesses raised 'loans for the Treasury whenever the government required them') which ensured that 'business profits or business capital attracted almost no tax' (Cousins 2018, pp 165– 167). This cosiness meant that Pitt ultimately chose a 'tolerant system' which was 'easy to work around and was in effect voluntary'. Taxable income was self-declared; inspectors could not ask to see books; section 96 of the Act allowed commercial parties to be assessed by a commercial commissioner rather than the general commissioner; and returns were secret and anonymous, 'marked only by a number that matched that on the assessment certificate, rendering external checks almost impossible' (Cousins 2018, p 172). Unsurprisingly, the Act failed in part because of the level of tax evasion it enabled on the part of business, and in part because of a determination on the part of those with wealth not to have their private affairs known. I will return to this in Chapter 4.

The contemporary site of analysis for the disposition of ignorance is the government of wealth and the wealthy undertaken through HMRC's WEF. The same discourse which enabled and then sustained the punitive turn in welfare policy in 2010 consolidated and accelerated a facilitative one at the other end of the spectrum: An HMRC-sponsored forum, the WEF was set up by the Labour government following the launch of the High Net Worth Unit (HNWU) in April 2009 and met for the first time in March 2010 shortly before the Coalition government came into power. The team 'deals with the personal tax affairs of the UK's wealthy individuals' – the so-called High Net Worth client group – identified as individuals with investable assets of at least £20 million. Its Terms of Reference characterise it as a 'consultation forum' between HMRC's 'Wealthy' Teams and professional bodies representing 'Wealthy' individuals. At its first meeting, the Chair of the meeting (the head of the HMRC HNWU) explained the main drive for setting up the WEF was 'to provide a focus for discussing, developing and promoting co-operative compliance strategies for dealing with the tax affairs of High Net Worth individuals'. The Chair noted that

> identifying other individuals is complicated by the fact that 'wealth' is difficult to measure from the information available to HMRC through tax returns etc., especially where individuals have low reportable income but high wealth. HNWU therefore envisages that the current customer base of around 5,000 High Net Worth individuals will be fluid to some extent and that further High Net Worth individuals will be identified through both internal research and recommendations from agents. (The National Archives n.d.)

In the minutes from September 2012, a representative from the industry body of wealth managers (the Society of Trust and Estate Practitioners [STEP]) asked to begin 'by mentioning the recent presentation by STEP to [the Chair of HMRC's Wealthy Unit] of the Geoffrey Shindler Award for Outstanding Contribution to the Profession'. He explained that this was in recognition of the value the Chair of HMRC's Wealthy Unit's leadership had brought to the improved relationships between HMRC, wealthy taxpayers and their advisers, and that he had 'set the standard for this approach around the world'. In her eight-year-long immersive ethnography with wealth managers, Harrington notes that STEP is 'active in offshore jurisdictions, where members regularly cooperate with elected officials to draft financial laws' (Harrington 2016, p 54). As noted earlier, STEP's publications acknowledge this aspect of its members' work, framing it as a defence of capitalists against 'the depredations of "confiscatory" states' (Harrington 2016, p 12).

Part II starts to think about how we have become what we are – how the level and texture of inequality described in the *state of wealth* section renews past inequalities. To do so, I explore specific institutions of the state – the thinking behind them, the mechanisms they use, and the identities they presuppose and/or seek to change. I'm seeking to reveal the emergence of governmental dispositions that continue to govern lives like those of Ms J and Madiyar Ablyazov through the long history of differential governmental dispositions of scrutiny towards the poor and ignorance towards the rich in social and fiscal policy making. I suggest that these parallel dispositions have served to naturalise and legitimise discrete legislative and policy approaches from the state to people with different amounts of wealth, and in Part III, I think about what these discrete approaches look like now. In Dean's genealogy *The Constitution of Poverty*, he states his purposes as being to reveal the 'theoretical basis of the statements and treatments of poverty at a particular time and place' (1991, p 7) through looking at the 'complex interlacing of knowledge, policy and practice' (1991, p 25). Parts II and III of this book together try to focus on this 'complex interlacing' of knowledge, policy and practice in the context of *wealtherty* in a temporally and socially extensive way. I look at the ways in which knowledge, policy and practice bring into being and then enshrine a particular relationship between the rich and the state, the poor and the state, and the rich and the poor.

PART II

How have we become what we are?

3

Knowing: how the state came to know richer and poorer people differently

In this chapter I start to address the genealogical question introduced in Chapter 1 – 'How have we become what we are?' – from the perspective of knowledge making and knowledge. How has the state come to know about richer and poorer people and wealth and poverty (the means of knowing) and what has it chosen to know? How have these ways of knowing and forms of knowledge shaped relations between the rich and the poor? What directions has the state chosen *not* to take knowledge in? In my definition of *wealtherty* in Chapter 1, I suggested that current levels of economic and social polarisation are sustained by distinct ways of thinking about poorer and richer people which are then embedded in legal, political and cultural norms and 'code': they are concretised in the way in which government itself is structured (HM Treasury, HMRC, the DWP, social and fiscal policy); and they are made material through the translation of wealth into political privilege (for example, party donations and funding think tanks). I presented these ways of knowing and acting as current manifestations of enduring governmental dispositions of scrutiny and ignorance.

Here, I start by looking at the relationship between the state and the poor. I look at three phases: making the problem; articulating the problem to a crisis; and making the policy 'character'. I then look at the relationship between the rich and the state. I preface this with some observations about political – or 'state'– numbers to illustrate shifts in, or awkward continuity between, the two periods I am looking at, by way of repoliticising state means of knowing (producing) a population.

Political numbers

It is almost impossible in the 21st century to imagine government without statistics and data. They are a primary means of justification for policy: levels of poverty; degrees of compliance; rates of inflation; numbers of immigrants, foodbanks, scroungers and entrepreneurs; the cost of the National Health Service (NHS); percentage of homeowners; and the proportion of income or wealth subject to taxation. Political and public discourse is increasingly saturated with them and we have become sophisticated consumers of them, understanding them as proxies for real things in the world. Numbers and other forms of calculation are tools for establishing authority, and are inscription devices which constitute and naturalise the domains and phenomenon they appear to represent (Rose 1999). Endres, writing in 1985 about early political arithmeticians in the late 17th century, observed that: 'The techniques of measuring, observing and counting *are tied to the use to which data are put* ... Use of data presupposes intentions, purposes, interests, and value judgements on the part of the interpreter' (Endres 1985, p 246, emphasis added). His observation is as true for the use of techniques of measuring by these early political arithmeticians as it is for the ways of measuring today, where 'the interests of those who govern [are] reflected in the very means of counting' and 'Data is constructed in such a way as to support the emergence of social structures that are more "governable"' (Cobham 2020, p 4). Numbers, when used politically, are 'political numbers': 'hundreds of small boats' is either the Henley Regatta or a national crisis.

Political numbers can abstract complex social experiences into proxy statistical indicators (Rose 1999). During this process of abstracting, as I suggested in Chapter 2 when introducing the Capabilities Approach (CA), 'lives can disappear'. Not just parts of lives – the more abstract senses, emotions, imagination and play that Nussbaum (2011) brings under her description of capabilities – but also the lives of whole groups of people: women and people of specific races and ethnicities. What parts of experience and whose experience is captured by political numbers, and what parts of experience and whose experience is not reflects the interests of those who govern: recall the ways introduced in Chapter 2 in which data collection methods hide women's economic agency, for example. As Bacchi proposes, we can deduce from this 'What the problem is represented to be' (2013) and, more broadly, who and what is held to matter. The original political arithmetic of the 17th century was considered to be 'the expression of political understanding in terms of "Number, Weight, and Measure"' (Horwell 2019, pp 45–46). Keeping this sense in mind as we progress of statistics being an expression of political understanding in numerical terms will be useful.

An example of the differentially applied (politicised) means of coming to know can be found in the use of surveying and mapping as a key form of political arithmetic in the service of empire in the 17th century. Mapping functioned as the epistemic phase of enclosure: knowing the lay of the land, its contours and populations was a necessary precursor to its 'theft' or transfer to the gentry or the state. Mapping was recognised as a precursor to expropriation by the mapped, who understood the relationship between knowing, and subduing, exploiting and extracting. The first attempt by England to survey Ireland in the 1650s, for example, led to violent local opposition and the beheading of the surveyor. Nevertheless, the Survey of 1655–1656 was eventually completed, measuring Ireland's shape and size accurately for the first time. The maps facilitated the eventual shift of seven million acres from Catholic to Protestant ownership, neatly demonstrating what Slack calls 'political arithmetic in action' (Slack 2004, p 36) and what Hacking less decorously calls 'the rape of Ireland' (cited in Rose 1999, p 215). Being seen was being known; being known effected an act of submission – consensual or otherwise – to a state whose evolving economic model was fundamentally extractive. This awareness of the link between being measured, mapped and surveyed – that is, known in numbers – triggered similar resistance at the other end of the wealth spectrum, although crucially this ended in concession to the rich rather than their submission (for example, through agreement to uphold customary privacy norms in the design of the 1798 income tax). The wealthy could draw a line which must not be crossed in terms of the intrusion of the state, but this was not to be tolerated on the part of subaltern Others. Although there was no national census in England until 1801, for example, 20 took place in the then North American colonies in the 1700s, largely to facilitate the levying of taxation to fund wars and to provide an understanding of how many men were available to be conscripted (Slack 1988). The application of a new, assessing gaze, and the quantification and translation of space and human behaviours into indicators were applied differently to people and groups of people with different amounts of wealth and power (Figure 1.1 and Table 3.1). This is an early example of the dispositions of scrutiny (in this context enacted through mapping/census) and ignorance (enacted through choosing not to map or scrutinise the financial affairs of the rich). In Table 3.1 I have visualised how these dispositions operate across the domains of knowing (the focus of this

Table 3.1: Dispositions of ignorance and scrutiny across the domains of knowing, governing and being in two contexts (historical and contemporary)

Disposition and population	Context	Way of coming to know	Way of governing	Way of being	Epistemic roles
Ignorance (the wealthy)	1790s/1800s (Income Tax Bill)	Concession; Cooperation; Co-production	Permissive: Acceding; Conceding; Ignoring	Direct	Governor Advisor; Inquirer.
	2000s (HMRC Wealthy External Forum)			Intermediated	
Scrutiny (the poor)	1790s/1800s (Workhouse system)	Abstraction; Calculation; Administration.	Disciplinary: Scrutinising; Demanding; Containing; Starving	Bare	Source of information
	2000s (Universal Credit)			Administrative	

chapter and Chapter 6), governing (the focus of Chapters 4 and 7) and being (the focus of Chapters 5 and 8) in historical and contemporary contexts. This figure can be referred back to as you read the book.

The state and the poor

Let's now add more detail to the function of the disposition of scrutiny in the area of 'coming to know' about poorer populations. The use of political numbers evolves and endures, as we will see in Chapter 6. My focus in this book is on understanding how, in the evolving relationships between the state and the poor as manifest in key social legislation between the 1500s and the 1800s (and particularly in the late 1700s), we came to naturalise a particular way of understanding the poor as dependent. The statistical methods that we now take for granted as underpinning contemporary modes of government (epidemiology, population data, mapping and national statistics) were an innovation of the 1600s, were regarded with scepticism by political economists in the 1700s (Endres 1985, p 246) and didn't become governmental norms until the 1820s and 1830s, when they were more routinely used to define and prioritise new social issues (and/or redefine old ones) and make them governable (Hoppit 1996; Slack 2004). In the later 18th and early 19th centuries, new forms of administrative accounting played a key role in individuating dependency (pauperism) from a broader conception of 'poverty' as the focus of policy reform, shepherding in the New Poor Law (NPL) in 1834. Particular ways of thinking made the new legislation 'intelligible'; other ways of thinking had to 'give way'. Prevailing understanding of the role of the poor in society up to the late 1700s viewed a large poor population as the engine of national wealth. The political use of numbers and the use of political numbers helped create the conditions under which it became possible to reshape the social problematisation and to consider new knowledge about the poor to be 'true'.

I'm going to give a bit of background here about the Old Poor Law (OPL) so that it is clearer what the nature of the shift in 1834 was, and so that the links between the ways of thinking that enabled the transition *then* and the ways of thinking that sustain wealtherty in our now become clearer. Poor law legislation is broadly conceived of in the historiography in two chunks: the OPL codified in the 1601 legislation and iterating almost continuously across the 17th and 18th centuries (albeit in peaks and troughs of punitivism), and the New Poor Law (NPL) from the passing of the 1834 Poor Law Amendment Act. The OPL up to the abolitionist debates in the late 1700s had an 'all-inclusive notion' of the poor which was superseded in the NPL by 'a new concept of poverty in which dependency and non-dependency were the organising principles' (Englander 1998, p 6). After this point, debate centred on the distinction between the 'pauper' and the 'poor', and poverty per se 'was considered inevitable and … any other position, at the time, could only have been held by "visionaries or cranks"' (Poynter 1969, p xiii). Poverty in and of itself, then, although widespread, was no longer 'facienda' (the business of the state) in this new concept. It was held to be the 'general and unchangeable state of man; that as labour is the source of wealth, so is poverty of labour' (ergo, poverty is necessary for wealth) (Edwin Chadwick, Secretary to the Poor Law Commissioners, cited in Dean 1991, p 175). The problem, newly conceived as dependency, found a new target in the dependent, able-bodied male. Here I draw out some key moments relating to shifts in ways of thinking that made the 1834 legislation possible, commencing my genealogy by 'zipping back and forth' between then and now to link our contemporary state of wealtherty with scenes from the past (Koram 2022, p 18). This involves engaging with and presenting in the context of wealtherty, some key work from the historiography of the poor law. The moments I am bringing together here form a 'semantic' bridge between the 1790s and contemporary ways of thinking in key regards. They mark moments of the emergence of the current problematisation – the idea of dependency as the primary social problem – and they bond the perception of dependency to, solely, the poor. If we are to think about wealth, poverty and enduring inequality, this demands not just an account of the wealth and poverty that endures in contemporary distributions (Chapter 2), but also the 'power' of those material resources (Robeyns 2019) that resides and endures in contemporary norms: capital drags ideas and norms with it as ballast.

Problematising the population

Dependency continues to be the social bad that social policy is seeking to address. I want to focus here on the ways in which this idea, which came to dominate political thinking in the 1790s and early 1800s, was brought into being, starting with the ideas articulated in Malthus' 1798 *An Essay on the Principle of Population*. This essay was fundamental in creating the rupture described earlier between a way of thinking that conceived of a large, poor, population as an asset and as fundamental to the wealth of a nation, and a way of thinking about (part of) that same population as a problem that social policy needed to solve. The key principle of the essay was that population had the propensity to outgrow the means to support it and needed to be managed through positive and negative checks: positive checks such as premature mortality through hunger; and negative checks such as prudential delays in marriage. These checks were necessary to prevent widespread famine or unrest (Poynter, 1969, p 146). Despite being 'almost entirely innocent of evidence' and a 'farrago of all available abolitionist arguments' (Poynter, 1969, pp 104, 155), the ideas did important political work in several ways, some related to the substantive content of the ideas and others to their means of communication. First of all, the idea was presented as a scientific calculation. This 'apparent scientificity' (Poynter 1969, p 104) gave it the status of objectivity. The simplicity of its central 'calculation' (based on two categorically distinct kinds of growth – arithmetic and geometric – which moved at different rates) helped it to gain political salience such that despite *empirical* studies undertaken in the late 1700s (Eden and Davies, cited in Horwell 2019) showing the cause of poverty to be 'rooted in the disparity between wages and subsistence', political opinion came into line behind the Malthusian principle and the so-called science of population. The essay cemented the use of 'scientificity' as a legitimation device, as something that produces 'truth' and, relatedly, it marked the growing ascendency of calculation and statistics over empirical work and/ or 'opinion' – a hierarchising of knowledge types. 'Apparent scientificity' endures as a means of conjuring 'objectivity' from deeply political numbers, as I will go on to explore in Chapter 6, and the diminishing of empirical and qualitative work has ratcheted to the extent that civil servants now lack capacity in government to understand and use *non* quantitative data in policy development and analysis (Monaghan and Ingold 2019).

The distinguishing between the relative status and utility of opinion versus calculation in political decision making was the outcome of a long-baking process which took place over centuries. Malthus' essay and subsequent early 19th-century Malthusia*nism* was a key moment of catalysis in this longer process. In the early 17th century, for example, 'political and mercantile pressure groups were *probably more influential in determining ... decision*[s]' (Slack 2004, p 53, emphasis added). In the later 17th century, as innovations were made in political arithmetic, new forms of political 'calculation' continued to exist *alongside conceptions of 'common sense'* (Endres 1985, emphasis added) and were not always the trump card in knowledge-making processes. By the 1770s, practices of government were shaped by new informational sources, including 'good, quantitative, long-run perception of public finances' (Hoppit 1996, p 531), but 'opinion' largely continued to constrain and/or complement their use. This melding of 'information' with 'opinion' endured in Malthus' essay in the 1790s and is evident in Chadwick's 1832 Poor Law Commission work. It is at work in contemporary knowledge production processes, characterised as 'decision-based evidence-making' (Slater 2008, p 955). So, while there is an observable shift between the relative status of types of knowledge between the Tudor-Stuart-Hanoverian period of the OPL (opinion) and the Victorian one in which the NPL came into being (political numbers), it was not a sudden switch from 'older' forms of knowledge with their roots in local relationships, customary practices and various forms of deference/tribute – both continued. However, the evolution of methods for analysing data enabled its more routine, executive use by the 1800s when *accumulation* of local records collected in the past (ecclesiastical and secular courts, dioceses, counties and parishes) gained new political value and their role evolved in response to new statistical methods and techniques. This enabled a shift away from the use of information to address immediate concerns of identifying who could be 'conscripted, taxed, prosecuted as an encloser, given poor relief, or isolated or avoided in a plague epidemic' (Slack 2004, p 40) to the *executive* use of population-level data (Rose 1999, p 35) as a mechanism of government. This is the context in which Malthus' ideas take seed – one in which population data is available for the first time (following the first census in 1801) along with new methods for data aggregation and analysis, but in which *opinion* can still explicitly subordinate the scientificity of numbers to political ends and scientificity can seem to rid political decision making of sentiment.

Malthusian ideas marked a key moment, a point of catalysis in a longer-durée problematisation of poverty that had been rumbling through the 18th century, as seen in a churn of enabling reforms (see Brundage [2002] for details of the 18th-century legislation), failed proposals (for example, Samuel Whitbread's 1795 proposal for a minimum wage bill) and a proliferation of pamphlets and essays expressing quite oppositional views (broadly humanist/evangelical reformers, and mercantilist abolitionists). Malthus' essay helped to legitimate and render scientific the reframing of the social problem away from a generalised one of the 'labouring poor' to one of the dependency of the idle able-bodied poor. At the point at which the 'radical reorganisation' of the poor laws come to be on the *parliamentary* agenda for the first time in the *1817 Report from the Select Committee on the Poor Laws*, (Dean 1991, p 95), its scientific basis was the flawed, contested, Malthusian 'science' of population. The developing belief in the sanctity of scientificity carried an unscientific policy over the line and in so doing made canonical and orthodox the idea of dependency.

Articulating the problem as a crisis and to a crisis

The crisis at the end of the 18th century was interesting as much for the data that helped to construct and inscribe it as for the factors whose convergence led to it, namely a population boom (the population doubled between 1750 and 1801); enclosure, which began in the 13th century and peaked between the 1760s and 1820s, creating a landless working class (Slack 1988, pp 4–5); unemployment and higher food prices which, in combination with the population boom, made poor rates soar from £1.5 million in 1776 to £4 million in 1803 and £18.6 million in 1813 (Brundage 2002, p 25). Data from the first national census of 1801 were married with this information about the poor rates and the numbers of OPL workhouses in operation (3,765 workhouses across 14,611 parishes with 83,468 indoor paupers, averaging 22 per house). These figures were presented by abolitionists and reformers as foretelling the imminent overwhelming of the services designed to relieve the poor (Driver 2004). The combination of these data – coupled with the rationale provided by the Malthusian population principle – gave the problem of the (specifically *dependent*) poor legislative tractability, legitimacy and, above all, urgency. The data seemed to *prove* the Malthusian hypothesis, creating a frame that it became impossible to think outside of: a new paradigm had come into being. A crisis legitimates forms of government that in noncrisis times would be intolerable and, as such, they are useful vehicles for initiating and/or accelerating unpopular or complex legislative change. They enable the 'suspension of temporal sovereignty' (Standring 2018, p 153) – one can act on the basis that the urgency of events demands it. The crisis helped shift opinion towards the need for reform: in 1790, reformer Samuel Whitbread had sought to pass minimum wage legislation; by 1807, he had been converted to Malthusianism and 'saw the tendency of relief ... to demoralise the poor and create overpopulation' (Brundage 2002, p 41). The problem of dependency had been articulated, and articulated *to* the fin-de-siècle crisis.

It is important to note that there were other ways in which the debate could have gone (for example, towards a minimum wage) at all points and including in the later 1790s and early 1800s. However, the overwhelming sense of crisis catalysed the more apocalyptic voices. Malthusian ideas benefited from the prevailing wind, but other ideas were 'in the soup' (Kingdom 2011). Kingdon's articulation of pre-policy making processes is a useful one to sketch out here. He uses the metaphor of the 'soup' to describe available solutions (in the form of policies) which float around waiting for a problem to be articulated in such a way that they can attach to it. The solutions *pre-exist* these problematisations. The scientificity of the idea of the 'population principle' plus the growing sense of crisis helped humanists and evangelicals who had felt unease in supporting radical reform or abolition of poor laws to get on board with a clear conscience: after all, reform was urgently needed in order to stop future suffering due to unsustainable population growth, and a solution was 'in the soup'. More radical/humanist ideas like the minimum wage failed to catalyse because the problem articulation had shifted to one of dependency and population crisis, and these solutions no longer fitted.

I now want to think about the information-gathering work of the 1832 Commission, whose existence, if not its findings, rationalised and shaped the 1834 Act itself. It is a manifestation of the governmental orientation of scrutiny. As I made the case for in Chapter 1, the governmental disposition of scrutiny is a form of administrative panopticism which we see renewed in Universal Credit: both the NPL and Universal Credit would be unthinkable and unachievable without it (Figure 1.1). There is never a sense when the poor come into contact with administrative processes related to the poor law or the administrative processes of contemporary welfare policy that compliance is a matter of personal discretion or that there is a provision for privacy or voluntarism. Indeed, in the context of Universal Credit, failure to disclose is subverted through the use of real time income data passing directly from HMRC to the DWP (Alston 2018), and is criminalised the through the aggressive pursuit of benefit fraud (Taxwatch 2021). In the context of the NPL, complete disclosure was mandatory and celebrated: Chadwick cited at length in the 1832 Commission report an example of 'depauperising' work undertaken in Nottinghamshire, which saw labourers proudly display their rent receipts in their windows as proof of their social contribution; and the forms used to collect information from labourers included the amount of savings held by each individual.

This brings us back to the shifting role and use of political numbers. The accuracy, reliability or integrity of political numbers can be less important than the process of their collection. For example, the Assistant Commissioners undertaking the parish-based research for the 1832–1834 Commission's work visited 3,000 of the 15,000 parishes and townships in England and Wales. They collected a breadth of data that was hitherto unprecedented: information on depositors (amount per annum) in the savings bank; a more comprehensive 'account of some labourers', with information on the number of children born and number living; wage; land ownership; savings; rent paid; and money from the parish (British Parliamentary Papers 1970). In addition, the Commission sought input from abroad, but didn't wait for the responses before writing the report (Poynter 1969, p 89). However, it was asked to release interim findings at a point at which replies had only been received from 10 per cent of respondents covering 20 per cent of the population of England and Wales, and before the material had been analysed (Englander 1998, p 10). Research was 'drawn upon selectively in defence of a pre-conceived project. Policy, in short, had become the determinant rather than the outcome of empirical inquiry' (Englander 1998, p 12). For Chadwick, the *act* of finding out was more politically valuable than the veracity of the results. Performing the act of 'knowing the population' in effect wrapped 'science' around sentiment.

In Chapter 6, I 'zip forward' to the 2000s and explore the production of dependency as technique of government in the work of the Centre for Social Justice, the use of it to legitimate its radical 'grassrootsism' which keeps the gaze down, and the related 'ideological reworking' of the collapse of the financial services sector in 2008 into the political problem of 'how to allocate blame and responsibility' (Clark and Newman 2012, p 300). This work helped to renew the problematics of so-called welfare dependency. This reworking focused on 'the unwieldly and expensive welfare state and public sector, rather than high risk strategies of banks, as the root cause of the crisis' (Bramall 2013, p 2). It enabled a shift away from the rich and towards the poor as a locus of both blame and reparation. And it legitimised otherwise intolerable levels of fiscal re-alignment by branding them as austerity in attempts to borrow moral and cultural cache from the post-war era (Bramall 2016). In short, Chapter 6 shows how in approach (articulating a problem, articulating the problem to a crisis) *and* focus (the dependent poor), the method of governing the poor, and their maintaining as the primary focus of social policy that characterised the NPL, is renewed in Universal Credit.

So far I have looked at an evolution in ways of 'coming to know' about a population in which calculation and opinion meld, and I have observed a trend towards ever-increasing degrees of politicisation, from 'These data are a numerical representation of truth in the world. They need no interpretation' in the 1600s, to 'What can we know by bringing X and Y sets of data together?' to 'What are they indicators of?' and 'What data could be used to present X as true?' in the 1800s. I'm now going to introduce how these ways of knowing both required and produced particular policy characters.

Making policy characters

The effect of forms of knowing and governing on *types of being* is a recurring theme in this book (Chapters 5 and 8 in particular). Finding out 'how a human being is envisaged ... and the social practices that constitute this human being' (Ball 2015, p 308) is the focus of this section. Then as now, the third ingredient that went alongside problem articulation and crisis articulation was the production of a character whose behaviours could be rendered problematic and whose discipline could be the legitimate focus of policy. In the context of the NPL, this was the pauper. The production of the pauper was crucial to the social legitimisation of harshening social policy.

Again, as I showed earlier, in tracing the shifting balance between opinion and calculation, these processes evolve over centuries: the 1834 legislation would not have been possible without a progressive vilification of the poor (in peaks and troughs) from the 16th century when the idea that the poor were in some way to blame for their own poverty had begun to emerge (Vallely 2020, p 229). By the 1820s and 1830s, the progressive vilification and stigmatisation of the poor was such that it was tolerable for abolitionists and reformers to unflinchingly conceive of the poor as 'swarming, indolent, improvident, discontented, dispirited, oppressed, degraded, vicious ... chiefly owning to the system of the Poor Laws' (Brundage 2002, p 41). Between these dates, the abstraction and then vilification of the poor was produced and reflected through, for example, a proliferation of 'rogue literature' like Harman's *Caveat for Common Cursetors* which individuates fine grain distinctions and variable moral judgement against rufflers, upright men, hooker or anglers, wyld rogues, pryggers or prancers, palliards, to name but a few (Thomas Harman in Tawny and Power 1951, pp 407–415; Aydelotte

1913), and through pamphlets that sought to 'warn the public about the threat of itinerant men and women'.

The vilification of the pauper that ultimately enabled the 1834 Act was an evolution of a much longer process of abstraction and stigmatisation over the course of the 17th century which changed social relations between richer and poorer people. It shaped relations between richer and poorer people socially in a systemic way, in the modification and eventual erosion of a tradition of 'tribute' – the idea that rich people and poor people existed in a mutualistic relationship in which the rich had an obligation towards the poor of charity and hospitality (Slack 1988, p 19). In times of poor harvest, for example, the rich were called back from town to look after 'their' poor, and at times of distress, the rich routinely subsidised food for the poor (Field and Frost Sutton 1884). In return, the poor in effect agreed to respect the property rights of the rich and maintain social order. In the 16th and early 17th centuries, there was a 'powerful impulse ... to the acts of mercy which Christ himself had recommended' (Slack 1988, p 19), but by the late 16th century, there was also a current of thinking that the poor could legitimately be denied tribute if they broke the 'reciprocal relationship' by exhibiting 'lewd behaviour' for example (1988, p 19). Over the course of the 18th century, opinions became harsher (although Christian currents coexisted with these opinions). It is important to note here that tribute was not unproblematic: Marxist historians interpret the tributary (or tribute) of the 18th century as a relationship operating on the basis of land ownership with its roots in enclosure and engrossment, and in (ethically) illegitimate hereditary land transfer (Hay 1975). Hay suggests that the 'benevolence of rich men to poor, and all the ramifications of patronage, were upheld by the sanction of the gallows and the rhetoric of the death sentence' (Hay 1975, pp 62–63). And postcolonial scholars, for example Mukherjee (2010, p 73), note that in the context of empire, the tribute was in effect the 'unrequited transfer of capital from the colony to the metropolis', referred to as the "drain" or "tribute" by early Indian nationalists. I don't wish to romanticise this here.

The progressive vilification of the poor and the reshaping of social relations were deeply connected, as was the embedding of the new, harsher attitudes into more or less punitive legislation. This included the brief legalisation of chattel slavery for the poor in England in 1547 (Brundage 2002), the Vagrancy Acts of the 16th century and the Settlement Acts of the 17th century, the latter resulting in truly desperate outcomes for populations often on the move for work or food (Vallely 2020, p 219). It also manifested in a recalibration of the balance between private charity and poor rates as sources of relief caused by the emergence of discriminatory philanthropic relief: Tudor philanthropy shifted towards providing for the 'true poor' and harshly punishing the 'thriftless poor' (Vallely 2020, p 209). Where private charity was the primary source of relief for the poor at the beginning of the

17th century, by the beginning of the 18th century, public relief from rates 'provided nearly half as much for the poor as endowed charity' (Slack 1988).

The effect of the rich increasingly not feeling beholden to the tribute relationship meant that both sides were cut free (or loose) from the ties that bind, with differing impacts on each side. This caused a shift from a 'softer' era of (mostly rural) 'paternalism and mutual obligations' in 'what was still a face-to-face society'. This was the context in which tribute, in the form of 'a mutual recognition of need and obligation ... gave the poor a respected place in the social hierarchy' (Fraser 2017, p 41). The shift was towards the 'harsh free-market individualism of Victorian urban England' (Fraser 2017, p 41), resulting from the 'gradual erosion' of the moral economy through, for example, 'enclosure, the loss of gleaning rights, stringent game laws, the curtailment of customary rights' (2017, p 42). The declining opinions about the poor and the severing of a sense of mutualism – however tenuous or strategic this mutualism was – was the final ingredient combining with 'science' and 'events' to usher in the 1834 legislation. It is this shift that we see 'concretised' by Malthus as lingering humanitarian and evangelical currents line up behind reform.

Who is left out?

I've looked at methods of coming to know, what the 'new' approaches to knowledge making were, who the focus of these methods were and how progressive vilification of the poor helped to modify social relationships to be less mutualistic. I now want to think in more detail about who is maintained *outside* of this new problematisation (the pauper) in addition to the 'industrious' poor. Which parts of the 'social enters the statistical' (Rose 1999, p 204) and which parts are left out? I am interested in who is conceived to be inside and outside 'the social': providing challenge to the enduring understanding of social policy as being a form of government *of the poor* rather than *of the social* is fundamental to the *wealtherty* manifesto (Chapter 9).

The reasons why not all of the social enters the statistical can be methodological: Poynter's observation in 1969 holds true today – 'not all the ingredients of poverty can be counted' (Poynter 1969, p xiii). But *because* the quantifying of the social is a productive act – its aim is to produce 'a governable social' (Cobham 2020) – the entity (in this case the state) undertaking the counting is able to maintain not just the things that can't be *counted* outside of the governable social; it can also maintain things that it does not wish to *fully govern* outside the governable social by not counting them or not making them count. This is a productive act and a political one. This works positively and negatively: some of the resources of the rich are held outside the calculative realm for the purposes of reducing tax liability on the wealthy (achieved through having an approach focused on voluntarism and self-declaration in the 1790s, and through the adoption of a 'cooperative compliance' in the 2000s). Women are held outside of the social problematisation of the 1790s–1830s by virtue of not being recognised as full economic agents. This manifests today in their subsidiary role within 'unitary households' for welfare purposes (Bennett 2021). Colonial populations are held inside for the purposes of (fiscal) extraction and outside for the purposes of (welfare) distribution in the later 18th and 19th centuries, and this continues in contemporary forms of enclosure and extraction (Federici 2019). I'm going to look at the example of women again here, before using this idea of the rich remaining outside of the social problematisation for calculative purposes, as a means of introducing the final part of this chapter.

I made the decision in writing this book to use the broad-brush terms 'the poor' and 'the rich' (see Chapter 1 fn 1). These are blunt heuristics. Populations of richer and poorer people are of course made up of different groups (women and men, people of different races and ethnicities, for example) and these groups fare differently within the same macroeconomic context, as I described briefly in Chapter 2. Within the broad evolutions of 'ways of thinking' about richer and poorer people sketched out previously are nested parallel evolutions of ways of thinking about groups, such that *wealtherty* is always gendered and racialised. For example, contemporary social policy disproportionately harms women. In a 2021 article, social policy sociologist Fran Bennett cited a comment attributed to Alston during his 2018 visit: 'There is a really remarkable gender dimension to many of the reforms ... If you got a group of misogynists together in a room and said "How can we make a system that works for men but not women?" they wouldn't have come up with too many other ideas than what's in place' (cited in Bennett , p 14). This is a renewal of norms that have shaped women's experience of fiscal and social policy, and that have defined the terms of their inclusion within policy – usually as dependants or subordinates. Himmelweit's recent work on gender and taxation, like the work of Thane (1978), and many others who look at the longer histories of the relationship between men and women within legal and policy systems, observes that public policy has usually 'assumed and reinforced a male breadwinner model ... in which women are treated as dependents [sic]' (p 182). It is startling to see how little evolving knowledge about the *actual* economic activities of women shifts institutional practice. For example, Booth found that in East London in the 1880s, one third of all families depended for survival on the earnings of the husband *and wife* (Thane 1978, p 33 emphasis added), and Rowntree (in York) revealed that the wages of wives and children 'frequently amount to more than the earnings of the head of the household' (Thane 1978, p 33). Notwithstanding these data, the National Insurance Act of 1911 'excluded married women out-workers from complex arrangements made for the unmarried, on the grounds that married women's earnings *were not essential to the family economy*' (Thane 1978, p 33, emphasis added). Even when data demonstrated a particular economic reality, the strength of prevailing restrictive norms prevented the recognition of what was often the *primacy* of women (and children's) economic contribution, the primacy of women and children as economic actors. There is a consistent and fundamental failure or refusal to know, characterised by a determination not to take knowledge in particular directions. The progressive peripheralisation of women as economic agents is documented in Federici's retelling of primitive accumulation from the 'viewpoint of the changes it introduced in the social position of women and the production of labour-power' (Federici 2000, pp 1–3). It ramifies in social and fiscal legislation. In tax policy, from the event of 'couveture' in the 1100s (the belief that married men and women are one financial entity), married women could not own property, but widows and spinsters could (McGee and Moore 2014). This idea is 'corrupted' over time into the view that 'women are the property of their husbands' (McGee and Moore 2014). This relationship of property is then embedded within tax law. In Pitt's 1798 Income Tax Bill – which I will explore in the next section of this chapter – a husband and wife were taxed as a single unit; in the 1842 Finance Act, the 'profits of any married woman living with her husband [were] deemed the profits of her husband'; in 1970,'a married woman's income chargeable to income tax' was deemed for income tax purposes to be [her husband's] income and not to be her income' (Barr 1980, p 478); women couldn't open a bank account without their husband's permission until 1975; independent taxation (where a married woman has a taxation status independent of her husband) was an innovation of 1990; and 'hangovers' from this joint status (like the Married Couples Allowance for older couples) still remain (Himmelweit 2023). In social policy, the same narrative becomes embedded and naturalised. The specific ways in which the 1832 Commission produced the governable population for the Poor Law Act of 1834 unsurprisingly affirmed the patriarchal norms of its era: the forms used to collect information for the 1832 census focused on husbands and children (living and dead). Wives were mentioned usually only if they were in the asylum, as evidence of a man living on his own. Chadwick and Senior (the Poor Law Commission Secretary and one of its Commissioners, respectively) proceeded with the 1832 Poor Law Commission's two-year factfinding based on an assumed norm of a stable two-parent family with a male breadwinner. The male breadwinner was the target of the legislation, and his wife was to be subject to the legislation as a dependant, *in the same way as a child* (Thane 1978). The report was sufficiently fixated on this household structure that it remained silent '[w]ith regard to the really baffling problems presented by the widow, the deserted wife, the wife of the absentee solder or sailor, the wife of a husband resident in another parish or another country – with or without children' (1978, p 31). We will see how the report and this particular 'gap' in it is defining in terms of the make-up of workhouse populations in Chapter 4. The 'responsibilisation of the male head of the household' and the tethering of the wife through conjugal dependence (Dean 1991, p 172) was *established by* rather than described within the 1834 amendments. The way in which the data were collected had material – often devastating (Englander 1998) – consequences for the many (types of) women who were not wives. The 'tethering' of women endures in the design of contemporary welfare policy through the concept of 'unitary' households and through the 'head of household' approach to disbursing benefits that was written into Universal Credit. The disregard of women as economic agents both in terms of their paid work and the economic value of their *unpaid* work is an enduring governmentality (Federici 2020, 2021) which is reproduced at both ends of the wealth spectrum: Glucksberg (2016, p 2) describes the ways in which women and their labour are key to the production of elites, and Bessière and Gollac, as noted in Chapter 1, observe that women's agency is calibrated to wealth: in poor families, 'money problems are women's problems', whereas in wealthy families, 'looking after capital is a man's prerogative' (Bessière and Gollac 2023, p 4). This section has sought to illustrate that within the same economic contexts, some groups fare worse. Consider the many women whose oral testimonies form part of Todd's *The People: The Rise and Fall of the Working Class, 1910–2010* (2015) and whose lives are distinguished from their male counterparts in the same social class and in the same macroeconomic context by the operation of restrictive norms relating to sex. This takes place at both ends of the wealth spectrum (as Glucksberg's work noted earlier attests to). The 'faring worse' of groups is an effect of the rendering legislative of prejudicial social norms.

Before I go on to look at the 1798 Income Tax Act as a moment in which the state's government of wealth and the rich is consolidated (through the disposition of ignorance), I want to comment on the way in which the *social* legislation of 1834 also consolidated some enduring *fiscal* norms. First, it cemented the idea of dependency *as only belonging to the poor*. Of course, as Poynter (1969) notes in another context, any other position at the time could have been held 'only by cranks'. But the political inviolability of this division endures. It remains almost impossible to make the idea of *fiscal* welfare dependency (the dependency of the rich on tax reliefs, for example) tractable, even though then as now, the estates of the rich *depended on* fiscal measures and principles of state-backed law (those of priority, durability, universality and convertibility) (Pistor 2019, p 3) to survive within and between generations. This bonding of dependency to *poverty* is a critical conceptual barrier to the effective problematisation of wealth and the recognition of forms of fiscal welfare dependency today (which I articulate more fully in Chapter 6). Second, the implementation of the NPL required forms of centralisation with which the landed gentry refused to comply. In the process of 'engrossing' parishes to unions and unions to districts, the Poor Law Commission tasked commissioners with defining district boundaries by using a compass to centre a country estate, and then drawing a perfect circle around it (Shave 2017). Landowners refused to have their local knowledge overridden by such formulaic impositions from a modernising centre, which they felt flattened local complexity and disregarded generations of local knowledge and customary relationships. The 'refusal to be governed' and its tolerance by the state is a facet of the disposition of ignorance that we will see rippling through forms of governance (Chapter 4) and forms of being (Chapter 5) as the book progresses. As well as affirming the power of localities (and thus the landed gentry) (Brundage 1972, 2002),[1] the NPL in effect also reproduced the idea of the independency of the wealthy and established a limitation to their consent in terms of being governed. This refusal to cede to authority based on knowledge originating from the centre (or implicitly from 'above') was a refusal by the gentry to cede epistemic primacy: they regularly and persistently took opportunities to reassert their dominance through correspondence with the Poor Law Commissioners and forms of what Ball et al would call policy 'refusal' (Ball et al 2012). This took the form of, for example, attempts to counter the perceived harshness of the central banning of outdoor relief – the foundation of the 1834 Act. In a series of letters, the inaugural Chair of the Southwell Union workhouse Magistrate R.H. Bromley asserted his wish to continue making decisions informed by his 'inter vivos' knowledge of his parishioners (TNA Source B, MH12/9525/282); he interceded to make the case for continuance of outdoor relief in cases of need (TNA Source B, MH12/9524/65 [1836]) and he worried that the cessation of out-relief for nonresident paupers would inflict 'moral degradation…upon the many deserving and industrious Families' (TNA Source B, MH12/9524/79). The Poor Law Commissioner ultimately responded by saying that 'the commission will take the points he raised into serious consideration. However, one of the chief objects of the Poor Law Amendment Act was *to take from individual overseers that control that can never be exercised with uniformity*' (TNA/ML16/Folio 236. Dated 23 February 1837, emphasis added).

The suggestion here, which proved contentious to many Workhouse Boards of Guardians whose members were used to being afforded unquestionable decision-making rights and status, was that the Poor Law Commission (three men based in Somerset House in London) was now the seat of privileged and *objective* power over and above that of the resident wealthy gentry (based in the 'localities'). The jostling for privilege between central and local forms of knowledge took place diffusely at this time both within the context of taxation and in relation to the role of the local gentry in the government of the poor. It manifest concerns with the changing nature of expertise and knowledge (which I introduced in the first section of this chapter), as well as concerns about the changing location of authority (from locality to centre), and the relationship between the two.

The state and the rich

I am now going to consider how the state made attempts to come to know the rich, through looking at debates surrounding the Income Tax, and forms of government that the state sought to impose, but that were refused. These two debates – the abolitionist debate of the late 1700s and the debates surrounding the 1798 income tax – are rarely considered in parallel, despite the anxieties they express/expressed being the same or related. I bring them together here as part of my commitment to thinking about the rich and the poor relationally (temporally and spatially in the way in which I described earlier using the concept of *Ma*). This is also a way of helping to consolidate the idea of the emergence of the state of *wealtherty* specifically in the context of ways of thinking about richer and poorer people, and their relationship to the state. At the end of the 18th century, taxation policy was governed by entrenched norms delimiting the inquisitorial claims of the state; the right to consent to taxation; the right to self-assess; and the right to submit returns locally and privately. In challenging but then eventually shoring up these norms, the 1798 Act legitimated 'privileged capabilities' whose operations today continue to shield wealth from the state: the governmental disposition of ignorance becomes embedded in legal code. I'm going to explore this under two themes: the right to consent/the right to privacy; and hierarchies of knowledge.

Legitimising consent and privacy

The same *ideational* climate that reached a peak in the 1790s and that paved the way for the 1834 Act also paved the way for Pitt's 1798 first direct tax on income. While Malthus and others were making the case for reform or abolition of the poor laws, passionate debates were taking place about the levying of a direct income tax after large-scale evasion thwarted the success of less onerous mean (property and visible wealth tax) of raising the money to fund the war with revolutionary France (Cousins 2018). Although tax administration is inquisitorial by nature, the proposed new income tax of 1798 was a legislative challenge to norms governing the inquisitorial limits of the state, and the fierceness of opposition was testimony to how dearly held the principle of minimally intrusive taxation was. The canons included the presupposition of a legitimate realm of private financial affairs for the wealthy. Challenge to these canons represented challenge to the limit of the state with regard to its right to know. Previous taxes had focused on 'visible wealth and badges of status' (carriages, houses, male servants and riding horses) (O'Brien 1988, p 10). In these taxes, the state knew its rich by their possessions and, as such, by what was visible. Opposition to the proposed *new* form of taxation levied against income focused less on the amount (which most agreed could be borne) than on the penetration of the state's gaze into hitherto private financial spheres of the lives of the rich. Its nature was declared 'unequal, unprincipled and unjust' (Kingsbury 1798, p 15). The common council of the city of London adopted a resolution in December 1798 stating that 'the said bill proposes to establish an inquisitorial power unknown in this country – inconsistent with the principles of the British Constitution – and repugnant to the feelings of Englishmen' (cited in Cousins 2018, p 161). An MP described a tax collector as a spy '[that] comes, not only into the House, but opens the bureau of every man, and becomes acquainted with his most secret concerns' (Cousins 2018, p 162). The mechanisms of the administration of the income tax were variously described as 'odious', 'arbitrary', 'immoral', 'cruel', 'harassing', 'disgusting' and 'impolitic' (cited in Stebbings 2009, pp 300–301). Its process was referred to as a 'system of espionage' and 'nefarious machinery', and its personnel as 'spies and informers'. 'A Northern Freeholder' in 1806 railed against 'the *disclosure of circumstances,* which ought not to be disclosed *at all*' (2009, pp 300–301). It was 'an abhorrent invasion of privacy which gratified either animosity or idle curiosity in those administering it, and the disclosure of a man's personal misfortunes to "a set of heartless functionaries" would lead to pain and humiliation' (various contemporary sources cited in Stebbings 2009, p 301). The eventual introduction of the Income Tax Act in 1799 'provided the state with both an enormous new source of revenue *and access to information regarding individual wealth and lifestyle that had never before been available*' (Levi 1989, p 122, emphasis added).

Alongside the resentment at having their incomes scrutinised, the preceding complaints reflect the 'perceived breach of consent' by government. Contemporaries believed themselves to possess a 'constitutional right to consent to taxation' and, as such, any centrally imposed taxation was considered to be at odds with ideas of 'liberty and constitutionality' (Stebbings 2009, p 164). The concerns indicate an assumption that there is a realm of private affairs and concerns which lie legitimately beyond state encroachment or knowledge, and that it is the role of the wealth holder rather than the state to decide where that encroachment must end. The resistance led to a neutered version of the Act and, more importantly, further formalised an enduring approach to the government of wealth and the wealthy of respectful caution on the part of the state (or what we now call 'cooperative compliance' [OECD 2009]), and righteous privacy on the part of the wealthy. This is key because it shows the consolidation of concession and permissiveness as a form of government of the rich. This enduring disposition is evident in the contemporary institutionalisation of cooperative compliance in the work of the HMRC Wealthy Unit (the focus of Chapter 8). The response of the rich to these attempts to derive knowledge through scrutiny secured a compromise: *voluntary* disclosure and compliance, not discipline or punishment. This represented an acknowledgement that the state was not the final arbiter of what the rich would or wouldn't (be made to) do. The rich secured a commitment that in effect 'personal financial information [would] remain[ed], as far as possible, secret' (Stebbings 2009, p 316), and, further, on repeal of the Act in 1816, a commitment was made to burn all the records (Horwell 2019, p 185). The idea that the rich were to be able to set the terms of their compliance is predicated on the assumption of a right to privacy in financial matters, which I introduced in Chapter 2 as a 'restricted privilege' and which I return to throughout the book. In making the case for his income tax in 1798, Pitt acknowledged that there was no way of ascertaining the amount of a man's property 'except such as were of a nature that could not be resorted to' (cited in Horwell 2019, pp 165–166). The means 'that could not be resorted to' constitute what he called 'improper disclosure' (2018, p 1139). The ideal was to tax according to means, but he felt unable to do so for fear of intruding on people's privacy. So, notwithstanding his belief that there was 'much income, much wealth, great means' that had not been reached through the assessment (2019, p 168), he was unable to access that income and wealth because of his fears of aggravating 'the entrenched opposition to inquisitorial powers, asserting that it was "an imprudent and dangerous request" to grant them' (2019, p 166). This reluctance to aggravate was behind concessions for 'declaration by oath without requiring evidence', that historical *practice* consistently showed (Beckett 1985) was subject to lies and concealment. In both instances – the NPL and the Income Tax Act – the response to noncompliance of behaviours on the part of the rich was concession: the rich ultimately got to draw the NPL district boundaries (Brundage 1972; Shave 2017), and they got to define the terms of their (partial) submission to being rated and assessed for income tax (Stebbings 2009; Horwell 2019). These concessions in 1799 and the 1830s were evidence of the state (albeit itself unproblematically composed of wealthy men) quietly acknowledging its impotence in the face of a governance refusal from the rich. State means of coming to know about richer and poorer people and resultant forms of knowledge manifest different orientations towards each group (and subgroups within them). These evolve in response to, for example, the forms of policy 'refusal' described earlier. However, the principles that were established in the later 1700s and early 1800s – the orientations – endure, as Part III of this book will show. Behaviour norms – privacy for the rich and disclosure on the part of the poor – started to become encoded in defining pieces of legislation at the end of the 18th and beginning of the 19th centuries, and these norms have been renewed in contemporary legislation.

Hierarchies of knowledge

The 'powerful ideological allegiance to local interests' (Stebbings 2009, p 310) and to locally led government that I discussed earlier in the context of the poor law was also a point of fierce debate in the income tax debates. This was not new: local landed forces had been instrumental in the 17th-century debates on taxation in resisting centralising moves around excises (Beckett 1985). In the debates leading up to the 1799 legislation, a key objection was central interference into what were widely held to be local matters. This had a power/knowledge aspect (as outlined earlier in the context of the 1834 Act) and a practical one: fear of the impact on newly credit-based trade relations if citizens came to know their neighbours' financial position (Jeffrey-Cook 2010). In the face of outrage about the idea of disclosing 'personal' financial information to a central authority, Pitt promised that the general declaration of income would be made not to a government official, but to specially appointed commissioners, who would be 'persons of a respectable situation in life; as far as possible removed from any suspicion of partiality, or any kind of undue influence; men of integrity and independence' (Stebbings 2009, p 159). Crucially, these were also to be *local* men. This commitment to local administration was reinforced by the imposition of a system of oaths of secrecy on the part of these local commissioners (2009, p 160). Perhaps predictably, despite the quite radical moves to increase revenue, revenue decreased: 'the assessors and collectors were still appointed locally, and the returns were notoriously incorrect and insufficient' (Jeffrey-Cook 2010, p 382).

In this chapter, I have described a shift in knowledge-making processes towards calculation and political numbers, but have noted the enduring influence of opinion in rendering data as 'evidence of …'. I have described tussles between centres and locality as traditional hierarchies of knowledge were threatened by new centralising administrative functions and the availability of new data and methods. And I have looked at the relationships between groups: the poor and the state; the rich and the state; the rich and the poor; women and the state. I considered what sense of obligation has existed between richer and poorer people in the past. This raises many questions for the state of that relationship now. What kind of relationship 'can be thought' between the rich and the poor in our now? What is the sense of obligation to one another? What is the role of the state in producing (calculating) and mediating these relationships? Is the state of contemporary modes of tribute requited or unrequited? How can we lament what was lost in the erosion of customary or 'tributary' relationships (the seeping away of humanitarianism which softened the implementation of the 1834 in certain contexts), without romanticising the extractive foundations (enclosure, engrossment and servitude) on which they were built? What can we learn about the need to work at the level of problem-*questioning* (Bacchi 2013) from the failure of radical ideas to make it onto the legislative agenda in the past (for example, Rickman's 1800 proposal for a tax on 'superflux', defined as the wealth of those 'who acquire improperly great property; who have infinitely more than is necessary for the elegancies and superfluities, as well as the comforts, of life; who wickedly hoard, or wickedly misapply the riches they have, and who make their exorbitant wealth the constant engine of public and private misery' [cited in Seligman 1914, p 86])? In looking at two debates taking place in the same period, debates in which the government of richer people and wealth, and poorer people and welfare were being negotiated, I have drawn attention to the very different orientations of the state in each case. I have also highlighted the sometimes startlingly similar currents that endure in our contemporary modes of governing these populations.

In 'How to read this book', I offered different pathways through the book for the reader. Chapter 4 continues the story by looking at how the ways of knowing described earlier were made material in policy for richer and poorer people in the late 1700s and early 1800s (and I start to draw more parallels and recognise renewals in contemporary practice). Alternatively, you might like to go directly to Chapter 6, in which I describe the work of a think tank in the 2000s, if you wish to continue the focus on knowledge making.

4

Governing: how the state came to govern richer and poorer people differently

Chapter 3 described the dispositions of scrutiny and ignorance at the level of knowledge making. This chapter looks at how these ways of thought are embedded in some of the practices and processes of policy making. For example, the disposition of ignorance is manifest in the principle of privacy described in Chapter 3. It becomes embedded in legal code which enshrines privacy in the law (Pistor 2019). The disposition of scrutiny is manifest in forms of mandatory disclosure. This becomes embedded in administrative and technical forms of 'total surveillance' through the real-time transfer of data from HMRC to the DWP for Universal Credit claimants. The enduring effect is a generalised legislative form of what the Committee of Public Accounts described in 2017 as 'one set of rules for the rich and another for everyone else' (PAC 2017, p 3).

This chapter looks at specific means and mechanism of governing in the state of wealtherty aligned to the dispositions of scrutiny and ignorance as described in Figure 1.1 and Table 2.1. It is divided into two sections. The first concerns itself with actions of government initiated by the state: these are the *means of restricting relief* to the poor on the one hand, and the *means of augmenting relief* to the rich on the other. I start with the workhouse and Universal Credit, which are framed as governing mechanisms that seek to restrict the provision of relief to the poor. I then look at the 1799 income tax and contemporary approaches to taxing the rich as means of 'augmenting relief', as mechanisms that seek to minimise the tax 'suffered' by the rich. The second section shifts its focus to *mechanisms of punishment and discipline*, specifically, the use of food and hunger, mobility and work, and a range of what I'm calling 'less sensational' forms of cruelty (after Henriques 1968, p 365) in the government of the poor. Henriques' essay was a response to a seam of work in the 1960s which had suggested that charges of cruelty and punitivism about the workhouse system were exaggerated or caricatured. She insisted that the law was 'oppressive in ways which were real, if less sensational than they were made out to be', insensitive rather than sadistic (1968, p 365). I then consider the relevance and meaning of sanctions for the rich. As with Chapter 3, I am not searching for a recognisable past faithfully reproduced in our now, but rather I am seeking to recognise forms of government in our now as *new instances of enduring governmental dispositions*. In keeping with my sensibility to *Ma*, I am also trying to reveal and bring to the surface *more* of the mechanisms of governing the rich, even if these are sometimes, like some of Tōhaku's trees in Figure 1.2, enabling and in the shadows. I will focus on compliance, and on space and mobility.

Securing fiscal and social relief

Let's begin with the NPL. As I discussed in Chapter 3, the aim of the NPL was to narrow the focus of social policy to the problem of dependency. I am interested here in the mechanisms through which the state mobilised this newly restricted focus. I focus primarily on relief *within the house*, while acknowledging that the role of the house was overwhelmingly totemic within the wider system of relief and that most people continued to receive outdoor relief (that is, relief outside of the workhouse, often in their local communities). Nonetheless, the house in some ways established the limits of what forms of disciplinary and punitive government were morally and politically 'intelligible' at the time. Correspondence relating to the process of securing of relief in the *old* system (the OPL) reveals welfare to have been 'genuinely negotiated', and the poor to have had 'a distinctive agency' (Carter and King 2021, p 119): people often remained in their homes and communities, and decisions were based on local relationships and knowledge. The process changed in 1834, not just with the 'sorting mechanism' that was the workhouse test, but also through the scaling from parishes to unions and districts through so-called 'engrossing'. This shift constituted a 'breach[ing] of the connection between local poverty and local relief' (Carter and King 2021, p 118). In aggregating to unions and districts, and in imposing a central authority, complexity was flattened out and systems were redesigned to operate at a national scale. The changes shifted the model of claiming welfare from one of genuine negotiation to something altogether less human and more formulaic: Within a decade of the law coming into being, letters between the PLC and individual paupers had changed from almost entirely individually written to almost entirely pro forma (Carter and King 2021). The first item at each meeting of the Southwell Workhouse Board of Guardians meetings, for example, was the same: 'The paupers in waiting were called in and questioned', with paupers from distant parishes being questioned and assessed by a singular board with whom they had no history (Nottinghamshire Archives Source B). The process was felt by those attempting to navigate it to be harsher than its antecedent and was thus the source of frequent appeals. Between 1836 and 1845, the PLC received an average of 29,954 letters per annum (576 per week and around 300,000 in the whole period) (Shave 2017, p 175). A significant number of these concerned attempts by paupers to try to avoid the house and continue with outdoor relief in some form (Carter and King 2021, p 126).

The complexity of the process of applying for Universal Credit is a deterrent. It puts off the very people who need support most from applying (Wright and Dwyer 2020). This is in part because of its 'digital by default' approach, which reduces uptake from the many digitally marginalised groups in the UK: In 2018, the ONS found that 10 per cent of adults in the UK (5.3 million people) were not users of the internet and the DWP's own survey revealed that 25 per cent of people were unable to make a claim online, with take-up of its online Universal Support service 'a third of what it expected' (PAC 2018, p 14). The 2019 Select Committee on Universal Credit and Survival Sex (WPC 2019a, b) heard directly from women with complex physical and mental health needs, like Ms J in Chapter 2, who found the digital application process so daunting that they simply 'chose' not to apply (WPC 2019a, 2019b). A second feature which many experience as punitive is the mandatory five-week waiting period, resulting in endemic late payments. To mitigate hardship during the waiting period, claimants are able to apply for an advance payment, to be recovered from future payments up to a value of 40 per cent of the claim each month. Repayment pushes people into debt, leaving them 'with little to live on, undermining their ability to cover the cost of essentials' (JRF 2020b, para 16). WPC (2019b) heard from two women who were using survival sex to cover basic needs who cited either the debt cycle resulting from their use of the advanced payment, or fear of it, as a reason for their 'choice' to sell sex (Witness UCX 002 in WPC 2019b, and third and public sector bodies at the evidence session confirmed this as a wider trend. National charity Changing Lives reported that three quarters of its services had supported clients who named Universal Credit as the reason for their involvement in survival sex or sex work. Further, most of their clients referenced particular features of the policy – benefit sanctions, waiting for payment to be processed, debts accrued due to Universal Credit – as the reason behind their financial hardship. (Witness UCX 0013 Changing Lives in WPC 2019a).

More generally, the complexity of the design process prevented engagement from already vulnerable groups. Cheetham et al interviewed 33 Universal Credit claimants who experienced the system variously as 'complicated, difficult and demeaning' and 'hostile, punitive and difficult to navigate' (Cheetham et al 2018, p 3). Foodbank charity the Trussell Trust's research found 'strong evidence that the design and delivery of Universal Credit is causing hardship, particularly to vulnerable groups such as disabled people and families' (WPC 2018, UCR0002 [written evidence submitted by the Trussell Trust] 2018). It reported a 52 per cent increase in foodbank use in areas where Universal Credit had been rolled out for 12 months or more (compared to a 13 per cent rise in areas where Universal Credit had not been rolled out) (WPC 2018). The Trussell Trust (2021) found that almost half of all foodbank users were in debt to the DWP.

The design of both systems – the NPL and Universal Credit – represented for users a diminution of quality of service compared to the preceding system, a newly complex or more 'irksome' application process, fewer resources and a sense of loss of status. Both included a performatively punitive element (the workhouse and the regime within it, the five-week wait and digital by default); both systems showed a lack of interest in the radically different effects of the new systems on different women (Thane 1978; Englander 1998; Bennett 2021). In its fervour to end out-relief in the later 19th century, for example, the Charity Organisation Society (COS) focused its activity on women, who made up the majority of out-relief recipients. They were placed under surveillance to see if they were cohabiting and were pressured to hand their children over to the workhouse and seek work (Englander 1998); Bennett (2021) shows that after a preliminary (albeit limited in scope) equality impact assessment of Universal Credit in 2011, there has not been a further one, despite mounting evidence of its gendered impacts. It is by now well acknowledged that the single household payment, for example, risks endangering women by 'giving control of the payments to a financially or physically abusive partner' (Alston 2018). Contemporary means of securing relief for people living in poverty manifest an enduring use of making processes of accessing help part of the deterrent function of the policy. The process becomes a punishment.

Let's now turn to the means of securing *fiscal* relief. We are used to reading about 'securing relief' in the context of social policy, as a way of describing the processes that poor people have been subject to in order to access money, shelter or food to prevent material suffering. We are *less* used to thinking about forms of relief for the rich in the same way, in part because for the poor, it is relief from suffering, and for the rich, it is relief in support of privilege (for instance, tax relief which allows the already wealthy to retain more of their money [Sinfield 2023]) and is often hidden. The means of securing relief are also not performatively visible: there are no requirements to turn up at an office to 'sign on' for them. In this chapter, I aim to make visible more of the processes of acquiring fiscal relief, by which I mean all forms of relief from 'suffering taxation' through any action that helps to limit the amount of wealth a rich individual contributes to the resources of the state via taxation. For example, tolerance of avoidance or evasion, which we saw to be endemic in the late 18th and early 19th centuries and which is evident in contemporary forms of the government of wealthy and the wealthy, allows individuals and corporations to pay less tax (Siddons 2024) and as such might be considered a form of fiscal relief.

Starting with my historical example, we can see the evolution of a system of raising money through taxation that becomes progressively more regressive.

By the mid-16th century, the principle that wealthy individuals assessed themselves for tax purposes was well established (Beckett 1985); likewise, the principle that tax was levied exceptionally (to raise money for war, for example) rather than permanently (to sustain the normal functions of a peacetime state). Taxation generally took the form of land tax or excises (the indirect taxes paid by most people in the 18th century levied on basic commodities), scrupulously avoiding forms that might 'stick'. It was also considered voluntary and low compliance was generally tolerated 'in order that it should be collected in a routine and pedestrian manner' (Beckett 1985). In Chapter 3 I described the shift in the opinions held by richer people about poorer people from the 16th to the 18th centuries and the related erosion of *tributary* relationships. During this same period, a key change happened with regard to taxation. Poorer people had hitherto been more or less exempt 'in theory and practice' (Beckett 1985, p 305). The poll tax of 1641 was payable by *everyone* 'since each individual had rights which the state was protecting, each was bound to share in the cost of that maintenance'. Once this principle that all men should pay taxes was established, the state was able to call on this extended base more routinely to raise more revenue through excise – as long as it didn't apply to food and other necessities. For the rest of the 17th century, excises were the predominant revenue source for the state 'while the role of land and assessed taxes steadily declined' (Beckett 1985, p 306), meaning in effect that taxation began to become more regressive. By 1798, as a result of the cost of wars (with France and Spain), increases in stamp duties, customs and excises were insufficient to support the military aims of the state, and despite other measures to avoid imposing a tax on income, none managed to raise the anticipated level of revenue. The first direct tax on income was introduced in December 1798. I tell this (hugely truncated) story here to demonstrate quite how much legislative effort went into *avoiding* imposing a tax on the income of the wealthy. Tax policy sociologist Sinfield distinguishes between two forms of selectivity: means-enhancing, which applies to most income tax reliefs, provides more generously for those with higher incomes whose tax liabilities would be greater without these reliefs; and means-tested, which applies to an increasing proportion of working-age public spending benefits, limits benefits to those with resources beneath a certain level and often adds various behavioural extensions (Sinfield 2023, p 53). I suggest that the efforts to avoid taxing income in the 1700s were *means-enhancing* in ensuring that tax liabilities on the wealthy were kept to a minimum both through tolerance of noncompliance and through choosing to broaden the tax base rather than increase tax on those with more wealth and income. The eventual tax itself – despite the froth that accompanied its introduction, described in Chapters 2 and 3 – was also means-enhancing, in that it retained self-assessment and tolerated systemic under-reporting. While there was provision for detailed returns, this rarely happened as 'there were few officials to examine them' (Jeffrey-Cook 2010, p 387). Those subject to the new tax – those with annual incomes over £60 with a sliding scale between £0 and £200 – were simply asked to sign a short declaration: 'I do declare that I am willing to pay the sum of £x ... and I do declare that the said sum of £x is not less than one tenth part of my income, estimated according to the Directions and Rules prescribed' (cited in Jeffrey-Cook 2010, p 387). The light-touch approach to assessment and the failure to pursue detailed returns was in effect a concession to the principle of consent and an invitation to underdeclare. It embodies the state disposition of ignorance in choosing not to know and in sanctioning nondisclosure (see Figure 1.1).

What of the means of securing fiscal relief for wealth in the 21st century? First, the principles of voluntary disclosure and consent described in Chapter 3 endure. They continue to be entrenched within fiscal norms relating to the government of private and corporate wealth (Pistor 2019; Cobham 2020). Despite benefiting disproportionately from policies delivered through tax policy and tax expenditure, wealthy people are not envisaged as 'claimants' and a large part of the relief they benefit from is invisible and remains unarticulated (Sinfield 2023). They are also unencumbered by the responsibility of having to manage their lives as 'claimants': if unemployed, they aren't mandated to 36 hours job searching per week; if they have more than two children, this doesn't affect what benefits they are entitled to. Instead, the relationship between their fortunes and the state is mediated by a family office (Glucksberg and Burrows 2016) and/or a cast of paid advisors and professionals (independent financial advisors, specialist brokers and asset managers) who offer comprehensive wealth management services including 'asset protection; tax planning; estate and financial planning; investment planning; trusts; insurance; private annuities; investment banking; long-term care planning' (Beaverstock et al 2010, p 4). In addition, the rich benefit from the effects of the direct influence of paid advisors who lobby the government for a favourable tax environment (Harrington 2016) and, more broadly, through the fiscal provisions of 'accommodating jurisdictions' (Deneault 2018). The idea of an 'accommodating jurisdiction' can apply equally to mechanisms of influence like the WEF whose operation I will look at in more detail in Chapter 8, as it can to the various forms of tax haven originally included in Deneault's description. In short, relief is extensive (PAC 2017; Baker and Murphy 2020; Sinfield 2023), and is in the form of the advisors for the extremely wealthy having a direct engagement with the state in order to help design policy in their favour. This section has shown that processes of accessing relief for the poor were (and continue to be) performative, irksome, stigmatising and shaming. The processes of accessing relief for the rich were and continue to be enabling and enabled (by the state, and by advisors and the relationship between the two).

Discipline and punishment in social policy

I will now move on from the means of securing relief of one form or another to mechanisms of discipline and punishment, beginning with an introduction in each case to the general economy of discipline and punishment in each context, followed by an exploration of specific mechanisms (hunger, mobility and work for the poor; compliance and mobility for the rich). The workhouse system provided for progressive sanctions from one-off or low-grade offences which were badged 'disorderly', to repeat or high-level offences which were badged 'refractory'. Key punishment types were withdrawal or substitution of food, various forms of confinement and forced work. Carter et al (2019) assert that the NPL was not *intentionally* punitive; rather, excessive cruelty took place when the law was infringed, not fulfilled: Scandals like those at Andover (1844 – starving men eating 'green meat' from bones they were meant to be crushing) and Bridgwater (1836 – deaths caused by changes to the funding and deployment of medical officers) were the result of 'unsupervised local abuse, rather than a central policy direction' (Fraser 2017, p 60). In this reading, Andover and Bridgwater are presented as aberrations within a gentler economy of punishment. However, the collection of pauper letters to the Poor Law Commission (TNA Source A) suggests that punitive*ness*, if not punishment, was endemic and that extreme violations such as Andover and Bridgwater were the end of a spectrum of 'less sensational' forms of cruelty as defined by Henriques (1968). The 'flavour' of the time was one in which the worth of poor lives had been called into question by the progressive erosion of their status, and their vilification during the fin-de-siècle abolitionist debates, as described in Chapter 3. The scandals were undoubtedly against the letter of the law, but well within the spirit of its punitive intent. I will use the Southwell Workhouse Punishment Book (Nottinghamshire Archives Source A) as a source to illustrate this throughout the chapter.[1]

It is possible to trace the emergence of contemporary ways in which work, hunger and movement are used as techniques of government in the regimes within the workhouse. The economy of discipline and punishment within Universal Credit is delivered through conditionality and sanction. Conditionality embodies the principle that 'aspects of state support, usually financial or practical, are dependent on citizens meeting certain conditions which are invariably behavioural' (DWP 2008, p 1). Dwyer and Wright (2014) show that Universal Credit established a high watermark of conditionality and sanction as instruments of welfare policy. This built on the harshness of New Labour's New Deal for Young People in 2002, which at the time was considered to be 'the toughest sanction regime ever seen in the UK' (Dwyer 2018, p 5). New Deal sanctions included a 14-day loss of some or all their benefit for a first transgression, rising to 100 per cent loss of benefit for 182 days for a third offence. For Universal Credit,

Figure 4.1: Universal Credit Claimant Commitment form (sample excerpt)

Claimant Commitment

Joanne Brown
National Insurance number: AB123456C

1. **My commitment**

I'll do everything I can to get paid work, and will receive Universal Credit payments to support me in this. The things I'll do are set out in this Claimant Commitment.

2. **Finding and taking work**

I'll look for and take any work I'm able to do, that:
- pays £6.19 an hour or more
- is within 90 minutes' travel from my home

I'm available for work for 40 hours each week. I can work on any day at any time.

I will:
- apply for vacancies I'm told to apply for by my adviser
- attend and take part fully in job interviews I'm offered
- take up offers of paid work that I'm able to do

If, without good reason, I don't do all these things, my Universal Credit payments will be cut by £10.20 a day for up to 3 years.

I will be available to:
- attend a job interview immediately
- start work immediately

If, without good reason, I'm not available as described, my Universal Credit payments will be cut by £10.20 a day for up to 91 days.

3. **My actions for getting into work**

My work search and preparation plan lists the things I'll do to give me the best chance of finding work quickly. This means I will normally spend 35 hours each week looking and preparing for work.

I will:
- complete all the activities in Section 1 of my work search and preparation plan
- provide evidence that I've done my regular work search activities when required

Page 1 of 4

Source: https://assets.publishing.service.gov.uk/media/5a8084e840f0b62302693fb2/foi-3786-13-eg-claimant-commitment-annex1.pdf

a third 'high level offence' – which means failure to apply for a job or refusal of mandatory work activity (for instance, a violation of the Claimant Commitment [see Figure 4.1]) – earns a 1,095 day (three-year) reduction or potential cessation *of all benefits* until 're-compliance' (Fletcher and Wright 2018, p 333). Sanctions are now longer and more immediate and their use is routine (Dwyer 2018, p 5) – in 2001, around 300,000 benefit sanctions were imposed on JSA claimants. This had increased by 245 per cent by 2013 to a peak of 1,037,034 as part of the 'great sanctions drive' when around 25 per cent of JSA claimants were sanctioned between 2010 and 2015 (Dwyer

2018, p 5, and Webster 2016). As Englander (1998) said of the 'great drive' to abolish all out-relief in the mid-1880s, the suffering behind these numbers is hard to imagine. Supporters of welfare conditionality see it as the means to reduce dependency; opponents say that it is ethically unjustifiable and ineffective (Dwyer 2018, p 2). Recent empirical work shows that sanctions trigger negative financial, emotional and health impacts on individuals and their families (Wright 2016; Dwyer 2018). This is evident in the Work and Pensions Committee evidence session on Universal Credit and Childcare and Universal Credit and Survival Sex (WPC 2018a and b; WPC 2019a and b). At the same time, sanctions are 'fundamentally ineffective in initiating or sustaining movements into paid work among benefit recipients' (Dwyer 2018, p 9). Given that the punishments increase precarity but aren't successful in moving people into work, we might conclude that their function, like that of the workhouse, is (in part at least) semiotic. It is designed to establish and to signal the limits to which the state will go to coerce compliance.

Food and hunger

Disciplinary power is exercised through constant surveillance and 'presuppos[es] a closely meshed grid of material coercions' (Foucault 2003, pp 35–36). This idea of a 'closely meshed grid of material coercions' is a useful way of thinking about the many practices involved in the production of the *bare life* in the workhouse, of which hunger and the regulation of food as a form of subdual and coercion are key. The amount and variability of food was reduced through the adoption of one of six carefully calibrated dietaries; the policing of mealtimes (meals were eaten looking down and in silence [see Figure 4.2]) narrowed the experience of what it means to eat in a human, social manner (Sen 2017): The archives show the dietaries were felt to be insufficient to survive (TNA Source A).

The Southwell Union Punishment Book (Nottinghamshire Archives Source A) reveals the substitute of a meal for a measure of potatoes or bread as one of the most common punishments. The symbolic value of the substitute food was considered to be a source of shame: potatoes were considered an animal food, fit only for the socially reviled Irish; 'black bread' marked the eater out as socially marginal. The regime described in the book substantiates Agamben's argument that the central project of the Poor Law Report of 1834 was 'the production of the destitute subject who is recognised by the outer world and who achieves self-recognition as merely the bearer of "bare life"' (cited in Sen 2017, p 239). The dietaries were, he proposes, a 'conscious biopolitics' with the deployment of hunger a key part of 'forms of statecraft to ensure that the market could operate free of the entanglement of an earlier moral economy' (Sen 2017, p 239). It was already obvious by 1837 that the inmate population was *not*

Figure 4.2: 'Marylebone Workhouse Dining Hall'

Source: © Peter Higginbotham Collection/Mary Evans Picture Library

workshy able-bodied men whose behaviours were technically the target of the policy, but the old and the vulnerable who were subject to harsh discipline through the use and abuse of food (see Table 4.1). The enduring focus on the figure of the wilfully workless male, and the policy consensus achieved as a result of abhorrence towards him across the political spectrum, justified punitive sanctions in the 1834 Act. The misalignment between the deterrent nature of a policy and the populations who were pulled into its strictures is evident in Table 4.1. The high numbers of able-bodied women here testifies to the fact that they were often either forced into the house if their husbands were ill, or were single or widowed, and therefore one of the anomalies that the Act had not anticipated in its design, as discussed in Chapter 3. There are *no* able-bodied male inmates (the actual target of the deterrent policy).

This misalignment between deterrence and the vulnerability of populations that end up coming into the orbit of the policy continues under Universal Credit. Many groups have come under conditional regimes for the first time and/or are particularly vulnerable to sanctions which were designed for other target populations (women with very young children, the partners of Universal Credit claimants, those earning low wages and people with disabilities), and they become subject to the deterrence and sanctions designed to deter *other* populations.

Table 4.1: Inhabitants of the Southwell Union Workhouses in April 1837

	Week 18 April 1837	Week 25 April 1837
Men		
Able-bodied	0	0
Infirm	34	36
Total men	34	36
Boys		
Over 9	12	12
Under 9	24	19
Total boys	36	31
Women		
Able-bodied	10	11
Infirm	32	33
Total women	42	44
Girls		
Over 9	11	8
Under 9	8	10
Total girls	19	18
Infants	0	6
Totals	131	135

Source: Based on a handwritten table in the minutes from the Southwell Union Workhouse Board of Guardians in April 1837 (Nottinghamshire Archives Source B)

Other letters in the National Archives Poor Law collection attest to the quality, type and amount of food being experienced as punitive. For example, a letter to the local Board of Guardians for Poplar Workhouse on 23 November 1888 is accompanied by a potato as evidence of the rotten food that workhouse inmates were given (TNA Source A, MH12/7700). Although the main focus of the Andover Inquiry (HoC 1846) was the starving male inmates reduced to gnawing 'green meat' off bones they were preparing for bone crushing, the scandal revealed other indignities relating to food, agency and hunger: inmates were given no cutlery; female inmates had no extra food when breastfeeding; children were reduced to eating raw potatoes thrown out for pigs; milk was skimmed and the cream given to the master or shaken (by the inmates) and then carried to his table as butter (HoC 1846, lines 8964–8966). The authority was diffuse, creating fear of asking for more under pain of being beaten or locked up in 'a dark place' (HoC 1846, p 343). The result was that hunger was managed rather than relieved in the workhouse. Further, the inducing of hunger as a form of punishment was disproportionately used for female inmates in the Southwell Workhouse: in all categories of offence, over half of punishments for women related to food (withdrawal of substitution) compared to just over one fifth for men.

Hunger continues to be a form of government, a 'conscious biopolitics' in Agamben's terms (Sen 2017, p 239). In April 2023, the Trussell Trust revealed it had provided almost three million food parcels in the last year. JRF responded by stating that 'Hunger on this scale isn't normally associated with a society in peacetime' (JRF 2023). While in the NPL the imposition of hunger was both a part of the day-to-day 'irksome' conditions in operation in the house *and* a sanctioned and routine punishment for breaking behavioural codes with maximum prescribed limits in the General Orders 1847, hunger within Universal Credit is an 'effective' strategy – that is, a predictable but not articulated effect of the policy. Claimants often find foodbank use shaming: 'I've had to go out and go to a food bank and I'm working 40 hours a week … How embarrassing is that? … That is wrong' (Paul, forty-six, cited in Wright and Dwyer 2020, p 14). Accessing a foodbank or receiving food parcels constitutes a deviation from norms in line with the definitions of poverty and wealth explored in Chapter 1. In his observations on the link between food and the *bare life*, Sen (2017) notes that being unable to eat adequately or 'normally' within your social context marks you apart and confirms you 'unable to participate in the life of the community'. The photograph in Figure 4.3 by author Louisa Britain is of a free school meal half-term pack (during lockdown). It sparked outrage when she shared it on social media in 2021. Like the black bread and potatoes in the workhouse, it marks its recipients out as unable to eat adequately within their social context. In 1846, children were found to have been scrabbling among the food thrown out for the pigs; in 2019, a headteacher in Morecombe told the BBC that: 'We have children who have nothing in their lunch boxes and children who are just fixated upon food … When children are food deprived it alters their behaviour and they do become quite food obsessed, so we have some children who will be stealing fruit cores from the bins' (*BBC News* 2019). In 2024, hunger continues to be a contemporary means of government.

Space and movement

The design of, access to and confinement within space was a form of government in the workhouse system. The workhouse itself was designed as 'an instrument of surveillance', understood as 'a territorially-based process of administration designed to regulate the conduct of human beings' (Driver 2004, p 9). The models for workhouses, often cruciform to enable maximum segregation and surveillance, embodied the links assumed in the 19th century between design and moral reformation, which meant that 'to

Figure 4.3: Free School Meals holiday pack, January 2021

Source: @RoadsideMum Louisa Britain

each environment there was a corresponding form of life' (Driver 2004, p 14). The pauper population was physically separated by sex and age within separate wards and yards to facilitate the 'targeting [of] appropriate treatment', and to act as a 'barrier against contagion, moral as well as physical' (2004, p 65). Carter et al cite *The Times* from May 1834: 'Such a [workhouse] system amounts to a declaration that every pauper is a criminal, and that, under the name of workhouses, prisons shall be erected throughout the land for their safe custody and punishment' Carter et al 2019, p 163). The workhouse operated alongside other means to equivalise poverty with criminality. For example, the Anatomy Act 1832 provided for the bodies of paupers to be donated – without consent – to medical schools, supplementing the usual source of hung felons. The workhouse aesthetic, too, confirmed that 'poverty was to be treated as a crime' (Driver 2004, p 61), and, indeed, some accounts of experience in the houses clearly identify them as prison-like *or worse*. In *Down and Out in Paris and London*, for example, Orwell (2001) observes that the casuals (nonresident paupers using workhouses on a single-night basis) shared information with each other about the conditions in the houses around London, praising particular houses where the blankets were 'as good as those in prisons'.

What was the specific role of the workhouse in this regime of regulated movement? First of all, those who applied to the house had to first accept their dislocation or relocation: the 1834 Act displaced people from their communities and confined them in an area they were often unfamiliar with: women were returned not to their own parish, but to the parishes of their husbands, even if he was dead or they were separated. Inmates also had to accept effective imprisonment and then accept the harsh conditions – including restricted mobility – *within* the workhouse. Letters to the PLC bemoan the regular restrictions on access to outside space and clean air: 'the Duke of Northumberland (bequeathed) to the inmates of the Tynemouth Workhouse [for] a garden and recreation ground. Then why should it now be tabooed at the caprice of either master or guardians?' (TNA Source A, MH12/9163). Although technically allowed to leave, most inmates experienced the house as a prison. Henriques (1968) suggests that the idea of there being freedom to leave in the absence of practical alternatives was illusory, especially for women, who often had nowhere to go. Here is Catherine Lock, protesting this issue in 1866:

> Sir, I hope you will pardon me writing to you, but it is to solicit [seek] the favour of you to order the Guardians of Issing, to allow me support to myself and two small children, aged 5 ½ and 8 months … My husband is in a deep decline and being past recovery he is in Uppingham Union [workhouse]. I have a small comfortable home and do not wish to go into the Union. (TNA Source A, *A letter from a woman wanting to maintain her two children outside the workhouse*, 21 November 1866, MH12/9812)

Mobility was also a form of government for the population *outside* the house. Questions around the mobility of the poor had been the focus of legislation throughout the Tudor and Hanoverian periods through laws of settlement and those against vagrancy and vagabondage, which I referenced in Chapter 3 in the context of their role in the progressive vilification of the poor. These were designed not to fully arrest mobility, but to regulate it based on the exigencies of the labour market. The 1834 Act was in part an intervention of a similar nature, in effect, regulating population movement to be responsive to the spatial flow of capital (often rural south to industrialising north). Arresting or directing mobility, like the strategic use of hunger, contributes to the reducing of human experience to a 'bare life'.

While confinement *within a building* may have stopped with the closure of the workhouses, the spatial management of the poor continues both directly, through the requirements placed on individuals to always be available to attend meetings or to take up work, through the format of those meetings (which I will return to in Chapter 5) and indirectly through processes of territorial displacement: public sector workers are unlikely to be able to afford to live in the cities they service, for example, or will live in areas subject to forms of territorial stigmatisation (Wacquant et al 2014; Daniel 2019). I will leave a detailed exploration of the management of mobility under Universal Credit to Chapter 7, where I describe the flows of people through the Jobcentre Plus buildings, and the wider constraints on the movement of the poor in neoliberal urban contexts (Atkinson 2021; Savage 2021) as a modern semiotics of deterrence.

Work

Under the terms of the NPL, work within the workhouse was to be 'a source of deterrence rather than self-respect' (Englander 1998, pp 38–39). The system in effect 'legitimated the abuse of the poor through work' (Shave 2017, p 221). Workhouses were mandated to provide employment for able-bodied inmates, who were punished if they refused it: the Southwell punishment book registers 'refusal to work' as among its most often recorded offence, earning the harshest penalty (prison with hard labour). The workhouses chose employment that was not considered a threat to local private economies: oakum picking, stone breaking and bone crushing. Most male inmates were elderly or otherwise infirm (that is, not able-bodied [see Table 4.1]) and they found the work physically difficult and often personally humiliating: skilled craftsmen who were in the house for no other reason than having arthritis, for example, were made to break stones. Inmates tried to break a hand mill at the Southwell Union workhouse in 1844 which had been deliberately 'constructed *so as to perform no useful task*' (Carter et al 2019, p 170, emphasis added). The mill (see Figure 4.4) had been meticulously drawn to support replication in other unions, although it was ultimately rarely used after protest and eventual banning. However, it illustrates the energy with which *unproductive* labour was designed into the NPL. Although the mill undoubtedly represented the apotheosis of labour exploitation in the NPL, the oakum picking and stone breaking were not dissimilar in the refusal of dignity or purpose to labour. Thinking of *life* as the primary form of wealth as Ruskin did, writing when the workhouse system was at a high water mark ('There is no wealth but life': Ruskin 2010 [1862]), the reduction of the body to a physical force through its working of the unproductive mill, violates basic principles of a moral economy just as surely as it violates almost all of the central human capabilities necessary to a life worthy of human dignity defined by Nussbaum (2011). Key to Nussbaum's tenth capability, *control over one's environment*, is the idea of being

Figure 4.4: Section of a drawing for the machine that produces nothing – designed for vagrant labour in the Southwell Workhouse

Source: MH12/9360/303/2. Permissions secured from The National Archives.

able to 'work as a human being, exercising practical reason, and *entering into meaningful relationships of mutual recognition with other workers*' (Nussbaum 2011, p 34, emphasis added). This restates Ruskin's recognition of 'empathetic rather than merely instrumental links between economic actors' (Ruskin 2010 [1862]) and their desire, proven, he felt, in the ways in which people tend to act ethically towards one another, to act towards collective and not just personal wealth. The forced, fruitless work of bone crushing, oakum picking and milling for no purpose is not only a refusal of the dignity of work, but also disallows work as a form of collective participation in processes of shared wealth creation, and the related sense of fulfilment or wellbeing. Work continues to be a form of government in Universal Credit, albeit differently inflected. In their qualitative longitudinal study of claimant experiences of conditionality and benefit sanctions, Wright and Dwyer (2020) interviewed Joan, a woman in her sixties who had been a cleaner for eight years before claiming Universal Credit. She had arthritis and depression (since being widowed a decade earlier) and lived in social housing with her son. The authors follow Joan over a two-year period, during which she 'worked continuously and held down between three and five part-time cleaning contracts concurrently'. At the beginning of the two-year period, Joan was positive and upbeat. At the third and final interview, she had five jobs and was working full-time (34 hours a week), but was still required to seek more hours to get up to the requisite hours under threat of sanction, despite her ongoing impairments. Universal Credit adds cruel and constant pressure to take on more work and 'coerces working claimants into time-consuming unproductive job-seeking' (Wright and Dwyer 2020, p 12). It also produces work as an aggregate of hours rather than 'decent' work that coheres into a job and has meaning and value in anything but a bald economic way, reflecting the refusal of dignity through decent work we saw in the workhouse example given earlier (see Figure 4.4). Alston observed that the process of claiming makes 'many claimants ... feel that they are forced to jump through hoops for the sake of it, fill out pointless job applications for positions that do not match their qualifications, and take inappropriate low-paid, temporary work just to avoid debilitating sanctions' (Alston 2018, p 6). There is no option to choose work that is meaningful at an individual level. Instead, the sanction regime operates as a 'criminalisation strategy, which is sensitive to government control' (Fletcher and Wright 2018, p 334). Language around compliance is legalised (noncompliance is an 'offence'; sanction can be applied when the Claimant Commitment is 'breached'). When sanctioning rates are too low (that is, when the number of claimants being sanctioned doesn't hit the desired level), Jobcentre Plus staff are 'subject to an "improvement plan"' (Fletcher and Wright 2018, p 335). The mandatory 35–40 hours per week of job-searching for those on the top level of conditionality, in the absence of jobs paying wages sufficient to sustain life, is the contemporary equivalent of the machine that produces nothing. Here is the witness testimony of single mother-of-three Gaynor Rowles to the Work and Pensions Committee Inquiry into Universal Credit Roll-out and Childcare. It brings together several of these aspects that make up a bare life under the current welfare regime (low wages, long hours and an inability to partake in family life):

> [M]ore than anything, my parents have had to provide and pay for my children to go to nursery so that I can still go to work. Like I say, I have had my business for 15 years. I do not want to give that up. But my parents should not have to pay for my children to lead a normal life and for me to lead a normal life, but I would be better off not working ... I did an entitlement thing not long ago and I am only £9.37 a week better off working. That is it ... Since I have been on this [Universal Credit], I have changed as a person – I am not my normal happy self. It is quite sad to think about how it can affect people. (WPC 2018b, pp 28–32)

I want to finish this section by looking at some of the 'less sensational forms of cruelty' that become normalised as means of governing the poor through their use in the workhouse and that are manifest in contemporary repertoires of the state. I am interested in the ways in which these mechanisms of government undermine humanising capabilities as identified in Nussbaum (2011), and act as barriers to lives worthy of human dignity. The first is the act of being observed. As per Bentham's original intent in his panopticon prison design, hypervisibility was part of the regime of government in the workhouse, and this was manifest both physically (house, uniform and meals) and administratively (inspections forms and new administrative procedures) (Carter and Motlagh 2023). This hypervisibility is the motivation for Alston's comparison between the workhouse and the 'total surveillance' of the Universal Credit system. The second is the state of being unlistened to and unheard. The overwhelming sense when reading about the female inmates in the workhouse is of being unlistened to – of there not being a place or person within the system who will hear their story. I will explore this in more detail in a contemporary context in Chapter 8 (and I have written about it in Kerr [2023]) in the context of epistemic injustice. Here, Jane Grace attests to having been beaten by the master and the mistress on a regular basis. She didn't complain because: 'We were likely enough to have it again if we had.' This is an excerpt from her interview with the Committee (HoC 1846, p 344):

> Did any of the visiting guardians ever ask you if you had any complaint to make against any one in the establishment? No.

Have you ever had an opportunity of speaking to any of the visiting guardians, so that the master could not hear what you said? No.

There was no occasion on which you could have spoken to the visiting guardians without the master hearing what you said? No.

Had you expressed a wish to anybody that you would like to complain to the visiting guardians? No.

Did you ever hear any other girl express a wish to complain? No.

Did you ever hear them say they were ill-treated by Mr or Mrs McDougal? Not more than being beaten; all the girls have been beaten.

That frequently happened? Yes.

And did you ever hear any of the girls afterwards say they would complain of that? Sometimes they have said so, but they have not done it.

Third, when the policy produces perverse and harmful outcomes for certain subpopulations, these are treated as some kind of social 'rounding error' even when they affect many people or particular groups of people. In *Down and out in Paris and London,* for example, Orwell observed that the Poor Law – still in operation when he was writing in the 1930s – produced the vagrant population it allegedly aimed to suppress. The one-night rule for 'casuals' (nonresidents) meant that every morning thousands of men had to set off again on the road, seeking a new place to sleep the next night. The DWP responded to witness testimonies to the WPC Inquiry into Survival Sex and Universal Credit (of which Ms J's testimony cited in Chapter 2 is part), with rebuttals and counterevidence, suggesting that there was

> little *reliable* data to illustrate any specific cause and effect in this space ... [and] 'social security' or 'welfare' more broadly has long been blamed for a rise in prostitution or sex work ... On the basis of current evidence, it appears over simplistic is wrong to suggest that there is a direct causative link between Universal Credit specifically and an increase in prostitution or survival sex'. (DWP 2019b, pp 47–48, emphasis added)

In the 1840s, Louise Barnes is turned out of the workhouse two weeks before she gives birth, because she is about to give birth in a parish that is not hers, and under the new law, the parish she is in would be responsible for the cost. So despite being very ill, she is asked to leave 'the back way' and struggles to walk across the parish boundary with nowhere to go (HoC 1846, p 273). Fourth, there is disregard for bodily integrity, especially of women. This is shown respectively through tolerance of hunger as a form of control, the disproportionate confinement of women, and for the downplaying of sexual assault. When Hewill Williams is recorded as having 'indecently interfered with a female inmate' (Nottinghamshire Archives Source A, 2 September

1900), the punishment he receives is the same as William Corden gets for hitting a boy with a stick (Nottinghamshire Archives Source A, 7 July 1900) and is half the term inmates get for refusing to work (Nottinghamshire Archives Source A, 22 and 28 October 1901). In the context of Universal Credit, the tolerance of survival sex in effect establishes coerced sex as an acceptable means of minimising the welfare 'burden' on the state. Finally, the frugality and depersonalisation inherent in the space and processes of the workhouse caused mental harm. The barren white-wall aesthetic was only softened as the system matured *on the advice of the Lunacy Commission*, which recognised its effect on the mental health of the inmates. In the late 1860s, pictures were bought to relieve the white monotony (In Their Own Write 2021). I will pick up on this in the context of Universal Credit in Chapter 7.

It is clear that the contemporary punitive repertoires of government of the poor renew older punishment economies of the workhouse in the most general sense of 'abandon[ing] of concerns for meeting human needs in favour of maintaining a disciplined and orderly society' (Rodger, cited in Fletcher and Wright 2018, p 325). The increasing resilience of the state with regard to tolerating hunger, its retrenchment from some of the micropractices of, for example, adult social care (such as ear syringing [*BBC News* 2020]) and the likely cessation of government funding of the arts as local authorities make swinging cuts to absorb chronic underfunding (Thompson 2024) might undermine human dignity in ways we consider 'less sensational' than the workhouse, but which nonetheless are structurally designed to, or will tend to, produce a bare life.

Discipline and punishment in the context of wealth

The general economy of discipline and punishment in the context of wealth must be described as one that is reluctant, consistently permissive and highly responsive to refusal on the part of the rich to being seen or known. A prerequisite to discipline is to be able to *see*: recall the early political arithmetic focus on large-scale 'seeing' through censuses and mapping. But the tendency of the state towards wealth and the wealthy is to accede to limits set by them in terms of acceptable levels of inquisitorialism – that is, to accede to not seeing. Pitt's reluctance to move towards inquisitorialism in terms of income meant that he was forced to seek to reduce revenue fraud elsewhere in the system, namely through actions against smuggling. Smuggling (an umbrella term in the 18th century for most forms of fraud, bribery, forgery and nondisclosure of income) was endemic. One of the reasons it proved difficult to counter was that, although technically and legally criminal, it was not considered so by the population. It was a 'social crime', a 'criminal action which is legitimised by popular opinion' (Horwell 2019, p 257). Attempts to deal with it were rendered difficult because of deep-seated opposition to an intrusive state (as outlined in the introductions to Parts II and III of this book), a lack of appropriately robust administrative capability within government, strongly held public opinions on what could be taxed and how this might be collected, and the lack of a shared idea of what constituted just process (Horwell 2019, p 263). The overall effect was a limited scale and reach of sanctions and punishment.

Compliance

These barriers endure in the opposition to a perceived 'intrusive state' evidenced in the membership and nature of the participation of the Society of Trust and Estate Practitioners (STEP – the professional body of wealth managers who represent the superrich to the government) in the HMRC's WEF (which will be the focus of Chapter 8). It endures in the continuing limited administrative capability or interest of the state in coming to know about wealth and the wealthy: The ONS WAS only commenced in 2006, for example. It endures (although less straightforwardly) in public opinion where there is support for even very high levels of wealth if it is perceived to be an outcome of fair process and where there is a dislike for discourse that vilifies the rich (NEON et al 2018; Hebden and Palmer 2020), although there is also aversion to avoidance, which was not a feature of 18th-century public opinion. These factors help to limit the scale and reach of sanctions and punishment, which manifests as lightly for wealthy people in the 21st century as they did for the wealthy in the late 18th and early 19th centuries. Where a social welfare claimant who fails to comply with the Claimant Commitment can be 'fined' up to 100 per cent of their benefit income for up to 1,095 days, a HNWI who fails to comply with their tax liability is fined an average of £10,500 (PAC 2017, p 8) against a *minimum* investable asset to qualify as a HNWI of £20 million (discounting income and primary residence). This equates to a maximum fine of 0.05 per cent of this asset. The first is clearly a deterrent; the second is permission to continue.

Tolerance for revenue loss to tax avoidance, evasion and fraud as a result either of not having the means to know about it, or not pursuing it actively, continues to be a governmental strategy within the disposition of ignorance: not knowing is an active form of structural apathy, '... the deliberate choice not to engage knowledge in a particular direction (as it is presumed to be unimportant)' (Gross 2007 in Croissant 2014, p 12). If we attempted to deduce government policy in relation to the tax revenue of the very wealthy from its *effects*, we could confidently say that it wishes to minimise revenue or, at the very least, does not wish to optimise it. For example, tax evasion is illegal, whereas tax avoidance is legally compliant but has two poles – tax planning or optimisation, and aggressive or abusive avoidance which seeks to subvert the purpose of the law (Seely 2021, p 3) with a blurred line between the two. The tax gap is the difference between tax collected and tax due (against the letter and spirit of the law). In 2018/19, tax evasion (illegal activity) cost £5.5 billion and tax avoidance cost £1.5 billion. Despite evasion costing the economy much more than avoidance, the state prioritises avoidance, enacting sanctions (albeit minimally) against something that is legal over something that is illegal, and against something that has a much smaller financial impact. Tax fraud costs the Treasury nine times the amount lost to benefits fraud, but is pursued less enthusiastically (Taxwatch UK 2021).

In its 2015 Report, the Public Accounts Committee said that 'HMRC's failure to prosecute more than one individual from the Falciani list [a leaked list of HMRC customers using the bank for tax evasion purposes], HMRC having closed this case and the Financial Conduct Authority no longer taking further action, creates the impression that the rich can get away with tax fraud' (PAC 2016, p 3). In January 2017, the Committee questioned HMRC's strategy for dealing with the very wealthy, suggesting that the wealthy 'get help with their tax affairs that is not available to other taxpayers'. The Committee expressed alarm that 'the amount of tax paid by this very wealthy group of individuals *has actually fallen by £1 billion since the unit was set up* – from £4.4 billion in 2009–10 to £3.5 billion in 2014–15' (PAC 2017, p 4, emphasis added). Between 2018 and 2022, civil investigations by the offshore, corporate and wealthy unit, part of HMRC's fraud investigation service, fell from 1,417 to 627 (Siddons and Ungoed-Thomas 2024) – a decline of more than half. In the six years between 2017 (when it was introduced) and 2023, the HMRC 'has not charged a single company' with corporate tax evasion (Siddons 2024). Taxwatch UK (2021) found that tax fraud 'cost the Treasury an estimated £20bn in 2018/19 – 9x more than benefits fraud (£2.2bn)'. Despite this, 'DWP employs 3.5x more staff in compliance than HMRC'. And while there have been 85,745 criminal prosecutions for crimes relating to benefits since 2010, there have only been 3,665 prosecutions for tax crime of all types (3,665) – that is, 23 times less (Taxwatch UK 2021). We seem not to have come very much further than Pitt in terms of the lack of political will or capability to interrogate and scrutinise the rich and their riches, and the durability of assumptions of trustworthiness towards a group whose actual fiscal behaviours are characterised by endemic breaching of trust.

What can we know from these practices in terms of the government of wealth through policy? Wealth and its objects, the rich, are taxed (but not much) and pursued when they refuse to comply (but not energetically – recall the £10,500 average fine for fiscal noncompliance against assets of at least £20 million+ described earlier). The practical effects of governmental ignorance and privacy *there* (wealth) demands scrutiny and disclosure *here* (poverty), because the shortfall arising as a result of underpayment of taxes by the rich has to be made up from taxpayers lower down the fiscal chain. A 2015 Public Accounts Committee (PAC) report expressed concern that HMRC could not explain why income tax receipts from HNW individuals had fallen by £1 billion (20 per cent) since 2009–2010, while income tax from all taxpayers had increased by £23 billion (9 per cent) over the same period. While tax avoidance and evasion combined from a relatively small groups of very wealthy individuals and business cost the UK government £7 billion in 2020–2021 (financial loss from tax avoidance was £1.5 billion and the cost of tax evasion was £5.5 billion [House of Commons Library 2021]), the net loss to the DWP of benefit fraud *and error* for the year ending 2023 (including error *on the part of DWP itself* – error is not disaggregated from fraud in the figures), after accounting for recoveries, was 3.1 per cent (£7.3 billion) of total benefit expenditure (DWP 2023). The fact that the pursuit of the latter is resourced so much more comprehensively, and is pursued more aggressively, is a reflection of the balance between the two governmental dispositions (ignorance and scrutiny) of wealtherty.

Space and movement

I want now to reflect on how techniques of managing mobility or spatial confinement operate in relation to wealth. In Chapter 3, I looked at how the movement of the poor has been a constant source of anxiety to the state, and legislation has sought to manage it: from Vagrancy Acts in the 16th century, Settlement Acts in the 17th century and the workhouse system in the 19th century to Joan, trekking across London on the night buses mopping up an hour here and an hour there of low-paid work to ensure compliance with Universal Credit. The enduring distinction between the government of mobility for richer and poorer populations could not be more stark. In terms of space and movement of wealth and the wealthy, techniques of government are what Sinfield (2023) calls means-*enhancing*: they deliver maximal freedom and movement as is evident in the example of Madiyar Ablyazov in Chapter 2: one of the capacities that extreme wealth enables (Beckert 2023) is the opportunity to buy forms of mobility through residency.

Mobility as government under *wealtherty* is contrastive: Some people get to move and others become stuck. The management of the mobility of poorer people (very broadly conceived here as those who need to earn labour from work) is aligned with the needs of capital. This contrasts with the borderless, unregulated, smooth navigation of space available to the rich: Harrington's (2016) ethnography of wealth managers includes the story of one who flew outside Europe with her Chief Executive Officer (CEO) and did not need to produce her passport – they were literally beyond jurisdictions and law (Harrington 2016, p 244). Vandana Shiva contrasts the very different modes of mobility for the very wealthy, who are 'mobile on a world scale, with no country, no home, but the whole world as its property' (Ablyazov, as described in Chapter 2), with the arrested mobility of people living 'in refugee camps, resettlement colonies and reserves' (Vandana Shiva, cited in Braidotti 2011, p 7). This results in what Braidotti calls a form of urban imprisonment for some, a 'dense materiality' of bodies trapped in 'the very concrete conditions of advanced global societies' (Braidotti 2011, p 6). This dense materiality is countered by the easy fluidity of the very wealthy, like Ablyazov, who opts out of national identity to pursue a life free from taxation and other regulatory impositions. She concludes that 'the global city and the refugee camp are not dialectical or moral opposites: they are two sides of the same global coin' (Braidotti 2011, p 6). Cities play a particular role in this contrastive government of poorer and richer people's mobility. Hall and Savage (2015, in Savage 2021, p 241) present contemporary cities as 'elite urban vortexes', as engines of social mobility for those incoming from outside (Ablyazov), not for those born urban (Ms J) (Savage 2021, p 239). The vortex operates with a centripetal force, pulling towards it the weight of capital, anchoring this capital within real estate, while simultaneously flinging those without the weight of capital to ground them to the peripheries. This constitutes a refactoring of urban space to optimise the flow and the nesting/layering of capital as part of which cities are hollowed out in terms of their poorer populations. In 2017, 1,400 homes in London were sold for more than £5 million. Before the financial sector failure in 2008, the most expensive home in London was sold for £19 million. In 2016, three were sold for more than £90 million each. In 2020, a home in Knightsbridge was sold to a Chinese tycoon for £200 million (Atkinson 2021, p 61). This refactoring is sustained by specific and active techniques of government: 'lax regulatory environment, low property tax and a vision of the city as a place for investment and the wealthy' (Atkinson 2021, p 82). Hall and Savage (2015) see the starkly polarised forms of mobility and locations described by Vandana Shiva and Braidotti (access to the whole world versus the arrested mobility within refugee camps) reflected in a more geographically concentrated way *within* the cities of rich nations (Savage 2021).

What about the role of work? Atkinson observes that 'many of the rich don't work.[2] Their capital works for them' (Atkinson 2021, p 65). It is the *capital* against which the 'behaviour' norms are applied in the Tier 1 visa context. Checks on personal behaviours (mediated through 'politically exposed person' [PEP] checks), are secondary to the ownership of capital and to agreement that this capital will be made to behave in specific ways: as 'share or loan capital in active and trading UK companies' rather than as an investment stake in a property, for example. If the capital behaves in this way, investors will be enabled to bring their families to the UK to live and work. In this way, the behaviours of rich *individuals* escape discipline. This is of course a generalisation. Rich people are sanctioned, but not sufficiently for this to constitute a technique of government; fiscal behaviours are not shaped by these sanctions, as is evident in the PAC's scrutiny of HMRC's compliance work (PAC 2017). Further, pre-emptive policy tools – such as the WEF, as I will go on to show in Part III of this book – go to extreme lengths to prevent punishment from happening, creating plenty of prelegislative conversation space to help with accidental 'errors' that might otherwise be committed.

This chapter has described some of the mechanisms, procedures, instruments, tactics, techniques and technologies through which richer and poorer people have been governed and continue to be governed – the 'making material' of the ways of knowing and forms of knowledge described in Chapter 3. I have found moments of emergence of contemporary ways of governing in those of the past. This is true for the rich and the poor, and the maintenance of the (spatial, fiscal and social) distance between the two groups. For those who are poor, hunger is a contemporary form of discipline; displacement is still a form of government; the means of seeking social relief are still punitive and still reproduce patriarchal dependencies; and they still disproportionately damage women. The state operationalises its mistrust of the poor through mechanisms that amount to forms of 'total surveillance' (Alston 2018, p 11). Work is enforced through coercion. At the other end of the scale, privacy still protects the assets of the wealthy from 'suffering' tax through the operation of the 'confiscatory' state; absolute freedom of movement is the norm, and the state's approach to sanctioning wealth and the wealthy is highly permissive. In terms of the relationship *between* richer and poorer people, the sense of mutualism – of responsibility for collective wellbeing – that gradually eroded over the 17th and 18th centuries continues to be absent. There is not, for example, a shared understanding of the rich being responsible for providing revenue in exceptional circumstances (for example, deep poverty or impending environmental disaster). In the face of social instability and environmental emergency, calls from rich people to contribute more to collective wealth via taxation are the exception rather than the rule (for example, Patriotic Millionaires).

How these mechanisms and processes shaped the individuals who became subject to them is the focus of the next chapter. Alternatively, you might like to jump to Chapter 7, which looks at contemporary mechanisms of government in the spatial and visual field of *wealtherty*.

5

Being: how ways of thinking and governing enabled different forms of self for richer and poorer people

In 1845, Hannah Joyce enters the Andover workhouse with her very young baby. The baby is ill and struggling to breathe properly. Hannah is not local and she does not know any other women in the house. She is allocated a bed with another inmate – Jane Grace. They share a single bed with the young baby, which dies in the night. Hannah is accused of killing the baby by the mistress of the house, although the inquest later finds that the baby died of a chest infection. After having been asked to sleep in the 'dead room' with the baby's body overnight, which she ultimately refuses to do, Hannah is instead locked – newly grieving – in the infirmary. The following day, she is made to carry the coffin with her baby in it up to the church on her own. She walks through the town carrying the coffin under her arm, accompanied by the workhouse porter who has been given strict instructions not to help. Fellow inmate Sarah Muspratt tells the inquiry that on the instructions of the matron, the women 'rattled' a distraught Hannah out of the house a few days later (they took pots and pans and wooden spoons and banged them like drums as Hannah made her way out of the house and into town), all the time observed from a window by the Board of Guardians (which were typically composed of wealthy local landed men) (HoC 1846, pp 300–316). Hannah, Jane and Sarah gave evidence in an inquiry into irregularities at the Andover Workhouse, originally convened in response to the 'green meat' scandal that had arisen among male workers.

Identity formation does not take place separately from institutional formation/re-formation. Hannah, Jane and Sarah are inmates within an institution of the state, itself a materialisation of specific ideas and opinions about poor people, their motivations, their behaviours, and their role in wider imaginaries of the (wealth of the) nation and its costs. Different practices of government presuppose different forms of person, self and identity, and seek to transform these identities in different ways (Dean 2010). Governmental orientations of scrutiny and ignorance manifest ways of thinking and doing that I described in Chapters 3 and 4, and predispose certain ways of life, certain forms of self and certain policy identities, which are the focus of this chapter. One of the imperatives implicit in the definition of wealtherty is the need to articulate the coexistence of these radically divergent governmental orientations towards richer and poorer people. There is remarkable continuity in this regard between the historical periods I focus on in this book and contemporary practice. We meet the cruelty of Hannah's experience in the workhouse in the testimonies at the Work and Pensions Committee Inquiry into Universal Credit and Survival Sex, as women struggle within and against prevailing ways of thinking that stigmatise them, and prevailing institutional norms and practices which harm them. They find themselves in need of care and support in an institution designed as a deterrent. At the other end of the spectrum, norms and canons that enshrined means-enhancing concessions to privacy in the first direct tax on income (1798) are embedded in contemporary instruments of law and regulation (for example, OECD 2009) and in the very ways in which the state and the rich communicate. We see this reflected in the communicative practices of the HMRC WEF, in which rich people are represented by the wealth management industry, becoming – what I go on make the case for later on – 'intermediated' subjects.

Let me illustrate the ways in which the dispositions are anchored in and endure in ways of thinking, doing and how these shape ways of being. In terms of *ways of thinking and doing* (the focus of Chapters 3 and 4), a governmental orientation of scrutiny is revealed through the epistemological rationale behind technologies of bioadministration that came of age in the early 19th century. It is predicated on an overwhelming right to see, to inspect, to demand, to be told and to *know* the affairs of the poor in all their detail. These ideas are made material regimes of total surveillance – of the panopticonic workhouse or of the direct transfer of Universal Credit claimant data between HMRC and the DWP. It is delivered through starving, imprisoning, degrading, reducing, diminishing or coaching and coercing, investigating and sanctioning. These mechanisms produce a self (a way of being) who in order not to be subject to sanction, works, seeks work and documents work seeking. She plans, agrees and complies. She must reveal and disclose; she must not withhold; she must be honest.

The inverse to these ways of thinking and doing is revealed through the operation of the disposition of ignorance. In terms of ways of coming to know, this disposition is characterised by accession to the limits imposed on the inquiring gaze of the state by the wealthy. It is characterised by a predisposition to trust, to forgive, to ignore and to enable. Its mechanisms are the accommodating fiscal environments (of the 1790s or the 2000s). And it creates a self with various capacities (capacities that *only* the wealthy have [Beckert 2023]), including the capacity to limit the gaze of the state into private financial affairs. This is a self who is entitled to privacy, assumes that he is trusted, can legitimately refuse attempts to be known, can keep secrets and can conceal – a self who plans, who avoids, evades, hides and self-exiles, refuses to be seen, or orchestrates and negotiates the terms of his visibility.

Subjectivation under a disposition of scrutiny restricts available *repertoires of the self* (Skeggs 2005) and tends to coerce the specific forms of subjectivity necessary to the evolving shape of the market (McGimpsey et al 2017). Subjectivation under a disposition of ignorance, on the other hand, is acquiescing, coaxing, retreating and cooperating. It produces selves who are private, hidden, boldly noncompliant and, as I will show in, are themselves the governors, conducting the conduct of the state

The first section of this chapter looks at ways in which social identities come into being antagonistically – identified *against* others. The second section looks at oppositional pairings (versions of 'us and them'). I think about what contrastive statuses, capacities and attributes are assumed between those who exercise authority and those who are to be governed (Dean 2010). Relational identity making is foundational to wealtherty. It allows us to ask questions such as the following: 'How has it become acceptable that a person who works full-time but is dependent on Universal Credit to survive must be made to identify as a *claimant* when someone who doesn't work at all and is long-term dependent on fiscal welfare to maintain a dynastic fortune may be thought of as "independently" wealthy?' This chapter explores how the exercise of political privilege (which I will look at in Part III of this book) restricts 'repertoires of the self' for those who don't have that privilege. I will end by introducing the idea of the *intermediated self* – a self that is a particular response to processes of subjectivation that exist between the state and the superrich in the 21st century.

Self-making in a state of wealtherty

Self-making is spatially and temporally complex. I want to think about this in the context of *Ma*, which was introduced in Chapter 1. The point I am making in this book is that the dispositions I have articulated of scrutiny and ignorance *endure*. They are a force that presses onwards, in Savage's terms (2021). The spatial/social context shifts the ways in which the dispositions inflect and the forms of self they enable. But they remain the *same dispositions*, mobilising the same sensibilities and antagonisms, through different policy repertoires. Thinking about self-making in the context of duration requires a focus on both space and time. Spatially, identity making takes place across multiple sites, which are already precoded, in terms of being territorially marked by ownership or otherwise of wealth: housing; Jobcentre Plus offices; work; policy texts, discourse and practices; the media; the secret spaces of wealth exile; urban spaces; and rural spaces. Temporally, individual actions – claiming relief in all its forms (fiscal, corporate and social), avoiding or evading compliance – take place within *longue durée* histories of contrastive governmental orientations towards individuals and groups with more or less wealth. They are never complete innovations of a particular epoch.

Identity formation takes place within and against incumbent ways of thinking and doing, and the policy researcher's task to 'find out how a human being is envisaged … and the social practices that constitute this human being' (Ball 2015, p 308). How does government seek to modify the individual or her capacities? What practices of self are a necessary function of the system of welfare prescribed by Universal Credit or the strategy of 'deliberately engineered' secrecy (Cobham 2020) enabled by the state for HNWIs through the WEF? What traces of *past* ways of self-formation and *past* identities can we see modulating in our now? How are the governmental dispositions of scrutiny and ignorance performed at the level of identity making, and what are the sanctioned responses in each case (disclosure or concealment)?

In the late 18th century, moralising judgements about the worth, behaviours and social value of the poor (including views about their contribution to the common wealth of the nation) fundamentally shaped attempts to define and delineate dependency from a wider concept of poverty. As Chapter 3 has shown, getting the 1834 legislation over the line happened once *softer* attitudes espoused by humanists and evangelicals had been rendered subordinate to the 'weight' of influence of the Malthusian idea. These moralising judgements produced two populations at the same time. The attribution of negative values to one group resulted in positive attributions of value to the other (the higher status group). Tyler's history of stigma explores this doubly productive act, asking us to turn our attention upwards to the identity and operation of the *stigmatisers* (Tyler 2020, p 21), towards the group making the judgement. It is holding this power to allocate value that distinguishes the in-group from the out-group. Holding this position of judgement allows a person, a group of people or even an institution to attribute value and, in so doing, to 'assign the other as immoral, repellent, abject, worthless, disgusting, even disposable' (Skeggs 2005, pp 974–976; see also Bayly 2000; Mukherjee 2010; and Bhambra 2021c in the context of empire/nation states).

The example of Hannah I used earlier is important to this chapter because it illustrates the extent to which punitivism can be ratcheted once a population has been judged to be abject or disgusting in one way or another. The moralistic judgements which establish the belowness of specific populations constrain what Skeggs calls the available 'repertoires of the self' (Skeggs 2005, p 974). They enable more or less disciplinary forms of government. At the same time, they establish the aboveness of the other population, opening up new, enabling repertoires of the self: 'Disgust at that which is below functions to maintain the power relations between above and below, through which "aboveness" and "belowness" become properties of particular bodies, objects and spaces' (Ahmed 2004, p 88). Here it is worth recalling the idea of dependency being 'bonded' to the bodies of the poor through the 1834 Act.

Opportunities for self-making within types of institutions (for example, disciplinary ones like the workhouse or Universal Credit, or enabling ones like the WEF) are constrained in part by the objectives of those institutions, and in part by the degree and type of access to symbolic resources for self-making. The long history of 'enforced narratives' of the self (Steedman 2000) characteristic of early interactions between the poor and state institutions involved a process in which those seeking relief were made to 'tell [of] themselves in highly specific ways in order to receive welfare, instructed by legal interlocutors for whom narratives of redemption and respectability were necessary' (Vincent, cited in Skeggs 2005, pp 973–974). In the Southwell Workhouse, minutes from the meetings of Boards of Guardians start with the same item: 'The paupers were called in and questioned' (Nottinghamhire Archives Source B). Enforced narratives of the self are also a feature of contemporary social policy-making practices (the Claimant Journal, the Claimant Commitment and the interview, for example). This idea of forms of restricted (and sometimes coerced) selfhood is captured by Skeggs in the contrast between the 'ethical' self, who has access to or control of symbolic resources, and a self that is excessive, improper and, in not having access to or control of symbolic resources, must be content with being represented and defined by others – she loses representational agency. This is the case for Hannah Joyce, Jane Grace, and Sarah Muspratt. It is true in a different way for Ms J and the other witnesses to the WPC Inquiry into Universal Credit and Survival Sex (WPC 2019b) who are able to be represented (directly or reported), but whose epistemic agency (this will be explored in detail in Chapter 8) is rendered 'derivative' or secondary.

At the other end of the scale, occupying a position of judgement is a means of commanding representational agency: assigning low status to 'out' groups, as was suggested earlier, shores up the higher status of the 'in' group. I'm going to illustrate this process of relational identity making in the context of relationships between richer and poorer people, and richer and poorer people and the state, with two imbricating examples from the 19th century (Edwin Chadwick) and the 21st century (Iain Duncan Smith). In the context of an emergent and powerful civil service in the 1800s, Joshi (2004) explores the interplay between Edwin Chadwick (thwarted Poor Law Commissioner and ultimately Secretary to the Commissioners) and the Poor Law Commission (PLC). In Chapter 6 I will look at the interplay between thwarted Conservative Party leader Iain Duncan Smith and the operation of his think tank, the Centre for Social Justice (CSJ) among a proliferation of think tanks post 2000s, and specifically, its constitutive role in the development of the 2010 Coalition Party's new approach to social welfare. In each instance, men thwarted in their careers have sought redemption through an interest in the poor, specifically through becoming known for knowing about them. They are, or they work with, 'state bureaucrats or civil servants who used their knowledge and expertise to study, recommend, and enforce laws' (Joshi 2004, p 353). Joshi situates Chadwick as a byproduct of 'the fledgling but growing state bureaucracy' (Joshi 2004, p 356) and at the forefront of the historical moment of the emergence of the middle class in the early 1800s. He notes the specific way in which this class used a concern for the poor as a way of mapping out and distinguishing its own identity. During the first half of the 19th century, this group gained 'increasing social and political authority' (Joshi 2004, p 360) and proliferated in numbers: The Home Office had 29 employees in 1833 and 35,084 by 1851 (2004, p 356). The legislation that Chadwick oversaw distinguished not only dependent from independent poor, but also brought into being a technical class of administrators whose role was to rationalise and enforce the legislation that upheld these distinctions.

Duncan Smith's setting up of the CSJ after the collapse of his short-lived Conservative Party leadership was arguably a similar search for legitimacy and professional redemption through developing knowledge about the poor. He used the CSJ to establish what the party referred to as 'compassionate Conservativism', but which in effect repositioned effects of poverty as causes and underpinned a ratchet in an already punitive trajectory of social policy. The CSJ was established during a flourishing of think tanks and knowledge-producing bodies in the 2000s (Pautz and Heins 2016; Anstead 2018) which changed the relationship between the government and the civil service, interposing a new cadre of technocratic policy professionals, sidelining academics and civil servants, and forging new knowledge which was often at odds with the academic consensus (Slater 2012; McGimpsey et al 2016; Ross and Barnes 2021).

Both men contributed to, renewed and then concretised in legislation narratives that operated as stigmacraft (Tyler 2020). Both used the government of the poor 'as a way to enact distinction' (Joshi 2004). Both published high-level reports in which policy was 'the determinant rather than the outcome of empirical inquiry' (Englander [1998, p 12] on Chadwick; Slater [2012] on Duncan Smith). Both reports underpinned social legislation whose effects were directly correlated with an increase in suffering and, within that, the increased suffering of women in particular (Englander 1998; WPC 2019a and b; Bennett 2021). Both pieces of legislation relied on stigmatising classificatory practices and modes of intrusive scrutiny and surveillance. Both were operating at a time in which the legislative current for the government of wealth was flowing in the opposite direction – towards leniency and the facilitation (or at the very least tolerance of) secrecy and noncompliance (Jeffrey-Cook 2010; Zucman 2015; Horwell 2019; Cobham 2020). Chadwick and Duncan Smith used new methods (McGimpsey et al 2017; Shave 2017) to identify and distinguish as abject and apart from certain subpopulations of the poor, constituting 'deviant' subject groups who became the focus of era-defining social policies (for example, Troubled Families).

Table 5.1: Ways of being under governmental dispositions of scrutiny and ignorance

	Known through	Governed by	Governed behaviours	Types of self
Scrutiny	Observation and calculation	Social policy (discipline)	Disclosing	Administrative
Ignorance	Negotiation and cooperation	Fiscal policy (lenience)	Concealing	Intermediated

Through these processes of distinction based on ownership of authority to judge, to distance and to make themselves 'other' in relation to the population who were their objects of scrutiny, they shored up (in both contexts) the disposition of the state towards the poor. These different ways of being are summarised in Table 5.1.

Relational selves

I'm now going to look at ways of producing relational selves – 'us and them' – and I'm going to introduce some of the subjects of policy making and broader policy discourse. The challenge that wealtherty draws attention to is that the relationship between 'us and them' is a political calculation (as described in Chapter 3). It is a tool for producing a problematisation – an element of 'what the problem is represented to be (Bacchi 2013). And it is often significantly out of line with what the problem can empirically be shown to be: Hills identifies the 'challenge of bringing perceptions into line with reality as one of the central challenges facing those making and debating social policies' (Hills 2017, p 268). For example, the enduring use of 'us and them' works by defining an out-group against an in-group. It is based on the idea that two communities exist – two 'distinct and unchanging groups' (Hills 2017, p 1) to which moral judgements can be applied. In reality, people have *always* moved in and out of these groups over time, and the trend towards in work poverty also means that a lot of people do both simultaneously (Hills 2017; Horwell 2019). In both contexts explored in this book – the reforms of the early 1800s and the 2012 Welfare Reform Act – an 'us and them' narrative is based on conscious distortions of the facts and a determination to avoid shades of grey, namely a significant third group (the working poor), and other groups that are not working, but sustain themselves through 'rentier' activity or through the proceeds of 'illth' (Ruskin's term – see Chapter 1 in the section on defining wealth). By keeping the focus on a simple dyad (deserving poor and undeserving poor, workless and working, taxpayers and scroungers), other groups – however defining they might be to the state of wealtherty, are kept in the shadows.

They are the trees in the background of Tōhaku's image (see Figure 1.2). They are integral to the effect of the foreground trees, but are themselves ghostly. They exert active force from the past in our present (Savage 2021) by *not* participating in the symbolic and discursive representation of what the problem is represented to be.

Contrastive judgements enable different mechanisms of government. In processes of narrative chaining, once long-term welfare dependency is established as the singular problem, and people perceived as inappropriately dependent are identified as the target population for social policy ('them'), coercive and punitive solutions seem to fall naturally from it. The policy consensus achieved as a result of shared abhorrence towards perceived wilful worklessness has justified punitive sanctions as a means of reducing or disciplining this problem population. Contrastive judgements of (high net) worth have at the same time enabled a governmental obsequiousness towards the wealthy and private corporations, which has reimagined the incredible levels of benefits (legal, social and fiscal) they receive as variously necessary for national prosperity, as a legitimate reward for hard work and not as benefits at all. The strength of the discourse legitimating wealth ownership shapes contemporary public attitudes, which reflect (qualified) strong support for the wealthy, attitudes which contribute to the absence of a political voice for wealth taxation. As Hills (2017) says, myths have consequences.

Since 2000, the historical division between deserving and undeserving has been diligently revivified in order to soften the social imaginary for a punitive turn. It was evident in the evolution of New Labour rhetoric, with concern expressed around 'poor abject whites' (Skeggs 2005, pp 971–972). It underpinned the (rhetorical) build-up to the Welfare Reform Act of 2012 as the Coalition vilified sections of the working class in order to legitimate the pivoting of responsibility for national debt onto the poor (Jones 2011). Through repetition across different media, 'specific figures acquire accreted form and accrue affective value in ways that have significant social and political impact' (Castenda, cited in Tyler 2008, p 19): stigma is produced incrementally, as the weight of meaning accretes during the restatement of a single idea or image across different discursive fields and practices (and times [Koram 2022]). Over a broad range of media, in the decade following the 2008 financial crash, the public were in effect 'tutored' into 'believing that people in poverty had chosen their fates' and that their distress was deserved – a 'result of poor behaviours, indiscipline and shamelessness' (Tyler 2020, p 28). Increasingly 'improper' selves (Skeggs 2005) made their way into policy discourse, exemplified in the form of the contemporary 'rogue' Barry, who was the focus of the 2012 DWP White Paper *Social Justice: Transforming Lives* (DWP 2012a, p 5). The confluence of images of 'chavs' (Skeggs 2005; Tyler 2008; Jones 2011) and narratives like that of Barry were instrumental in producing in the social imaginary, a population who were troubled, had made bad choices and whose behaviours were (a) the cause of social harms, (b) the legitimate focus of policy and (c) in need of coercion to incentivise better choices:

1. Barry was drug dependent, as was his father before him. His mother, an alcoholic, split from Barry's father and met another man, at whose hands Barry was physically abused. Barry was taken into care.
2. Barry was drinking by the time he was 10, using cannabis by 11 and heroin at 15. Quickly turning to crime to fund his habit, he spent the next 17 years in and out of prison ... When not in prison he was *parked on* benefits, money spent either on feeding himself or feeding his habit.
3. Barry is not alone. We live in one of the richest countries in the world, yet we still see that inequality is rife and social problems endemic. Growing up in broken communities and facing multiple disadvantages, too many find themselves passing on their difficult circumstances from one generation to the next. ((DWP 2012, p 5, emphasis added)

A secondary effect of the 'us and them' dyad is the elision of differences *within* the in-group (the 'us'). Presenting a simple dyad renders the differences *within* the 'us' group subordinate to the differences between the 'us' group and the 'them'. The forming of an alliance of 'all who aspire, all who work; save and hope' (improbably, the Conservative Party leadership and all working people) against the 'next-door neighbour sleeping off a life on benefits' does not *reflect* reality; it produces one. The following is a quote from George Osbourne at the Conservative Party Conference in the year in which the Welfare Reform Act was passed, renewing the distinction:

'Where is the fairness, we ask, for the shift-worker, leaving home in the dark hours of the early morning, who looks up at the closed blinds of their next door neighbour sleeping off a life on benefits?
   When we say we're all in this together, we speak for that worker.
   We speak for all those who want to work hard and get on.
   This is the mission of the modern Conservative Party.
   We represent not the factional interest of organised labour; nor do we indulge in the lazy politics of envy.
   ... We modern Conservatives represent all those who aspire, all who work, save and hope, all who feel a responsibility to put in, not just take out.' (Osbourne 2012)

And the following quote is Osbourne again, revivifying another key element of the myth as part of the 2013 Spending Review (cited in Hills 2017, p 2) that one distinct set of people pay for the welfare system and another takes from it. Of course, as Sinfield and others working in the field of the sociology of tax have shown (Farnsworth 2023; Sinfield 2023), this is certainly true – but not in the way imagined by Osbourne.

> 'Two groups need to be satisfied with our welfare system. Those who need it – who are old, who are vulnerable, who are disabled, or have lost their job and who we as a compassionate society want to support. And there's a second group. The people who pay for this welfare system: who go out to work, who pay their taxes and expect it to be fair on them too.'

In individuating 'those who are old, who are vulnerable, who are disabled, or have lost their job' as the group for whom 'we' (the taxpaying workers) feel compassion and wish to support, this careful dyad ignores the spectre of in-work poverty which was crescendoing at this time. Working households comprised 37 per cent of those below the official poverty line in 1994–1995 and 58 per cent in 2017–2018 (Bourquin et al 2019). Wealtherty is about recognising dyads like this as political calculations – in this case, a product of some of the forms of wilful unknowing that I will go on to look at in Chapter 6 – and seeking to make visible the forces of the past and the complexities of context.

The administered/administrative self

I'm now going to explore in more detail some of the ways of being – the repertoires of the self – that the wealtherty governmental dispositions (scrutiny and ignorance) make available to richer and poorer people, starting with what I call the *administered and administrative self*. The pauper workhouse inmate of the 1830s was an effect in part a calculation and in part a product of processes of classification, segregation and social separation. Foucault sees in this a reversal – 'where those who were most individualised were no longer the sovereign, the lord, but the criminal, the mad person, the patient ...' (cited in Rose 1999, p 231) and, we might add, the pauper. Their conduct was made visible in the workhouse 'by being judged against institutional norms' (Rose 1999, p 214). They were written up in the punishment book under a case number (Nottinghamshire Archives Source A), their punishments being calibrated against a table of offences. A disorderly person became a refractory one based on the numbers of offences in a given period (or, occasionally, based on the severity of the offence). This is a form of administered self: a self produced incrementally through entries into a ledger. Under Universal Credit, this calculating governmentality remains, but the object of its scrutiny takes a digital form through a process of 'abstracting human bodies from their territorial settings and separating them into a series of discrete flows [which are then] reassembled into distinct "data doubles"' (Haggerty and Ericson 2000, p 606), or what Deleuze would call *dividuals*. An individual becomes an aggregation of data points – a variable in a calculation about amounts of benefit, sanctions and childcare support, to be algorithmically computed in order to optimise outcomes. She interfaces with a digital decision maker and work coach who variously nudge her decisions or coerce compliant behaviours. She is also administered in the sense described previously. However, the twist in the contemporary repertoires of self under a disposition of scrutiny is the marrying of scrutiny with the neoliberal injunction to become self-responsible. This is the self in Universal Credit. This witness testimony is from Vikki Waterman, a self-employed nail technician (previously a police call handler who had to give up her job because she couldn't make it work with the childcare element of Universal Credit), when she gave oral evidence to the Work and Pensions Committee Inquiry into Universal Credit Roll-out and Childcare (WPC 2018b, p 30). In 'inculcat[ing] calculative mentalities' (Rose 1999, p 214), Vikki becomes an administrative self, spending her 'free' time collecting receipts and submitting evidence:

> 'We [Vikki and the three other single mothers giving testimony] have been speaking among ourselves, and we spend a lot of time submitting evidence for childcare, taking pictures of invoices and bank statements, highlighting what we have paid and when, submitting them either to the jobcentre or to an online account, and remembering to do them on the right date and at the right time. It is a massive stress. I work 33 to 36 hours a week, normally over three days, so I have long hours on those three days and then I have two children the rest of the time. I am running a house and trying to work a full-time job. As well as all of that, I am having to remember that I need to do this on this date and that I need to submit these childcare costs and that I have to remember to ring the nursery to submit the invoice, because otherwise it is not going to get paid on time.'

The redeemed self

In Chapter 6 I will look at the effects of the CSJ on the ideational climate of the 2000s, noting the particular Christian-inflected ethos that shaped their approach through Iain Duncan Smith's 'clear view about what human nature is like and the power of redemption' (Sieghart 2010). Pathways to redemption through work are an implicit feature of Universal Credit, with individuals being 'supported' to make better choices through engagement with health and work coaching. The training materials used by the DWP for new work coaches (DWP 2020) strongly emphasise the role of the coach in building what I call 'operational' trust – that is, trust in the service of encouraging (persuading) people towards a particular end: that work is an inherent good, for example, aided by the rendering of complex issues (such as disability, bereavement or single parenthood) into routes back to work. The following quote is an excerpt from a training pack developed for new coaches taken on to support the increased demand generated by the pandemic. We are introduced to Jane, a recent widow with two children, who is depressed and anxious. We are told that the coach:

> built up a good rapport with this customer and as her confidence started increasing they promoted how work can be good for our health and wellbeing and started to discuss the benefits of working for example, meeting new people, giving her routine and providing her with stability and security … They demonstrated how her finances would improve if she worked. (DWP 2020, UC55 Complex Needs Part 2 07 Activity Sheet – illustrative examples)

Jane's story is typical of the 'redemption narratives' of other claimants used as examples in the pack, like Debbie, who has bipolar and disassociation disorder and has been sanctioned due to missing appointments. After her encounter with the work coach, she 'was like a totally different person from the timid young lady they originally saw' (DWP 2020). These are narratives in which mentally and physically ill and bereaved individuals are reimagined (and redeemed) as confident, active workseekers.

Troubled families and troubling families

The symbolic heavy lifting in the 'us and them' dyad is usually done by 'them': vilifying the out-group is an effective way of ensuring that the in-group is not itself implicated in villainy. In the 2010s, troubled families were positioned as a pathogen in the social fabric – spreading improper behaviour and risking contagion to surrounding communities. But what role do families at the other end of the wealth spectrum play in producing and sustaining *wealtherty*? What social trouble is caused by very wealthy families? The resurgence of the relevance of inheritance as a mechanism for wealth accumulation among elites since the 1980s (Piketty 2014) means that it is now 'a main driver of wealth inequalities at the top in western economies' (Fize et al 2022, p 2). Inheritances received between 1995 and 2005, for example, 'accounted for 30% of the increase in the wealth of inheritors' (Karagiannaki 2015, p x). Their wealth secures privilege across different domains: it can secure and reproduce advantages through purchasing private education (Henseke et al 2021) or valuable work experience (Cullinane and Montactue 2018) (both in Savage et al 2024). Wealthy parents are able to pass on advantage to their children in this way (recall the example of Madiyar Ablyazov from Chapter 2). These transfers also include 'the gendered patterns of ownership which suppress the equalising of wealth holdings between men and women' (Bessière and Gollac 2023, cited in Kerr and Vaughan 2024b). Inheritance mechanisms are reliant on work *within families* to 'transfer 'social contacts, knowledge, and norms associated with the management of great wealth' (Beckert 2022, p 240). Inheritance is also secured by work undertaken *between families and the wider society*. Sklair and Glucksberg (2021) describe the ways in which philanthropy styles wealthy families 'as custodians of both private capital and the common good' in a way which seeks to reconcile poverty alleviation with inheritance processes, for example. So although inheritance is a matter of luck, its longevity and maintenance within families is secured through legal code (Pistor 2019) and through the active building of human capital necessary to engage the younger generations is generated through 'bonding'-type work like philanthropy (Sklair and Glucksberg 2020).

The *material* consequences of this intergenerational hoarding of wealth aside, very rich families are troubling because the *social* consequences of inheritance now being the primary route to wealth can be destabilising. The sense I mentioned in Chapter 1 that the gaps between people and groups of people are not only large and growing, but also that the means of 'winning' in the game are unfair and cause social disengagement (Sandel 2020). The increased role of inheritance in wealth inequality undermines the very notion of merit and disrupts the link between hard work and economic success, and the sense that the game is rigged and unfair makes it less compelling to participate in. The intergenerational transfer and consolidation of wealth through and in troubling families contributes to economic inequality and social harm.

In Table 5.2 I articulated four ways of describing the relationship between the rich and the poor on a sliding scale of 'intelligibility' in our now – that is, from that which most closely aligns with a 'common sense' understanding of the status quo to that which is furthest from it. Row 1 describes the *common sense* relationship – reflecting 'what the problem is represented to be' by

Table 5.2: Four ways of describing the relationships between people with low or no wealth and people with high levels of wealth

	Poor	Rich
1	Welfare claimant/dependent	High or ultra high net worth individuals and 'value creators'
2	Social welfare claimant	Fiscal welfare claimant
3	Low or no net worth	High or ultra high net worth
4	Low or no net worth and 'value creators'	Fiscal welfare claimant and extractive rentiers

the state and many parts of the media. Row 4 is the way in which we are *not* to understand this relationship socially and in policy terms, the version that could only be spoken by 'cranks' – that is, not intelligible within the current terms of debate.

These are all in effect ways of describing the same relationship, but their inscription gives different moral legitimacy to the 'claimants' and the 'value creators' in each case (especially rows 1 and 4). Recalibrating towards row 4 should be part of a reparative agenda; it reattaches Ruskin's 'moral sign' to wealth and the wealthy.

The intermediated self

I want to end this chapter by thinking about a form of self that is only available to rich people (however we choose to describe them): this is the *intermediated self* as a form of identity that further enables them to avoid moral and financial scrutiny and accountability. The intermediated self has access to the symbolic resources to *choose* repertoires of the self (as Skeggs' 'ethical' self does), *and yet refuses to participate in public processes of self-making* (or to participate publicly in processes of self-making). This can take many forms. They might conceal elements of the self and instead performs in other classes' clothes (often quite literally) to hide their privilege – Littler's *normcore plutocrats*, for example (Littler 2018, 2019) – or they may simply remain invisible. Mayrit's 2015 *You Haven't Seen Their Faces* made this exact point (see Figure 7.8). He visualised the 100 most influential people in the city of London, who are notable as a group for their greyness (and whiteness) and relative anonymity. The ways of self-making for this group are the inverse of the 'extraordinary public subjectivity' described by Skeggs (2005, p 974): they take place in some of the private, gated space I mentioned in Chapter 4 and will go on to talk about in Chapter 7. Far from the 'compulsory' individuality described by Strathern (cited in Skeggs 2005, p 974), choices can be made *not to exercise choice* or not to performatively enact the self. This is the individual who is represented in the HMRC's WEF by intermediaries (see Chapter 8) and who could exist for a lifetime with no direct encounters with the state, a restricted capability available only to those with the highest levels of wealth (Beckert 2023). This is a concealed form of self-making, which I present here as *the intermediated self*. The intermediated self is the sanctioned response to the disposition of ignorance just like the administrative self and the redeemed self (and others we could cite from previous chapters – for example, the bare self, the destitute self or the dividual) are the sanctioned responses to the disposition of scrutiny (see Table 5.1). What are the implications of this concealed form of identity making in terms of the 'realignment of associations between social groups and moral value' that Skeggs discusses (2005, pp 974–975)? How does 'telling yourself' in the way described by Skeggs operate if you aren't talking? What is it about your self you are telling if you choose not to speak, and what about *its* self is the state telling you if it lets you? In terms of *Ma*, these silent 'wealthy' produce the landscape in which the self-formation of others is foregrounded.

Reorienting to a more lucid, clear-eyed description of the processes of wealth production and protection and to a clear understanding of the target of a potential wealth tax policy (the super-rich) has the potential to concatenate a new logic of identity formation. If the problem is the idleness of the poor (1800s) or drug-dependent Barry 'parked' on benefits (DWP 2012a, p 5), then the question is 'How do we make people more active in the labour market?' and the policy object, once again, is the independent able-bodied worker (the NPL) or the coerced worker-claimant or versions thereof (Wright and Fletcher 2018). If the problem is the hoarding of global resources by the economic elite, then the questions are: how can we know more about the processes that enable this to happen? Who/what are the enablers? What can be done to stop them/it? If the problem is low availability of resources to fund public services resources because of chronic avoidance

Figure 5.1: An image of page 2 from the HMRC 2017

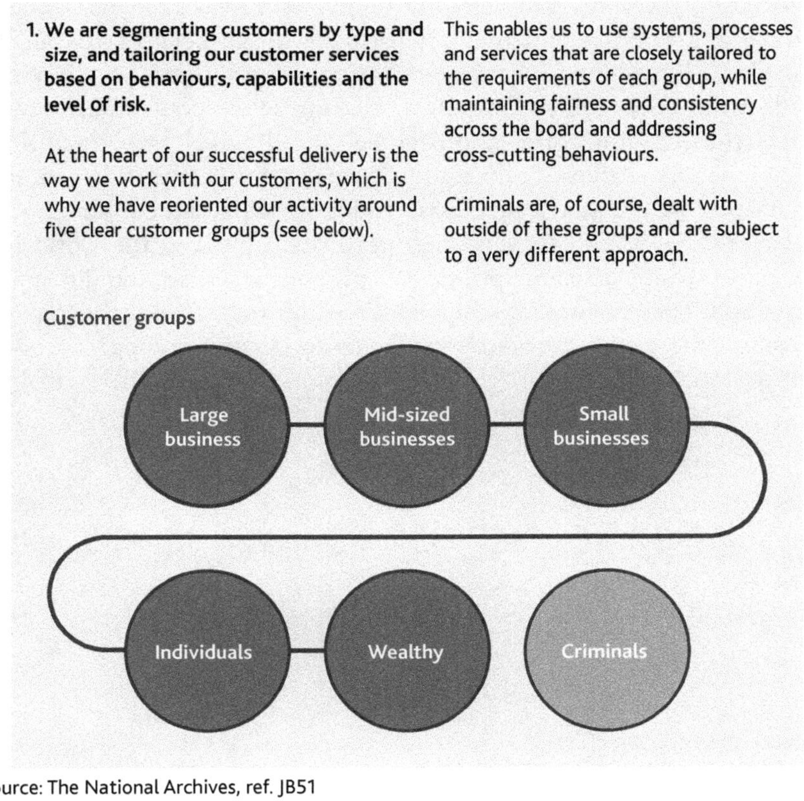

1. We are segmenting customers by type and size, and tailoring our customer services based on behaviours, capabilities and the level of risk.

At the heart of our successful delivery is the way we work with our customers, which is why we have reoriented our activity around five clear customer groups (see below).

This enables us to use systems, processes and services that are closely tailored to the requirements of each group, while maintaining fairness and consistency across the board and addressing cross-cutting behaviours.

Criminals are, of course, dealt with outside of these groups and are subject to a very different approach.

Customer groups

- Large business
- Mid-sized businesses
- Small businesses
- Individuals
- Wealthy
- Criminals

Source: The National Archives, ref. JB51

and evasion at the top, reworded and reimaged (see Figures 7.7–7.11) as tax abuse or revenue theft, then the questions become: who has committed a crime? Who is the criminal? Who are the victims and what should the processes of redress and reparation look like? However the subjects are defined, they are surely more complicated than this strategic document from HMRC suggests, with 'Wealthy' customers pictured as their own category, distinct from individuals and criminals (see Figure 5.1).

If the problem is that we have urgent unmet needs that could be resolved with more money available to the state, then the policy object is the 'deviant' tax abuser. Similarly, if the problem is reworded as one of wide-scale fiscal abuse, then the policy object might be the troubling family (office), or it might be nation states 'racing to the bottom'. The challenge in the context of *wealtherty* around identity formation, then, is multifold. What is the problem? Who are the objects of scrutiny (who should they be)? Who *aren't* the objects of policy (and why should they become them)? How can we provide more resources for self-making? How can we hold *all* practices of self-making to account rather than just those that we see?

In the next part of the book, I re-engage with some of the currents I've explored so far and consider how they are renewed in contemporary ways of thinking, governing and being. In Chapter 6 I reflect the discussion in Chapter 3, looking at contemporary ways in which process of making and using knowledge politically renew unequal relationships. In Chapter 7 I reflect the discussion in Chapter 4, looking at the contemporary ways in which mechanisms of government (specifically visual and spatial ones) renew unequal relationships. And in Chapter 8 I reflect the discussion in this chapter by looking at processes of subjectivation and considering the processes through which individuals negotiate a place in the world in a context of wealth-based inequalities of epistemic resources and differential attributions of credibility. You might wish to jump straight there if you wish to continue to explore *wealtherty* in relation to identity making.

PART III

What sustains the problem?

6

Producing knowledge: think tanks, policy networks

> The political genius of those who benefit ... lies in creating the impression that it is others who profit.
> Corwin and Miller, cited in Sinfield (2023, p 54)

What is stopping us making more effective narratives for social change? And why do the ones we have seem so 'sticky'? In this chapter I look at the role played in this stickiness by knowledge work undertaken by think tanks to promote and sustain *singular* narratives. Having the resources and influence to ensure that one particular understanding of 'what is wrong' predominates constricts the range of tractable solutions. This operates on two levels – one *offensive*, the other *defensive*. On the one hand, it makes a case *for* a particular frame (for example, worklessness and economic dependency [the Centre for Social Justice (CSJ)] rather than unemployment and low-paid jobs lacking prospects and security [Joseph Rowntree Foundation (JRF)]). And on the other hand, it protects against the destabilising of this preferred narrative by ensuring that knowledge is *not* taken in directions that could disrupt it: the drive to gain ascendency for a single narrative for which 'there is no alternative' means that others must be supressed, ignored or their credibility undermined. In the process, norms that might ordinarily govern the production processes of knowledge must be sidelined or ignored to enable a selective use of data; forms of scrutiny that might otherwise expose flaws or inconsistencies must be avoided. Such 'evidence-making' (Slater 2011, p 111) constitutes a form of agnogenesis (the production of ignorance) and it takes place both at the level of the frame itself and in the politicisation of the frame. I am reminded of and motivated by the following quote from Bishop Jones, made in a very different context – the 2017 Hillsborough tragedy report – which he entitled *The Patronising Disposition of Unaccountable Power*: 'the public narrative, once established, is difficult to change. *A false public narrative is an injustice in itself*' (Bishop Jones 2017, p 36, emphasis added).

This chapter reconceptualises some knowledge-making work undertaken by a particular think tank – the CSJ – as a 'false public narrative and an injustice in itself'. It might read like a conspiracy theory – 'those pesky rich people controlling the narrative on poverty!' – but a conspiracy theory is a belief that a secret yet influential organisation is behind key events or phenomena. The case I make here isn't that. There is nothing secret about the influential organisations I am talking about, but they are indeed in part responsible for sustaining and strengthening narratives and frames which actively distort the realities of inequality, dependency and value creation. In so doing, they produce a false public narrative which is both an injustice in itself and which lays the foundation for a myriad of economic and social injustices that ramify in the types of inequality discussed in this book. Concerns about what *isn't* known and the means by which knowledge *is not taken* in specific directions, and concerns about the revivification of frames that are unsupported by empirical evidence are not peripheral to wider considerations of social justice: a focus on social justice demands that we attend to the directions in which knowledge is or isn't taken and the 'grand narratives' which are sustained or challenged in the process (Bhambra 2021c).

The following section describes aspects of a policy network in the first decades of the 21st century. It highlights the closed nature of policy knowledge making at a particular point in time, and its saturation with private funding and partisan policy professionals who circulate within a network of largely private interests. Specifically, it follows the fortunes of key 'interlockers' (defined in Ball and Exley [2010] as highly networked and boundary-straddling individuals) working between the CSJ and the DWP at this time. The subsequent section starts from the premise that a network constitutes 'a history of on-going effort' (Ball 2020, p 550). I look at the network described in the following text and ask: 'For whom has this effort been expended?' If we were to deduce the strategy and the identity of the intended beneficiaries from the effort by looking at what the *actor does do and what he doesn't do*, then what was the *effective* strategy? What directions has knowledge been taken in and what directions has it not been taken in? I suggest that the history of ideological and agnotological effort manifest in the CSJ's activity can be interpreted as a fiscal welfare strategy, in which a particular problematisation of society (broken Britain; pathways to poverty) has been used to sustain *wealtherty*. Together, the two sections explore how wealth converts to power through funding knowledge work in think tanks; it looks at what *isn't* being talked about (and how that 'not being talked about' is achieved) when problems and solutions are always down among the weeds, and it asks who benefits from the policy *effect* of the CSJ's work and why it is important to make this explicit.

Knowledge-making networks

A policy network combines and interconnects physical and social structures with relational processes (Dicken et al, cited in Ball and Exley 2010, p 155) and is animated by flows of ideas and people (actors). Network actors produce and circulate meaning and value(s), and lobby or advocate for the translation of these meanings and values into policy. As such, network effects include 'the institutionalisation of beliefs, values, cultures and particular forms of behaviour' (Marsh and Smith 2000, p 6). The nature of policy knowledge making changed significantly in the 1980s. The inauguration of a 'marketplace' for knowledge applied market principles to the ideas landscape and effectively outsourced policy production, shifting politicians away from an almost total reliance on senior civil servants for policy ideas and research to private sector sources increasingly located within think tanks (Slater 2012; 2013). This had the effect of supplanting nonpartisan civil servants with partisan unelected individuals and organisations that were able to assume the position of 'amplifiers and even originators of [official Conservative] discourse' (Pautz 2013, p 373). I am not implying an absolute distinction between partisan and nonpartisan here, more a general principle. Even when not directly involved with solution development, these think tanks had a 'role in shaping the ideational climate in which politics take place' (Stone, cited in Anstead 2018, p 291). This shift in knowledge-production processes and personnel represents the contemporary version of the shift in the knowledge production landscape in the early 1800s effected by the rapid growth and professionalising of the civil service and traced in the story of Edwin Chadwick described in Chapter 5. The same principles – a new assertion of ownership of particular knowledge production processes and a recourse to claims of scientificity as discussed in Chapter 3 – were at work in both contexts. The shift in the 2000s removed several protective layers of transparency, accountability and reliability, ultimately 'subordinat[ing] … knowledge to political and economic demand' (Slater 2018, p 893). It produced a system of 'network governance' (Pal, cited in Junemann et al 2015, p 537) in which 'relations and boundaries between state, economy, and civil society are … reconfigured' (Junemann et al 2015, p 544). This reconfiguration has important ramifications for ethical standards. The Nolan Principles (Committee on Standards in Public Life [1995)] and Philp [2014]), which were produced by way of clarifying the difference between personal and public ethics, were established to govern the behaviours of public servants and to ensure that 'those engaged in political life of the country [need to] recognise that the ethical requirements of politics demand serious public deliberation and reflection' (Lord Paul Bew in Philp 2014, p 3). The civil servants who used to be the source of policy ideas, and of policy evidence (in partnership with academics where necessary) were bound by these standards. The new private sector evidence producers were not, despite their evidence sometimes funnelling directly (as we shall see shortly) into government. Data and evidence in this shift towards the privatisation of the knowledge sector become more explicitly politicised numbers, more explicitly *political* numbers. The CSJ's work – 'persuading the Government to change its policies and laws' (CSJ Annual Report 2019–2020, p 35) – constitutes lobbying, which is defined as the actions of an individual or a group trying to persuade someone in Parliament to support a particular policy or campaign (UK Parliament n.d.). This reflection from a senior Conservative think tank officer illustrates the point well: 'We published, we sent the stuff out, had it raised in Parliament ... If you do it in public over weeks, people are prepared for it – journalists and whatever. By the time the minister gets around to the idea, *it's already familiar. He's won* part of *the battle of public acceptance*' (cited in Peck and Tickell 2007, p 42, emphasis added).

Think tanks have a privileged position in the knowledge economy for policy. Funding think tanks is acknowledged to be a key form of political influence by the wealthy (Ruane 2012; Robeyns 2017b; Beckert 2023). My focus on the CSJ in particular is based on its decisive intervention in 2006/7 to effect a shift in degree, if not in type, in the Conservative Party's ratcheting of worklessness and dependency as the primary social problematic, and the translation of this problematic into a comprehensive welfare reform strategy. The CSJ came into being in 2004 within the knowledge marketplace described earlier. It was founded by Iain Duncan Smith, Philippa Stroud, Tim Montgomerie and Mark Florman as an 'independent not-for-profit think tank' whose expressed aim was 'to seek effective solutions to the poverty that blights parts of Britain' (Slater 2012, p 953). The motivation for the founding of the CSJ was Duncan Smith's notorious 2002 visit to the Easterhouse estate in Glasgow in his capacity as Leader of the Opposition, during which he came face to face with people living in dire poverty and was observed to be visibly upset (Collins 2012). His personal revelation took place in a wider political context in which the Conservatives had been out of office for seven years and were perceived to be in the political wilderness. Articulating a compelling and credible strategy for social justice was part of its attempt to shed the reputation as 'the nasty party' and to occupy the centre ground lost to New Labour. On his election as party leader in 2005, David Cameron asked the CSJ to undertake a policy review into social justice. The CSJ used the review process to cement the *pathways to poverty* into the Cameron and then Coalition agenda. The defining of the pathways effected a narrowing in two key ways: first, by ignoring inexpedient 'facts' (it was widely academically discredited [Slater 2012]); and, secondly, by making the site of intervention the behaviours of the social welfare recipient, and 'moving on' from money. Pautz (2013) cites an interview with a CSJ staffer who described the aim of the review and the wider social responsibility discourse as helping to "change the debate about the root causes of poverty, we want *to shift the focus of debate about poverty from money* to poor schools, family, dependency, debt, addiction" (CSJ Interview 2011, p 371 cited in Pautz 2013, emphasis added). Its work provided the ideological rationale and idiolect that helped smooth public and political assent for the subsequent punitive turn in welfare policy (in a way which mirrors the work done by the Malthusians at the end of the 1700s, as was described in Chapter 3). In shifting the debate about poverty *from money*, it entrenched a grassrootsist approach. Thus, when austerity led some to ask questions about the equity of the fiscal measures taken to reduce debt and to advocate for redistribution, the question of redistribution had become detached from the 'solving' of poverty, as both the problem itself and the solutions to it were within communities and individual behaviours, not with 'money'. The CSJ's work directly shaped Conservative and Coalition welfare policy making and, as importantly, rationalised the separation between the fortunes of the rich and the misfortune of the poor.

How was the ideational work so influential? This was achieved in part by the work of key interlockers in the CSJ network: Duncan Smith, Stroud and Brien. Mark Florman, Christian Guy and Tim Montgomerie constitute a second tier of key 'transfer agents' (Stone 2004). They are instrumental, but in a less continuous way than my three primary actors. The interlockers (Duncan Smith, Stroud and Brien) acted as a bridge between other actors and organisations with a shared mission (if not *ideological* alignment – for example, JRF), corporations and trusts (acting as funders, such as Deutsche Bank)[1] and the government, by virtue of their radical proximity to and sometimes coexistence with it. In 2010 and 2011, Duncan Smith, Stroud and Brien were all simultaneously involved with both the CSJ *and* directly employed by the government.[2] Stroud was paid £94,000 per annum in her role as Special Advisor to Duncan Smith at the DWP between 2010 and 2015, and continued to receive her CSJ salary for her role as Co-chair of the Board of Advisors (Jowitt 2012). So although Duncan Smith cut remunerated ties with the CSJ in 2010 when he joined the DWP as Secretary of State for Work and Pensions, instead becoming a Life Patron, he ensured a frictionless relationship with the organisation through the roles of Brien and Stroud. This blurring of boundaries was felt by many to have been a breach of the code of conduct and the Nolan Principles. Lord Oakshott said '[i]t's totally wrong to take money from a pressure group lobbying your own department', while Mark Serwotka, General Secretary of the Public and Commercial Services Union, said: 'We're very concerned about the increased politicisation of work that ought to be done by impartial civil servants' (Jowitt 2012). Text in Boxes 6.1, 6.2 and 6.3 give narrative detail about these primary interlockers, highlighting their values and motivations, ahead of looking at the work they did.

The indivisibility between the CSJ and the DWP enabled the frictionless passage of their ideas into government policy. Duncan Smith acknowledged this during an interview in 2016 in which he described how civil servants in DWP would typically have drafted policy for the Minister, but on hearing of his appointment in 2010, they simply downloaded the reports from the CSJ website and began to formulate policy based on them (Hughes and

Box 6.1: Iain Duncan Smith select biography

Duncan Smith effectively created a policy programme and then was brought into government to deliver it, leaving his ex-Senior Advisor (Philippa Stroud) to head up his think tank. Information from multiple sources (Sieghart 2010; They Work for You [https://www.theyworkforyou.com/mp/10180/iain_duncan_smith/chingford_and_woodford_green]; Hughes and Riddell 2016).

Iain Duncan Smith has been a member of the Conservative Party since 1981. He had a military career and then became an MP in 1992. He served as Leader of the Opposition between 2001 and 2003 (but lost a vote of no confidence in 2003. He co-founded the CSJ in 2004 along with Tim Montgomerie, Mark Florman and Philippa Stroud. He handed over the reins of the CSJ to Philippa Stroud in 2010, who had been his assistant at the DWP. He was Secretary of State for Work and Pensions from 2010 to 2016, during which time he saw through the 2012 Welfare Reform Act discussed in the previous chapter. He is a Catholic.

Duncan Smith's former press secretary, Nick Wood: 'Undeniably what has damaged the Conservative Party is this idea that they are only in it for the rich and to a degree the middle classes ... Duncan Smith's great achievement in politics has been to associate the conservative party with policies to help the poor' (Sieghart 2010, 1:00–1:11).

Duncan Smith knew that the Tories had to shake off the image of being the so-called 'nasty party'. His response was to shift the focus to public services, health, education and tackling poverty.

Bernard Jenkin (fellow member of the Shadow Cabinet): 'the Shadow Cab looked sort of bemused as he tried to explain about the struggle that really decent people were having. To be decent people really in an environment of real social deprivation and drugs and crime and I think he underestimated perhaps what a struggle it was to get the British political establishment to connect with *this very other world*' (Sieghart 2010, 8:47 to 9:02, emphasis added).

'After losing the leadership, he decided to devote himself to improving the lot of the poor. He set up the CSJ, whose work became the cornerstone of Conservative policy on welfare reform ... His belief is that the best way to alleviate poverty is to get people off benefits and into work' (Sieghart 2010, 11:30 to 11:54). Hughes and Riddell (2016) note that in the years between losing the leadership election and starting the CSJ, and re-entering government as Secretary of State, Duncan Smith had been 'a kind of freelancer, generating ideas ... but not part of the team.'

Sieghart suggests he is motivated by his Catholicism Sieghart (2010, 11:54 to 11:59) which Frank Field MP corroborates: 'Being a good Catholic…he has a clear view about what human nature is like…and [that] one is able to be redeeemed' (cited in Sieghart 2010, 12:03 to 12:13).

Box 6.2: Stephen Brien select biography

This information is intended to illustrate the penetration of Brien as an unelected, non-expert (by his own admission) policy professional into the heart of government policy-making processes, from formation to implementation, to scrutiny and review.

1. *Brien wrote the concept for Universal Credit in the mid-1990s, having read a book on compassionate economics*

    In his September 2020 interview for Chair of the Social Security Advisory Committee (WPC 2020), Brien describes the moment he mapped out the blueprint for what would ultimately become Universal Credit: 'It's like one of these apocryphal-type restaurant napkin type conversations where I actually laid out to a friend of mine, an American friend, in Oxford at the time, the structure which ultimately ended up being Universal Credit, inspired ... erm ... actually by a book by ... erm ... Samuel Brittan on *Capitalism with a Human Face*, which is very much bringing in those ideas of how do you provide the safety blanket, the support within a capitalist system' (9:32:14 to 9:32:41) Eltis (1997, p 252) noted that an important element in Brittan's political philosophy was 'that individuals should be at liberty to take the decisions which concern their welfare without coercion of any kind by those who work for the central or local government'. It is interesting to note the parts of the book Brien chooses to embed in his napkin blueprint and those he chooses to leave out. Coercion of course ends up being a cornerstone of the Universal Credit – from coercing the disabled to work, to coercing claimants to commit to the unachievable in their claimant commitments (as discussed in Chapter 4). He continues that: 'The opportunity arose in the 2010 Coalition government to make the ideas real' (WPC 2020, 9:33:26).

2. *Brien's then employer (the Legatum Institute) peremptorily bought in cover to replace Brien, anticipating he would gain the position of Chair of the Social Security Advisory Committee*

    When asked about managing conflicts of interest relating to time, Brien reported that the Legatum Institute (his primary employer) put a role in place to cover him: 'Interestingly enough, coincidentally, very serendipitously, we are hiring a very experienced managing director...specifically to allow people like myself to spend more time outside in roles that are complimentary to the mission of the Legatum Institute, which is to create pathways form poverty to prosperity' (WPC 2020, 9:38:43 to 9:39:04).

3. *Brien admits to not being an expert*

    Question (Steve McCabe MP): 'Would it be right to describe you as an expert on social security?' (WPC 2020, 9:55).
    Answer: 'I ... I think I have some expertise in certain areas of it. I wouldn't put myself forward as being, you know, a ... err, an expert on a very wide range of areas. I erm ... But I would say I think I have enough familiarity to be able to commence a role as chair knowing that the committee as a whole has a very wide range of expertise that I would want to be informed by and learn from and draw on' (WPC 2020, 9:56).

Box 6.3: Philippa Stroud select biography

Philippa Stroud co-founded the CSJ with Iain Duncan Smith in 2004 (along with Tim Montgomerie and Mark Forman). She worked closely with Duncan Smith to provide continuity between the DWP and the CSJ. She then worked with Stephen Brien at Legatum.

Like Duncan Smith, Stroud is a Christian (he is a Catholic, she an Evangelical), and her CSJ work is inspired by an interest/fascination with the poor and with poverty. In her ghostwritten autobiography, she recalls that: Friends bought her a subscription to *National Geographic* for her eighth birthday and she remembers 'lying across a massive Queen Anne armchair in our house in France, transfixed for a good couple of hours by photographs of famine victims in Bangladesh' (Stroud and Leonard 1999, p 25).

Later in her life, she said that she 'assumed I'd follow my father into a career in the financial world ... but ... banking didn't fill me with passion'. By contrast, she noted of her time in Hong Kong: 'nothing stopped my love of being in the Walled city. I loved it when rats ran across my feet in the dank darkness of sewer-like alleyways. I'd never felt this elation working in a bank' (Stroud and Leonard 1999, p 33).

Stroud was Director of the CSJ and was brought into government in 2010 when Duncan Smith was made Secretary of State. Duncan Smith says that: 'Philippa ... was already different from most advisors as we had worked together for some years and her remarkable qualities, I knew complimented my agenda.' She was highly interventionist: 'Philippa read everything that was going to be in my box before I got it, tidying up and deleting any shoddy work. She would just put a line through ill-thought-through sections. If a document was due for a decision from me she would know me well enough to know that I would reject it if it wasn't right. Sometimes a member of the private office, being chased by a more senior official might ignore her warning and sneak one into the box. What was amusing was I almost invariably did what Philippa said, I would return it, without having discussed it with her' (cited in Hughes and Riddell 2016).

Stroud became Director of the Legatum Institute in 2016, part of a group of organisations funded by the Legatum Foundation, which was founded and is chaired by New Zealand billionaire Christopher Chandler. The Foundation also funds GB News, the End Fund and Freedom Fund, and is one of two key investors in the conservative/Christian Alliance for Responsible Citizenship, of which Stroud was the founding CEO in 2023.

Riddell 2016). Duncan Smith, Stroud and Brien variously moved between the government (at the DWP and in Number 10) and two particular organisations in the private sector – the Legatum Institute (Stroud became CEO in 2015 and employed Brien as her Head of Policy in 2017) and the CSJ – alongside other roles. Duncan Smith in particular also worked for and received money from media outlets and private sector directorships (as reported in the publicly accessible register of MPs' interests data). In 2013, Duncan Smith was Secretary of State and CSJ Life Patron, Stroud was his Special Advisor and Co-chair of the CSJ Board of Advisors, and Brien was an expert advisor to the DWP and a CSJ Board Member. The individuals tracked each other, employed each other and promoted each other, in a tangle if not a conflict of interests (see Table 6.1).

Funding knowledge making: influence as corporate welfare

I made the case earlier that CSJ's grassrootsist narrative enabled it to shift the poverty debate on from 'money'. I want to develop that idea further here by making the case that the CSJ in effect delivers a corporate welfare agenda in a social justice wrapper. To be clear – the same could be said for other right-leaning think tanks. I am using the CSJ as an example of this kind of approach rather than suggesting that this is a singular practice, and I am not suggesting that this is the explicit or intentional strategy of the CSJ, but more that it is an *effective* strategy (that is, an outcome of the CSJ's work). What does this mean in practice? Corporate welfare includes disbursements, grants and other forms of financial distributions, and the tax expenditures (Sinfield 2023) to which I return at the end of this chapter. It also applies to processes of political influence which allow wealthy people to advocate for propitious regulatory conditions for themselves and their wealth. It is a restricted resource for the wealthy – a privileged capability as I outlined in Chapter 4 and expand on in Chapter 8 when thinking about the role of the Society of Trust and Estate Practitioners (STEP) within the WEF in HMRC. Ruane articulates this as 'shaping the policy framework', an activity that 'does not lend itself to easy measurement in terms of financial value, but *nonetheless comprises a highly significant element in enhancing the conditions in which corporations can flourish*' (Ruane 2012, p 25, emphasis added). Funding research is a more acceptable face of buying influence than direct lobbying or corporate gifting. It is a way of influencing and promoting specific causes. As Burt (2007) suggests, business sector 'bridge connectors' may gain certain advantages in terms of information access and brokerage rewards' (cited in Ball and Exley 2010, p 166), as I will explore shortly through a description of the 'flavour' of the wider networks surrounding think tanks (see Tables 6.2 and 6.3). As a result of these links and bridging individuals and mechanisms, corporations can obtain privileged access to policy makers and policy making, which makes it more likely that their concerns will be listened to and addressed. They are able to engage directly 'via networks of "dialogue" and discussion', and by virtue of the 'revolving door' between policy making and corporations which helps to shape ideas in the wider policy environment (Ruane 2012, p 24). This is a good description of the network effects described in Table 6.1.

Table 6.1: Career map of CSJ interlockers

	Iain Duncan Smith	Philippa Stroud	Stephen Brien
2010	CSJ (Life Patron); DWP (Secretary of State); Global Data Centre Management (NED – proportion of fee goes to the CSJ); Nlyte Software Ltd (share options held); Byotrol PLC (unremunerated director, share options held)	CSJ Consultancy Ltd (Director); CSJ Co-Chair Board of Advisors; DWP (Special Advisor to Duncan Smith); Sutton and Cheam Constituency parliamentary candidate (unsuccessful); Social Finance Limited (Director)	CSJ (Director); CSJ (board member); CSJ (member of the Policy Implementation Group); DWP (Secondment/ Expert Advisor); Oliver Wyman (OW) (Management Consultancy) (partner and lead member of firm's Consumer Products Practice)
2011	CSJ (Life Patron); DWP (Secretary of State)	CSJ Consultancy Ltd (Director); CSJ Co-chair Board of Advisors; DWP (Special Advisor to Duncan Smith); Social Finance Limited (Director),	CSJ (Director); CSJ (board member); CSJ (Publication author for 'Outcome-based Government' report); DWP (Secondment/ Expert Advisor); OW (Partner), OW (lead member of firm's Consumer Products Practice)
2012	DWP (Secretary of State); CSJ (Life Patron)	CSJ Co-chair Board of Advisors; DWP (Special Advisor to Duncan Smith), No. 10 Downing Street (Special Advisor on Welfare)	OW (partner); OW (lead member of firm's Consumer Products Practice); DWP (Secondment/Expert Advisor)
2013	CSJ (Life Patron), DWP (Secretary of State)	CSJ Co-chair Board of Advisors; DWP (Special Advisor to Duncan Smith), No. 10 Downing Street (Special Advisor on Welfare), CSJ Consultancy Ltd (Director)	CSJ (board member); DWP (Secondment/ Expert Advisor); UK Payments Council (Richer Data Task Force member)
2014	CSJ (Life Patron), DWP (Secretary of State)	House of Lords (Life Peer), DWP (Special Advisor to Duncan Smith), CSJ (Executive Director), Number 10 Downing Street (Special Advisor on Welfare), CSJ Consultancy Ltd (Director); CSJ (Director); CSJ Co-chair Board of Advisors	CSJ (board member); UK Payments Council (Richer Data Task Force member); Social Finance UK (Director)
2015	CSJ (Life Patron), DWP (Secretary of State); Byotrol PLC (share options held)	Legatum (CEO), Number 10 Downing Street (Special Advisor on Welfare), LIF Trading Ltd (CEO); CSJ (Director); CSJ Consultancy Ltd (Director); CSJ (Director); CSJ Co-chair Board of Advisors	CSJ (board member); Social Finance UK (Director); Ministry of Economy and Planning Saudi Arabia (Senior Advisor)

Table 6.1: Career map of CSJ interlockers (continued)

	Iain Duncan Smith	Philippa Stroud	Stephen Brien
2016	CSJ (Life Patron), DWP (Secretary of State); Speakers Corner Ltd (speaker); Target Jobs GTI Media Ltd; Scottish Widows Bank (not specified); YouGov (Speaker); *The Sun* (article writer)	Legatum (CEO), Number 10 Downing Street (Special Advisor on Welfare), LIF Trading Ltd (CEO); CSJ (Director); CSJ Consultancy Ltd (Director); CSJ (Director)	CSJ (board member); Ministry of Economy and Planning Saudi Arabia (Senior Advisor); Legatum Institute Social Metrics Commission (Steering Group member)
2017	CSJ (Life Patron); London Speaker Bureau (speaker); 2Plan Wealth Management Ltd (unspecified); Champions Loughborough (speaker); Leicester Tigers Rugby Club (unspecified); *Daily Mail* (article writer x4); Mallow Street (Speaker); Retail Week (Speaker); National Landlord Investment Show (Speaker); *Daily Telegraph* (article writer x4); BBC (presenter – *The Jeremy Vine Show*); Fisher Energy PLC (speaker); Oxygen Finance (speaker); Aktar Group (unspecified); journalism (articles various paid); Propertydrum Ltd (unspecified); London Authorities (unspecified)	Legatum (CEO), Number 10 Downing Street (Special Advisor on Welfare), CSJ (Director)	CSJ (board member); Ministry of Economy and Planning Saudi Arabia (Senior Advisor); Legatum Institute Social Metrics Commission (Steering Group member); Legatum Institute (Director of Policy)

In its annual reports, the CSJ acknowledges its reliance on individual private supporters, corporate sponsors and trusts and foundations 'who share our commitment to putting social justice at the heart of British politics' (CSJ 2016). The CSJ produced its first public-facing annual report in 2016. Data manually extracted from the Finance sections of CSJ annual reports between 2016 and 2021 show that on average between these years, 55 per cent of its funding came from private donations (amounting to £6.6 million), 30 per cent from trusts and foundations (£4 million), 11 per cent from corporates (£1.6 million) and 2 per cent from charities (£198,000). It is important to state here that the data presented in the finance sections are inconsistent, which makes it difficult to offer the data in this paragraph as anything other than illustrative. This is not evenly spread: overall, what is classed as 'private donations' have decreased (from a high of 71 per cent in 2016 to 45 per cent in 2021) in parallel with a marked increase in donations from corporations (from 5 per cent in 2016 to 18 per cent in 2021). The combination of private donations with donations from trusts and foundations (the latter sometimes acting as vehicles for individual or corporate endowments and thus proxy private donations) constitutes an average of 85 per cent of all income year on year, totalling £10.7 million between 2016 and 2021. The CSJ identifies four primary spend categories – Policy; Core Costs; Alliance; and Impact – with a fifth – Grant Administration – being added in 2021. The distinction between policy and impact categories is not clear, and the text reporting is inconsistent in terms of the activities it reports as falling into each. Out of the four spend categories, policy absorbs the most money, averaging 50 per cent of spending. Excluding core costs, funding is distributed in this order of priority: policy, impact and alliance. Between them, policy and impact account for between two thirds and three quarters of all spend.

So what does this activity buy for donors? What does it amount to as a 'history of on-going effort?' In 2022, the £1,339,661 spent on 'policy' included the production of 20 papers, 189 recommendations, 30 events, appearance on three Select Committees, and hosting ten roundtables and caucus events 'where we presented our ideas to keynote speakers including then prime minister Boris Johnson, and then Secretaries of State including Dominic Raab, Nadhim Zahawi, Sajid Javid, Priti Patel, and Rishi Sunak' (CSJ 2022, p 36). Fairfield defines instrumental power as involving 'capacity for deliberate and often collective action in the political arena' (cited in Clark et al 2020, p 7), and being related to political power and resources of elites. Structural power 'derives from the privileged position that businesses have in capitalist societies which assumes that they perform crucial public functions in the market system' (2020, p 7). The resources used to operate instrumental power include lobbying, participation in working groups; partisan links, technical expertise, media coverage and money (2020, p 7). Between 2016 and 2021, the CSJ hosted MPs and ministers 471 times, published 133 papers, hosted 106 events, made 1,310 recommendations and had 132 policy recommendations accepted, hosted 28 roundtables, made 18 Select Committee appearances and launched an All-Party Parliamentary Group (APPG). In that time, it undertook x4 polls involving (collectively) 35,000 members of the public. A total of 507 charities are now engaged in its alliance, a CSJ-convened network of charities, social enterprises and other organisations (up from 50 in 2016), and 82 of those members have participated in working groups or high-level roundtables or panels. It has opened three regional offices. As an effect of this work, it claims to have diverted more than £19 billion of funding to policy areas that it campaigned for. Data manually extracted from CSJ publications up to 2020 reveal that the disproportionate focus of its work is on what it refers to as worklessness and economic dependency – both as a workstream (41 per cent of all CSJ reports fall under this area) and as a target of donor interventions. Family is the next most-prolific publication stream (at 22 per cent, with debt and housing at 6 per cent, addiction at 7 per cent, education at 11 per cent and criminal justice at 12 per cent), which is very much in line with the CSJ orthodoxy in terms of problem articulation being the nexus between dysfunctional families and economic dependency.

I want to return now to the problematic of influence. In his *The Constitution of Poverty*, Mitchell Dean asks the reader to 'abandon an analytic framework which presupposes an opposition between the weight of institutions, laws and established social practices *and the intersubjective agency of ideas, the problematic of influence* (Dean 1991, p 87, emphasis added). A network can invigorate the agency of ideas. Through processes of 'soft transfer' (Stone 2004), ideas circulating within a network can revivify myths in the service of political ends, providing the 'ideological lubrication' for punitivism, for example (Peck and Theodore 2010). These myths might be temporally proximate or distant – they can and do draw on narratives of dependency from the 18th and 19th centuries, for example. At the same time, they can serve to hide, obfuscate and distract. In both cases they *influence* by either putting a spotlight on an issue or a community (for example, pathways to poverty) or by keeping that issue or that community in the shadows (for example, 'money' as something that must be 'moved on from').

Whose funding influences the CSJ? When think tanks play such a decisive role in our politics, it is reasonable to want to know who funds them, who they are and whose values they represent. Funding operates as influence in a network and can be a key vector for the bleed between financial and political power as cautioned by Robeyns in her work on limitarianism (Robeyns 2019, 2024). It is not possible to know from the financial data that the CSJ makes public who funds it. The CSJ scores poorly on financial transparency (E in 2021 on a scale of A–E).[3] The breakdown of donations is not included in its annual reports or its filings to Companies House, where the documents state that 'directors of the company have elected not to include a copy of the income and expenditure account within the financial statement' – as is their right as a small company. It is not unusual to not disclose information of course, and it is not illegal. But nor is it the norm: several progressive think tasks disclose all donations over £5,000. The lack of transparency about funding sources *is* problematic in a context where there are in effect 'revolving doors' (Ruane 2012) between CSJ staff and government departments (Anstead 2018, pp 290–291; see also Table 6.1).

Funding is a key form of influence, but values can enter the network through means other than funding. As think tanks proliferated after 2000, connections between them catalysed, and the reach of the network grew as new directors moved in and out, bringing with them their own values, and carrying too the interests of the many other companies in which they held contemporaneous directorships. Tables 6.2 and 6.3 show the companies in which directors of leading right and left-leaning think tanks (Compass, Demos, the Institute for Public Policy Research [IPPR] and Progress [Progressive Britain from 2021], the Adam Smith Institute, the Bow Group, the Centre for Policy Studies, the Centre for Social Justice, the Institute of Economic Affairs (IEA), Policy Exchange, Reform and the Legatum Institute) held contemporaneous directorships using data from companies house to identify the standard industrial classification (SIC) codes of these companies (the business areas in which they operated) (see Tables 6.2 and 6.3). The 'flavour' of this expanded network can be seen to indicate *degrees and types of private sector* connectivity, and identify differences between the corporate influences that infuse right and left-leaning organisations. It is reasonable to assume that the companies in which an individual has directorships can be legitimately conceived to represent their *corporate* interests. Between January 2000 and December 2004, officers of right-leaning think tanks held directorships in 111 management consultancy-type firms, 76 in financial and insurance activities, and 32 in real estate. By 2020, these directorships had proliferated and consolidated (see Tables 6.2 and 6.3).

What we can see from these tables is that beyond the first tier of directors, the networks of think tanks are 'animated by values and meanings' that reflect interests in private sector industries whose substantive areas of focus might be at odds with the professed social justice mission of the think tanks. If we think about the network as a history of ongoing effort, then these tables might help us to reflect on who and what this effort is expended for. This leads me on to the next section of this chapter.

A history of effort for whom?

Here I'm going to explore this question through the lens of *agnotology* – the making and unmaking of ignorance (Proctor and Schiebinger 2008). Proctor and Schiebinger conceive of agnotology as 'the conscious, unconscious, and

Table 6.2: Standard Industrial Classification (SIC) codes of companies in which directors of left-leaning and right-leaning think tanks held contemporaneous directorships between 2000 and 2005

SIC code category	LL	SIC code category	RL
Professional, scientific and technical activities	126	Professional, scientific and technical activities	111
Education	64	Financial and insurance activities	76
Other service activities	37	Education	51
Arts, entertainment and recreation	32	Administrative and support service activities	48
Information and communication	31	Information and communication	44
Administrative and support service activities	26	Real estate activities	32
Human health and social work activities	24	Human health and social work activities	27
Financial and insurance activities	19	Arts, entertainment and recreation	23
Accommodation and food service activities	9	Accommodation and food service activities	21
Construction	7	Other service activities	18
Transportation and storage	7	Construction	13
Wholesale and retail trade; repair of motor vehicles and motorcycles	6	Wholesale and retail trade; repair of motor vehicles and motorcycles	8

structural production of ignorance, its diverse causes and conformations, whether brought about by neglect, forgetfulness, myopia, extinction, secrecy or suppression (2008, p 3). My focus here is on what they refer to as 'active agnoses' – those which are the production of strategy and intent rather than those which are either inevitable or necessary (2008, pp 27–28). They suggest that: 'Ignorance has a history and is always unevenly distributed; the geography of ignorance has mountains and valleys, just like the geography of knowledge does' (2008, p 26). Thus, as historians of now (genealogists), we should ask not only 'what is the problem?', but also 'what *isn't* the problem?' What is left *un*problematised in current articulations? Agnotology is a way of focusing on knowledge that, for various reasons, 'could have been but wasn't, or should be but isn't' (Proctor 2008, p vii). It describes knowledge about ignorance. It has been successfully used as a tool to explore how governments successfully 'set aside' some knowledge to allow a singular focus on one issue. Slater presented the 'Broken Britain' narrative perpetuated by the CSJ as having produced 'institutional ignorance' about the causes of poverty, for example, successfully diverting attention away from structural and institutional failures, and ignoring alternatives' (Slater 2012, p 961) – an analysis that this chapter is

Table 6.3: Standard Industrial Classification (SIC) codes of companies in which directors of left-leaning and right-leaning think tanks held contemporaneous directorships between 2015 and 2020

SIC code category	LL	SIC code category	RL
Professional, scientific and technical activities	123	Professional, scientific and technical activities	167
Education	78	Administrative and support service activities	146
Administrative and support service activities	59	Real estate activities	142
Other service activities	48	Financial and insurance activities	116
Information and communication	39	Education	112
Human health and social work activities	31	Information and communication	85
Arts, entertainment and recreation	26	Human health and social work activities	40
Financial and insurance activities	22	Arts, entertainment and recreation	37
Accommodation and food service activities	14	Other service activities	35
Wholesale and retail trade; repair of motor vehicles and motorcycles	9	Construction	22
Real estate activities	6	Accommodation and food service activities	21
Agriculture, forestry and fishing	5	Wholesale and retail trade; repair of motor vehicles and motorcycles	12

indebted to and builds on. He made the case that this institutional ignorance was not a state of 'blissful unawareness or innocent absence of knowledge', but rather an outcome of 'rational calculation' (2012, p 960). Recall Chapter 3, in which I described the quantifying of the social as a productive act whose aim was to produce a governable social. I suggested that it maintains not just the things that can't be *counted* outside of the governable social, but also the things that it does not wish to *fully govern* outside the governable social by not counting them or not making them count.

Producing 'strategic ignorance'

If knowledge is for cutting (Foucault 1984, pp 97–98), then we might ask: what is ignorance for? Ignorance can be a means of preventing political action. This is a facet explored by Magnus (2008) in the context of the tobacco industry and climate denial activity through an exploration of what he calls *construct agnogenesis*. Construct agnogenesis achieves its aims by 'hyping and exaggerating ... scientific uncertainty' (Mooney, cited in Magnus 2008, p 250). Magnus describes how the Tobacco Industry Research Council (TIRC) and the Marshall Institute (MI) in the field of climate science functioned as producers of 'red herring' or 'distraction' research which allowed key industrial actors to continue harmful but profitable behaviours unfettered by regulation and unburnished by class action (Magnus 2008, p 251). The CSJ operated to produce enabling evidence for the Coalition government in the 2000s to simultaneously legitimate a punitive turn in social policy and to shore up a radical free market ideology in the face of challenges posed by the events of 2008. The ideological reworking (Clarke and Neman 2012) of the crash as a public sector debt crisis resolvable only through austerity was pivotal to this shoring-up process. The CSJ's *Breakdown Britain* report (2006) and *Breakthrough Britain* (2007) in which it articulated five *'pathways to poverty'* were fundamental to the implementation of that reworking. These two reports together situated the problem in individual behaviours, and solutions primarily in the voluntary operations of the 'Big Society' and the power of community, activated through their alliance. The effect was to produce not uncertainty, but artificial certainty: there is no alternative. This phrase (shortened to TINA) was made popular by Margaret Thatcher and is periodically revivified (for example, by Cameron in 2013 [*BBC News* 2013]). Table 6.4 summarises the agnotological aims, mechanisms and objectives in each of the examples described here.

The CSJ network sustains a particular problematisation of the state we are in. Active agnogenesis matters precisely because of the weight and agency of the ideas it constructs and reifies, and those it marginalises or diminishes. Network effects matter as agnotological *mechanisms* because of the motility they give to these 'filtered' ideas and the influence they deploy through the work of interlockers and processes of hard and soft transfer. Ideas intervene actively *in defence of* a certain way of life. Narratives persist because they are repeated, refuelled and renewed. They become 'grand narratives' that are presented as natural and inevitable. So-called 'fluency heuristics' (Smithson 2008, pp 220–221), the accretive force provided by discursive repetition, operates interdiscursively (between different 'orders' of discourse) and intertextually (between visual and written texts). This happens at different, longer frequencies too, as we reach back through history to revivify old tropes and deploy them in contemporary frames – see Bramall (2016) on the borrowing of moral and cultural cache from the postwar 'in it together' era to rework swingeing cuts to public services as 'austerity', for example. Savage suggests that once 'information is made portable and transparent, it becomes a resource for powerful agents to deploy' (Savage 2021, p 272). The process of the production, accumulation, circulation and deployment

Table 6.4: Summary of agnotological mechanisms in three sectors

Sector	Aim	Mechanism	Objective
Tobacco	Continue to generate profit from the sale of cigarettes	Tobacco Industry Research Council	Generate doubt
Climate science	Avoidance of environmental regulation of large energy producers	Marshall Institute	Produce uncertainty
Social welfare	Justify punitivism and avoid problem articulations that raise the spectre of equality or the idea of redistribution	Centre for Social Justice	Produce certainty – one problem, one solution: there is no alternative (TINA)

of information is not agnostic. It is shaped by determination *not* to know as much as desire to know. And it mobilises the force of past forms of distinction, like deserving/undeserving; dependency/nondependency as described in different ways in Chapters 3, 4 and 5, in contemporary narratives. In so doing, it becomes 'part of the process of accumulation itself' (Savage 2021, p 272).

Magnus suggested that the TIRC and the MI were engaged in *construct agnogenesis* as a means of distracting from harmful but profitable practices. What is the CSJ's construct agnogenesis distracting from? What does the history of effort reflected in the (net)work of the CSJ prevent from being known? I want to draw attention to some key points that Sinfield makes about the scale of 'tax expenditure' and the extraordinary efforts made by successive governments not to take knowledge in directions that might reveal it. This 'failure to know' or 'institutionalised neglect' (Sinfield 2023, p 48) about the scale, purpose and impact of tax expenditure is another form of 'strategic ignorance' – a form of 'non-disclosure tactically deployed to avoid repercussions of inconvenient evidence' (McGoey 2019, pp 2–3). Its revealing would risk destabilising the 'moving on from money' approach that the CSJ worked so hard to put in place. After all, if we are to 'move on from money' with regard to poverty, should we not also address the hugely costly fiscal welfare dependency issue at the other end of the wealth spectrum and 'move on' from money there too? Tax reliefs include things like allowances, exemptions, reductions, deferral and credits which 'tend to increase inequalities' (Sinfield 2023, p 47). Surrey describes them as 'upside-down-benefits' helping those paying higher-rate taxes (Surrey, cited in Sinfield 2023, p 47). They are a form of government policy being run through tax relief, 'deliberately created by government to be used for specific purposes' (Murphy, cited in Sinfield 2023, p 47). They 'take effect *before governments make budgetary allocations to their own spending departments*' (Surrey and McDaniel, cited in Sinfield 2023, p 54, emphasis added) and result in large-scale predistribution upwards which is invisible to the public – a form of fiscal welfare to higher-rate taxpayers. And they cost the UK government hundreds of billions a year: the National Audit Office (NAO) reported in 2020 that 'HMRC [under sustained pressure] identified 1,190 reliefs for all taxes, and provided costs for 196 of them, amounting to £426bn' (cited in Sinfield 2023, p 50). Tax expenditures constitute policy and yet remain unavailable to democratic scrutiny. Having the influence to ensure the continued obscuring of tax relief delivers fiscal benefits to the rich: as Surrey asks, could 'the upside-down benefits of tax reliefs ... possibly be introduced if their real nature were spelt out' (cited in Sinfield 2023, p 54). If their real nature were spelt out, it would be clear that higher-rate tax payers are the recipients of lucrative fiscal welfare. *They* are the beneficiaries of the system. Any social problematisation that keeps the focus downwards contributes to a failure to scrutinise the social role and effects of wealth and the wealthy, and their cost to the nation. Proctor notes that ignorance can be created through the production of knowledge (Proctor 2008, p 24). This was the approach of the TIRC, for example. The CSJ's social problematisation is such a form of distraction research or 'red herring' research (Proctor 2008, p 14). It foregrounds poverty (in a very particular way) and leaves wealth untroubled.

Sometimes we don't know what we don't know because prevailing historical cultural and political norms rendered it not necessary to be known at a particular time. Tuana describes this form of ignorance as an outcome of *structural apathy* (2008), a phrase I have used elsewhere in this book. The result is an absence of certain forms of knowledge and certain knowledge producers, and the effective subjugation of knowledges, a subjugation which affects our contemporary 'geography' of ignorance by producing and reproducing specific 'patterns of silence' (Medina 2011, p 91). Persistent structural apathy causes negative knowledge, 'the deliberate choice not to engage knowledge in a particular direction (as it is presumed to be unimportant)' (Gross, cited in Croissant 2014, p 12). But structural apathy doesn't just work to socially repress knowledge about the poor, women or other marginalised communities and certain knowers; the landscape of ignorance can reveal the 'cognitive and theoretical assumptions about the world which limit the policy alternatives that policymakers would consider' and 'the normative concepts that elites deliberately employ to justify policy programmes' (Campbell's definition of, respectively, paradigms and frames as types of idea [cited in Clark et al 2020, p 9]). The failure to recognise and account for corporate and fiscal welfare in a wider conceptualisation of welfare is *also* an effect of structural apathy. It constitutes a failure to bring into being knowledge about the actual relationship between 'givers and takers', and actual relationships of welfare dependency. It serves to maintain the gaze of the state on the small (and diminishing) amounts of support that the many are entitled to and away from the secret slices of the cake extracted for the few. It keeps in the shade the reality of what is in effect an encompassing welfare state (which I will return to in Chapters 8 and 9) which currently disproportionately benefits those who already have plenty.

I want to conclude by suggesting that *corporate* welfare ends can be achieved through *social* welfare advocacy in certain conditions. The pursuit of an explicitly *low welfare budget* social justice agenda such as that advocated by the CSJ – its Universal Credit policy (recall Duncan Smith's comments in Hughes and Riddell [2016)] about his team in the DWP printing off the CSJ's documents to start drafting the policy once he was made Secretary of State) was explicitly designed to deliver efficiencies by reducing the numbers of claimants. This can and does deliver corporate welfare outcomes (outcomes that benefit corporations and richer individuals too): reducing social welfare expenditure makes more resources available for corporate welfare (for example, the bank bailout, which represented 35 per cent of GDP in 2011). In less tangible ways, the CSJ version of social justice and the policies which are based on it provide other corporate welfare effects, such as preparing the workforce for precarity and 'flexibility' (and, of course, low wages).

Corporations are in effect dependent on state welfare in all the forms discussed earlier. This dependency is rarely articulated in media and political discourse (Kerr and Vaughan 2024a). The act of the making invisible of corporate welfare dependency constitutes an inverted form of Tyler's (2020) *stigmacraft* with the unmarked group (wealthy) distracting from their status as welfare-dependent claimants. This failure to know, appraise, regulate, tax and legislate corporate and HNWI welfare dependency has significant consequences. On a practical level, it creates 'a fundamental problem for social welfare' in the form of 'the decline of the corporate tax base, accelerated by government policy and the influence of corporations on shaping the tax rules' (Ruane 2012, p 27). But on an ethical level, the manifest unevenness it embodies in terms of different forms of government applying to the rich and to corporations is an injustice in and of itself. In the context of the CSJ, we need to move away from the idea that its primary or singular policy stance relates to social justice and identify its other policy stances that are *operative by omission*. How might we identify these stances? The CSJ is very much the vision of its founding CEO, Duncan Smith. Its policy stance is in part an embodiment of his values. These are manifest in his voting record:[4] he is against the mansion tax, but in favour of the spare room tax; against taxing bankers' bonuses, but in favour of increases to VAT; against welfare benefits rising at least in line with prices, and against and against paying higher benefits to those unable to work due to illness or disability, but in favour of reducing corporation tax and capital gains tax. And out of 65 opportunities to vote for a general reduction in spend on welfare benefits between 2010 and 2022, he has taken the opportunity to vote in favour 50 times and against once (he was absent for 14 votes). Evincing a socially compassionate agenda does not necessarily mean voting in what would be considered a fiscally compassionate way. This expanded conceptualisation of the CSJ's agenda as pro-'fiscal welfare' but anti-'social welfare' is reflected in its ideological prioritisation of addressing supposed fiscally damaging impacts of the social behaviours of the poor at the exclusion of addressing socially damaging impacts of the fiscal behaviours of the rich.

The fundamental question is this: what does 'the history of on-going effort' revealed through the operation of the CSJ's network outlined earlier, effort which has allegedly 'diverted £19 billion' over seven years to causes that the CSJ supports, mean in the context of fiscal relief for the rich that diverts at least £426 billion (Sinfield 2023) annually the other way? Given that the government has resisted providing an account of tax reliefs and management for years, and still has not provided costings for the major part of the 1,190 reliefs it identified in 2020, how can we possibly know who is contributing more and who is taking more? And on that basis, how can we know which social group is 'parked on benefits' and which is creating value? It becomes legitimate to interpret the CSJ's social justice agenda as what Proctor calls 'distraction research'. Grassrootsism starts to look very instrumental indeed.

In Chapter 3 I made the case that specific ways of knowing and forms of knowledge could be recognised as moments of the emergence of *wealtherty*. In this chapter I have re-engaged with ways of coming to know in the work of think tanks in the 2000s: the *dubious scientificity* of the Malthusian argument iterates now in the contested *pathways to poverty* concept (the CSJ); the *disregard for evidence* in the development of the NPL (evidenced by Chadwick's writing of the 1832 Commission report before the evidence came in) is reflected not just in the CSJ rebuttal of academic counterarguments to its foundational narratives (for example, the rebuttal to Thane [2010] on the issue of family stability) or in Duncan Smith's persistent misuse of statistics (Ball 2013; Wintour and Butler 2013), but also in the CSJ's determined ignoring of the symbolically inconvenient in-work poverty, as acknowledged by CSJ Director Christian Guy in 2012 (Gentleman 2012), despite its escalation in the 2010s (Bourquin et al 2019). I have made the case that the CSJ's role in reproducing the (behaviours of the) poor as our social problem functions as 'distraction research', enabling a persistent 'looking down' to find causes and solutions in the grassroots. I suggested that the CSJ produces knowledge and ignorance which helps to sustain the unequal state we are in.

In the next chapter I consider how the visual and spatial field of wealtherty sustains the dispositions of scrutiny and ignorance. I think about how we might mobilise images politically to help us visualise and talk about processes of the accumulation of great wealth and its relationship to the production of great poverty.

7

Shaping behaviours: space and the visual as tools of government

This chapter considers the field of visibility of wealtherty through some of the visual and spatial means that make it 'possible to picture who and what is to be governed, how relations of authority and obedience are constituted in space, how different locales and agents are to be connected with one another, what problems are to be solved and what objectives are to be sought' (Dean 2010, p 41). It asks the following questions: 'What is the field of visibility that characterises a regime of government?' and 'By what kind of light does it illuminate and define certain objects and with what shadows and darkness does it obscure and hide others?' (Dean 2010, p 41). These questions are useful to the overall sensibility in this book to using the concept of *Ma* as a way of thinking the integral, always-relational dynamic between *wealth here poverty there* (Bhambra in LSE 2021), and to thinking in a temporally and spatially extended way. The questions are as much about what we can see and know as they about that which we can't see and therefore can't know. And they require us to think about how the visual field – like the textual one discussed in Chapter 6 – mobilises the past in the present.

The governmental disposition of ignorance applied to wealth and the wealthy is one that doesn't seek to know and therefore it doesn't seek to see (or more actively seeks not to see). As such, the issue of visibility with regard to wealth is vexed – something to which I drew attention to in Part I of this book when I looked at the relatively recent attempts to understand wealth dynamics through the ONS Wealth and Assets Survey and the work of the World Inequality Lab. The governmental disposition of scrutiny, on the other hand, is predicated on Alston's 'total surveillance' (Alston 2018, p 11) which manifested in the 19th century in the workhouse system and manifests in the technologies of Universal Credit: everything is visible. The disclosure imperative is totalising.

Secrecy, manifest in a lack of visibility, has made visual engagement with wealth problematic. As Chapters 3 and 4 made clear, there was little tolerance for the state having oversight of a gentleman's private financial affairs in the 19th century, and little has changed since: the OECD's *Engaging with High Net Worth Individuals on Tax Compliance* (2009) is in effect an acknowledgement of the intransigence of the wealthy in this regard and their preference for remaining unseen. In Chapter 1 I described the focus of genealogy being *processes and procedures*, the 'apparatuses by which truth and knowledge are produced' (Tamboukou 1999, p 3) rather than 'only the objects that reify it in our eyes' (Veyne 1997, pp 149–150); here I look at the visual and spatial apparatuses by which knowledge about wealtherty is produced. In Chapter 4 I looked at the spatial, territorial and visual regimes of the workhouse; here I focus on the spatial practices of social welfare in Jobcentre Plus buildings, alongside the spaces of the wealthy in our now. The chapter concludes by introducing some critical photography which seeks to expand the visual field of wealth and implicitly engages with facets of my definition of wealtherty.

Rancière argues that 'the political is always aesthetic, in the sense that regimes of representation and perception delimit "the visible and invisible" and "speech and noise" in ways that shape "the place and the stakes of politics as a form of experience"' (Rancière, cited in Tyler 2013, p 25). The political is also always spatial. The continuity between Booth's maps of the parts of London inhabited by the vicious and semi-criminal or the upper class and wealthy, and the function of contemporary 'territorial stigmatisation' present in contemporary zoning of London testifies to this (Atkinson 2015; Slater 2018; Dorling 2023). The concept of the visual in this chapter is broad for this purpose: it needs to accommodate the things that we see and the spaces in which we see them.

Jobcentre Plus as a semiotics of deterrence

In Chapter 4 I looked at the regimes of the workhouse as a deterrent. I deferred an engagement with contemporary spaces of discipline for poorer people as I wanted to include this analysis alongside a more fulsome consideration of the contemporary spatial and visual field of wealtherty. That is the task I attempt here. The Jobcentre Plus network of buildings operates as a modern semiotics of deterrence. The 19th-century design made a link between moral reformation and environmental design, which meant that 'to each environment there was a corresponding form of life' (Driver 2004, p 14). The two principles of 'associational functionalism' (the relationships between sensation, perception and behaviour) and 'spatial functionalism' (the notion that moral improvement and social control could be achieved through the manipulation of space) governed approaches to the design of the workhouses. The spaces of welfare in the mechanism of Universal Credit are also disciplinary, mobilising associational and spatial functionalism to conduct and to encourage some of the 'sanctioned' ways of being or repertoires of the self that I introduced in Chapter 5. It is a nudge (or sometimes a shove) environment. Rigorous design engineering seeks to guide the mood and movements of claimants. Conduct is conducted here.

The claim and support processes for Universal Credit take place in a regulated network of Jobcentre Plus offices. The offices are not

Figure 7.1: The Jobcentre Plus sign

Source: Used with permission of Consultants in Design

subject to the same territorial setting apart as the workhouses: they are not on the edge of town, nor are they larger or carceral in design. But they are nonetheless Benthamite in their attention to environmental design principles, and they are intentionally and rigorously disciplinary. Jobcentre Plus formed when the Employment Service merged with the Benefits Agency in 2002. The offices host the initial customer interviews, the stage of a claim immediately following the mandatorily online application, and they are the locus for job search advice and reviews of progress. The offices are part of the 'technologies' of delivery of Universal Credit and are also a key part of its field of visibility. Through a meticulously designed experience, claimant and staff conduct is subject to spatial government in ways that support the objectives of the Universal Credit programme with regard to activation. Just like with the workhouse system, these buildings are part of an architecture of surveillance, a 'territorially-based process of administration, designed to regulate the conduct of human beings (Driver 2004, p 9). The administration of social welfare, now as then, 'requires ... the monitoring of conduct and compliance' (ibid, pp 9–10) and in both contexts – the workhouse and Universal Credit – enforced attendance at a building is a condition of relief. Once inside, claimants' movement is governed. There are zones. There is classification. There is a journey. And although technically you could choose not to go, these are often illusory choices now as they were in the workhouse system: nonattendance results in sanctions.

The building itself and the disciplinary tactics enacted within it perform a central role in contemporary regimes of government.

Using a web archive relating to the Jobcentre Plus network held by the National Archive (DWP 2012b), I am now going to explore the use of environmental design in the spatial government of people claiming welfare today, making the case that the nudge ethos that infused the wider Cameronian policy landscape following the establishment of the Behavioural Insights Team (BIT) within the Cabinet Office in 2010, is baked into the design of the Jobcentre Plus buildings. Behavioural change approaches to government proliferated in the 2010s, with between 300 and 400 government-led trials relating to behavioural change taking place between 2010 and 2016 alone (Halpern and Sanders 2016, p 62). The approach infused the wider policy landscape beyond the formal interventions led by the BIT itself. The Jobcentre Plus building interior design constitutes an antecedent behaviour change strategy and that of sanctions a consequence strategy. Cash et al characterise contemporary behavioural design as 'designing for antecedent behaviour change strategies using implicit interventions to impact behaviour' (Cash et al 2017, p 2). They distinguish between 'antecedent strategies' which use interventions that occur prior to a behaviour, influencing it in a desired direction (Abrahmsen et al, cited in Cash et al 2017, p 98), and 'consequence strategies', which use interventions that occur during or after behaviour has been performed (for example, using rewards, fees, and feedback) (Cash et al 2017, p 98). This is a useful lens to distinguish the overlapping forms of government which characterise contemporary processes of securing relief. The Jobcentre Plus field of visibility is highly regulated, nationally uniform and subject to rigorous compliance with hyperdetailed style sheets: from the type of lighting for the welcome point (spotlights), to the angle of the welcome banners (45°), to the linking of zones through circulation routes, the types of chairs in the staff mess, the colour and finish of the walls, the coating for exposed metal areas of banner stands, the attention to the impact of the environment on the behaviours of those moving through is forensic in its detail. These mandatory design features are communicated through a style guide called JPEG (Jobcentre Plus Environment Guide), which itself complies with a 63-page *Jobcentre Plus Designers' Handbook* (DWP 2012b). This handbook lets us know that the Jobcentre Plus brand is based on three fundamental principles: (1) inspiring; (2) straightforward; and (3) personal. Reflecting the dominant welfare-claimant-as-customer approach, the design concept is described as 'part civic, part retail' and 'wholly supports the business process and organisational structure'.

Whereas *surveillance* can be done from afar, *scrutiny* involves the close and critical observation or examination of a person or a thing. The panopticon principle is about surveillance or perception thereof: the people in the cells think there may be someone in the tower, so they behave in a certain way – they behave 'as if surveilled'. The modulation of the surveillance principle in our now has come closer to the individual. The possibility of being seen has become a certainty. Scrutiny as a governmental disposition is less about the governors having the option of seeing than it is about them having the right of knowing. We start to see the removal of voluntary offering of information, to information extracted at source, for example, through the operation of HMRC's Real Time Information (RTI) system that sends information about income for Universal Credit claimants directly to the DWP, as was discussed in Chapter 4. The Jobcentre Plus field of visibility explicitly enables scrutiny.

There are 30 different zone types in a Jobcentre Plus office, and each has its own detailed design specification tailored to provide 'the most appropriate surrounding for a specific service or office function'. These are spaces designed for 'visitors', 'customers' and 'members of the public'. The claimant journey is managed by and mirrored in these areas. The guidance notes that 'while the size and shape of zones may vary, the relationships between them should be consistent'. The journey starts with the *forum*, which is located immediately inside the main entrance, and then proceeds through the relevant zones. The behaviours of staff and 'customers' is to be regulated by the environment, with colours calibrated for maximum hope and optimism, and angles measured for swift intervention should the colours and angles fail to prevent conflict.

The value of privacy to those afforded it comes in part from the fact that they can decide what the limits of that privacy are. They get to decide where and when it starts and ends. For example, wealth holders told Pitt what they would and wouldn't accept in terms of state intrusion; Cameron gave evidence at the Select Committee on his dealings with failed company Greensill, but stopped short of disclosing how much he stood to gain, on the basis of its being a 'private matter' (Allegretti 2021a). Privacy is a restricted capability reserved for those with capital: it is a sanctioned response to the application of the governmental disposition of ignorance. In the management of space within the Jobcentre Plus environment, there is a denial of this autonomy – (partial) privacy is granted when someone other than the claimant decides it is necessary and the glass-fronted offices attest to the continuing primacy of the governmental disposition of scrutiny (with the sanctioned response of disclosure) (see Figure 7.2).

Privacy is at once to be 'maximised' by locating advice areas at the back of the space, and at the same time denied, by having glass fronts to 'private' interview rooms (PIRs) so that staff can monitor private activity within. Sightlines 'must not be blocked by other desks or banners'. PIRs 'require both customer access from the FoH [front of house] area and a separate staff exit to the BoH [back of house] or secure "backline" behind the staff desks'. Being observed while in a private meeting – and knowing that one

Figure 7.2: An image of a Jobcentre Plus screened private interview room

Source: Used with permission of Consultants in Design

is being observed – is a denial of respect, dignity and, indeed, privacy! The complex cases for which work coaches are trained (as evidenced in the training material for new coaches [DWP 2020]), including terminal illness, surviving sexual and domestic abuse, long-term mental and physical illness, and multiple caring responsibilities), require – *demand* – a private space and sufficient time for their disclosure. Failure to provide this constitutes a collapse of agency (Wright 2016). It manifests as 'disrespect, humiliation and an assault on dignity and self-esteem, shame and stigma, powerlessness, denial of rights and diminished citizenship' (Lister, cited in Wright 2016, p 238). It is a violation too of several of Nussbaum's core capabilities – most directly, the capability of affiliation, of 'Having the social bases of self-respect and non-humiliation; being able to be treated as a dignified being whose worth is equal to that of others' (Nussbaum 2011).

In the dominant deficit model, welfare subjects are conceived of as 'naturally inactive and in need of activation – either because of their perceived incompetency or immorality' (Wright 2016, p 236). The spatial and visual environment of Jobcentre Plus offices are designed as part of a wider system of 'coerced self-improvement' (Wright 2016, p 236), which includes other techniques such as monthly payments (to teach people how to budget like workers); the savings bank (which teaches frugality and the benefits of saving on low incomes); and the two-child cap (which teaches restraint and the principle of making responsible decisions about family size). The deficit model sees being active as 'a transformative state produced by coercive, punitive or quasi-market intervention' (Wright 2016, p 238), a model which Wright and Dwyer 2020 go on to describe as producing the 'coerced worker-claimant'. The Jobcentre Plus architecture and spatial management are part of this deficit model, designed to activate and transform (or redeem, as I suggested in Chapter 5), and its coercively calming pastel hues belie the threat of sanction for failure to do so.

There is no specific architectural plan for the Jobcentre Plus offices. The design continuity comes from how existing buildings are adapted and form a uniform 'brand' in terms of external signage, office zones and communications. The company's brand values are 'welcoming, dynamic, friendly and informative', but the design in reality *anticipates* hostility. Designers must make sure 'when planning Welcome Points that staff behind the lectern are not confined in an enclosed area in the event of confrontation with a member of the public. There should be a clear route away from a "flashpoint", or to move to assist others, on either side of the lectern'. The screened interview rooms (see Figure 7.2) are reminiscent of secure visiting units at prisons. They are described as 'multi-purpose spaces, typically used for functions such as Social Fund crisis loan or *other potentially confrontational interviews*' (DWP 2012b, emphasis added). The colour palette has been designed to be 'optimistic', but also calming – a form of pastel discipline. This again, assumes a welfare subject whose disposition and mood needs optimising for work. It assumes its opposites (pessimistic and agitated), and in so doing is a 'nudge' version of the more explicit conflict management apparatuses described earlier. The 'correct interpretation' of the colours is ensured by the provision of a bespoke pantone colour guide. The pastel discipline enacted through the Jobcentre Plus journey is an example of Henriques' (1968) punitive government in 'less sensational' ways.

The field of visibility is part of the delivery mechanism for the values and ultimately the objective of Universal Credit – to convert the unemployed or underemployed into workers; to produce an active welfare subject. Posters and banners 'sell' work to customers and suggest that – very much in line with the post-neoliberal injunction towards self-responsibility and freedom (McGimpsey et al 2017) – the state is providing the support needed to be

Figure 7.3: Jobcentre Plus office zones

Source: Used with permission of Consultants in Design

successful (the help and the jobs). In order to succeed, you simply need to take it.

Relations of authority and obedience are established, reinforced and enacted through the spatial design. The intention of the design is to manage the behaviour of the claimant in the building and to regulate her interaction with staff. It is to separate staff from customers and to ensure that staff, effectively, have escape routes to their secure 'backline' (a *truly* private space). It is to reinforce – to produce – the claimant as an active, optimistic workseeker, to minimise antagonism and to position the staff as helpful 'coaches' supporting claimants to make good choices. The claimant's movement in space is directed (she is on a journey, which will have a positive end!). Her behaviour is monitored and observed to minimise possible 'flashpoints'. Lighting design and colour schemes map out her journey and influence her mood. The case study content of training materials for new work coaches (DWP 2020) describes 'redeemed' claimants as being delighted with their experience: 'Peter phoned his work coach recently and made him cry as he stated that they were the first person in his life that had shown him real compassion and empathy, listening to him and giving him the help he needed' (DWP 2020, UC55 07 Illustrative Examples V.34, p 4).

The 'journey' is not just spatial of course; it is also temporal. This was captured in the analysis of mobility as a form of government in Chapter 4.

Figure 7.4: Jobcentre Plus welcome poster

Source: Used with permission of Consultants in Design

Mobility implies both dimensions. Time and its management are key to the form of discipline in Universal Credit: the five-week wait, the 36 hours per week job search and the three-year sanctions. Even the journal is a form of temporal tyranny, as are the administrative processes that I described in Chapter 4, which absorb so much time for the mothers interviewed as part of the inquiry into Universal Credit rollout (WPC 2018b) (cited in earlier chapters). Gokmenoglu, writing on the political sociology of time, observes how it is 'intertwined with power relations'; it is a 'dimension of power' (Gokmenoglu 2022, p 644). The examples he uses include the way in which 'states make certain social groups wait as a form of subjugation' (Schwartz 1974), such as 'the working class for social services' (Auyero, cited in Gokmenoglu 2022, p 644). The 'journey' envisaged in the Jobcentre Plus design manages the claimants along both dimensions.

So far, I have presented the Jobcentre Plus network of buildings as a visual and spatial means of establishing relations of authority and obedience (through glass-fronted privacy, pastel discipline and 'secure back lines' for staff); like the workhouses, I have described how the Jobcentre Plus buildings make up a coherent national network of adapted buildings with a consistent recognisable design that sequences the claimant/customer's journey through zones, on her way to activation. I have thought about what problems the spaces are trying to solve (labour market inactivity) and what objectives are to be sought (labour market activation). I will now move on to think about these questions in the context of wealth.

The spaces of wealth

How we choose to represent things and people *visually* reflects the values of the dominant discourse and is constitutive of it ('politics is always aesthetic'). Images and the wider visual field of architectural plans, buildings and photographs – the broadly conceived field of visibility of wealth, like other forms of discourse – 'form[s] the objects of which it speaks' (Foucault 1972, p 49). The question of fields of visibility for the wealthy, for wealth management and for the infrastructure of government which attempts to shape their/its conduct is a more complex one, in large part because of a culture of secrecy which manifests itself in successful attempts to hide on the part of the rich and (albeit qualified) acceptance of this on the part of state. The workhouse was built as a disciplinary mechanism. Jobcentres were adapted from existing buildings to perform new, disciplinary functions, nudging claimant behaviour towards greater economic productivity. The visual and spatial field of wealth has no explicitly carceral buildings. There is no comparable network of state-produced, or adapted, buildings relating to the *disciplinary* government of wealth, buildings in which active means are taken to shape the conduct of the rich and discipline (and, more specifically, punish) rich bodies. There are no explicit antecedent or consequence behavioural design strategies (Cash et al 2017), although a compelling case might be made for private schools' architectural opulence being a form of antecedent behavioural design strategy, and the gated 'ghettos' (Savage 2021) of the wealthy in cities being a 'consequence' design strategy. But the more general absence of disciplinary spaces is in large part because the governmental disposition is one of ignorance and choosing not to see. It is enabling and permissive. So, where the disposition of scrutiny relies on coerced visibility and disclosure, and assumes a radically visible subject (think Alston's 'total surveillance' or the principles of Bentham's panopticon), the disposition of ignorance chooses not to see, and its objects of government are able to choose uncoerced *in*visibility (gentlemen's clubs and masonic lodges, but also tax avoidance and offshoring). Inequality endures in the spatial and visual field just as surely as it does in the ways of thinking and governing that were the focus of Part II of this book. As a way of looking at our social situation, wealtherty is an effect of the relationship between all the trees on the canvas (see Figure 1.2), including those that came before and after. It is not just the story of those visualised in the foreground and the present. As was suggested in Chapter 1, wealtherty is about being simultaneously interested in what the actor does and does not do.

I made the case that the government of wealth and the wealthy is an enabling one, and that this is produced and reflected in the spatial field. Despite there not being a network of carceral buildings, as suggested earlier, there *are* buildings which conduct conduct. These buildings govern in ways that inscribe, produce and communicate wealthed rationalities and which subjectivate *wealthed relationships*: buildings in which poor (mainly) immigrant female domestic workers are imprisoned in conditions of modern slavery, performing services for the wealthy (Grant and Kelly 2016); buildings in which relationships of wealth and power are explicitly reproduced through conversations between men (notably in gentlemen's clubs), behind closed doors; Iain Duncan Smith, whose work I looked at in Chapter 6, has declared lifetime membership of two such clubs in his returns to the register of members' interests. These are often sexed relationships between wealth and power, with women included in these spaces in the first instance as either spouses or partners of Masons (and then only through separate weekend spouses' clubs) and in the latter through their roles as hostesses and escorts. The role of women in the construction and performance of (predominantly) male wealth is a well-trodden field, which will be engaged with through some of the critical photography I will look at shortly (Figures 7.6–7.10). Then there are the semio-techniques of explicitly wealth-zoned spaces, in which the super-rich colonise space through mechanisms of exclusion and exclusionary zones (Serafini and Maguire 2019, p 7): the 'scandal' of vacant property in an era of rising homelessness, where the property is not conceived of as a home, or even somewhere to live, but as an investment or a pension fund (Bullough 2018; Atkinson 2021). The practice of permitting property companies to build new developments with so-called 'Poor Doors', which perpetuates a distinction that manifests as a physical separation between individuals and communities based on wealth. A housing scheme in Hornsey, North London, has separate entrances for social housing tenants, located 'down a bin alley' (Wall and Osbourne 2018), while a scheme in South London – on the site of an old comprehensive school – blocks children from the *social* housing element of the luxury complex from playing in the communal play areas; they can *see* the areas, but have been prevented from accessing them by the conversion of gates into hedges (see Figure 7.5) (Grant and Michael 2019). These examples hit 'scandal' threshold because of their concentration within one housing development in a way that the more diffuse zoning of school catchment areas by housing type and housing ownership status doesn't, for example, despite reproducing the same divisions. These explicit wealth-based segregations are simply a more visible and concentrated version of existing wealth-differentiated housing provision and wealth-differentiated access to space, repeated 'less sensationally' across the city. These spatial privileges are 'capacities' of extreme wealth (Beckert 2023) which afford opportunities to use space in ways that are simply not available to those without wealth – or even those with Hecht et al's 'ordinary' wealth (2022). The buying of spatial exclusion in the ways described earlier undermines the available 'doings and beings' of those with no or low wealth: it restricts in a very direct way the capability of play (being able to

Figure 7.5: Salvatora Rea looks out at the communal play area and garden his children are not allowed to use

Source: Photograph by Graeme Robertson

laugh, to play, to enjoy recreational activities) and takes away the capability of control over one's environment.

What looks like wealtherty/what does wealtherty look like?

I'm now going to present some contemporary photographic image making as a form of critique of wealtherty. While the visual field of poverty has a long history, that of problematic wealth less so. Serafini and Maguire (2019) contrast 'surfaces' with 'structures' approaches to calling the rich into being in visual and textual media discourse. They note that the difficulty of gaining an inside view 'of the machinations and mind-sets, infrastructures, and ideologies at work in the perpetuation of the super-rich' can mean that the gaze tends to stay at the surface, on the ostentatiousness, lifestyles, accoutrements of super-rich individuals rather than 'the institutional, ideological and conventional bases on which rest the reproduction of inequality' (Serafini and Maguire 2019, p 2). The individualising and naturalising of inequality in this way constitutes what they call 'discursive misdirection' in which 'the structural processes that reproduce advantage are obscured' (2019, p 5) leaving the role that the wealthy have in 'shaping the processes that sustain them' (2019, p 5) underexplored. Discursive misdirection could be articulated as a form of agnosis – a form of ignorance making allied to the rhetorical misdirection that I attributed to the CSJ in Chapter 6. Positive representations of the wealthy, often based on narratives of hard work leading to extreme wealth (rags-to-riches-type stories) tend to gain public approval (Hebden and Palmer 2020); narratives about 'fat cats' or about tax dodging (where processes of accumulation are felt to be an outcome of not playing by the rules, as reflected in Ruskin's concept of 'illth' – see Chapter 1) do not. But even when wealthy people are held up for criticism for their excessive consumption behaviours through what Jaworski and Thurlow call a 'derisive stance', this focus on individuals rather than systems results in a 'fully decontextualized, de-historicised account of the Super-Rich' (Jaworski and Thurlow 2017, p 284). New analysis of a corpus of images attached to Facebook posts between 2014 and 2023 and used by UK civil society and news media to communicate the problem of wealth inequality illustrates a prevailing tendency to use images of wealth that are uncritical and that represent wealth as (physically) distanced from processes of accumulation and/or its (negative) effects (Vaughan and Kerr 2024). However, in some fine art critical photography and documentary photography, there has been an evolving engagement since the 2000s as photographers seek a richer and more critical engagement with wealth inequality through an explicit effort to shift from surfaces to structures. This shift takes us to quieter parts of the visual field, to the 'grey spaces' of genealogical sources described in Chapter 1, towards sources that extend beyond the restricted range identified in Vaughan and Kerr (2024). This is a shift from images *of* wealth (the objects that reify it in our eyes – the 'surface') to images *about* wealth (the processes and procedures of its production, and its social life). In a special edition of the *British Journal of Photography* in 2016 on photographing the wealthy called 'Shooting the Rich', the editorial noted that 'the world of the mega-wealthy [is] notoriously camera-shy' (Smyth 2016, p 4). The projects in the journal are fraught with problems, 'not least of which is access because while the poor may be willing to be photographed in the hope that things can change, the mega rich have much more invested in ensuring they stay the same' (Smyth 2016, p 19). Smyth described the work in the late 19th century of Jacob Riis whose *How the Other Half Lives* was the start of the long trend of photographing the poor 'in a bid to improve their lot' (2016, p 19), a genre which she notes has been accused of 'serving up the dispossessed for consumption, while making little actual difference' (2016, p 19). Some forms of photography of the poor are deeply 'extractive' and nonconsensual, and, I suggest amount to a visual counterpart of Steedman's enforced narratives of the self (Steedman 2000): the images of criminalised young women selling sex, for example, included as part of Booth's mapping of London (Booth 2019); the images of 'Chavs' which proliferated in the mid-2000s (typified by the image of Karen Matthews, discussed in Jones [2011]). Motivations for photographing the poor are not always beneficent and are often harmful. Picturing the rich has its own long tradition, which a visit to the National Portrait Gallery will attest to. However, a critical photographic engagement with the *processes of wealth accumulation* and with its effects at both ends of the wealth spectrum is new.

How can images that engage with wealth critique the idea that wealth is benign or distinct from the poverty that sustains it? As a recap, my working definition of wealtherty as the state we are in is one of a hyperconcentration of prosperity in terms of an abundance of possessions or riches, with a stark polarisation between the rich and the rest; the perpetuation of social and policy divisions based on this distinction (fiscal and social policy, winners and losers, claimants and customers, and the other classifications discussed in Chapter 5); concomitant unequal access to political power and influence (with rich voices predominating and gatekeeping) and resultant risks to the democratic process and social justice; constraints on full human flourishing of poorer people via the operation of privileged *restricted capabilities* (for example, media and political influence) and policy-induced lack of opportunity to exercise basic human capabilities (for example, alleviating hunger). The idea of *Ma*, where both time and space are a focus, and that enables us to think 'duration' back into the images we are looking at, means that we can see wealtherty in images of what we might traditionally think of as poverty images (see Figure 7.10) as much as in images of decadence and opulence (see Figure 7.6).

I suggest that there is a subtle distinction in degree if not in type between images *of* wealth and the wealthy (typified by Dougie Wallace's *Harrodsburg* series [see Figure 7.6]) and images *about* wealth and the wealthy, such as Mayrit (see Figure 7.7), Bush (see Figure 7.8) and Galimberti and Woods (see Figure 7.9). These distinctions mirror the methodological tension raised in different ways in Chapters 2 and 3 between the effects of data showing macroeconomic trends (WIR 2022), data focusing on individuals

Figure 7.6: Dougie Wallace, *Harrodsburg* (2012)

Source: Wallace (2012)

Figure 7.7: Daniel Mayrit (2012) – still from *You Haven't Seen Their Faces*

Source: https://www.danielmayrit.com/blank

(*The Times* Rich List, for example), and the desire embodied in the CA to know more of the doings and beings enabled by wealth through a focus on multidimensional ends. They represent a shift towards the more phenomenological engagements with wealth inequality (Hecht et al 2022) that focus on the experience of it – that is, why it matters. Figure 7.6 (an image by photographer Dougie Wallace [2012]) is also about wealth – and explicitly so. But the entry point in his series is largely the bodies of the rich (surface), and often the bodies of rich women, rather than the processes of wealth creation. The latter can be read on the former without doubt, but the bodies can tend to distract from the actual target of critique. The bodies are the tip of the iceberg. Bush's 'privatised public assets' (Figure 7.8) are its underbelly.

In Mayrit's work, the people featured 'represent a sector which is arguably regarded in the collective perception as highly responsible for the current economic situation, but nevertheless still live in a comfortable anonymity' (Mayrit 2015). Mayrit contrasts the treatment of the 2011 'rioters' with this top 100: 'I lived around 500 yards from the place where Mark Duggan was shot by the police', he says, 'when the ensuing riots spread, the media focused on the rioting but never addressed the causes. The police distributed photos of suspects in our mailboxes and the format resembled "Wanted" posters. The presumption of guilt was there.' He contrasts this with financial scandals that were coming to light around the same time, such as the Lux Leaks: 'In these cases it was as if those acts couldn't be directly attributed to specific people ... Meanwhile, some people were being arrested for stealing a pair of trainers' (Mayrit 2015).

Figure 7.8: Still from *Eleven Privatised Public Assets*

Source: Bush (2019)

In Chapter 3, I suggested that in the process of rendering poverty and wealth into graphs and charts, they are 'transformed into their statistical indicators', and in the process 'lives can disappear' behind percentages and their decimal points (Rose 1999, p 205). The photographs here rebuild a bridge between wealth and the body. They give a (visual) account of the 'material conditions that sustain ... different subject positions'. Through these images, the photographers engage in and with a 'politics of location, a politics of 'becoming situated' (Braidotti 2011, p 15). The images provide a starting point in materialising the diverse cast, the global network of cities and havens, and the procedures, processes and interrelationships that form the habitus of wealtherty.

Figure 7.9: Richard J. Geisenberger (standing), Delaware's Chief Deputy Secretary of State. He is photographed in the Wilmington State Building, overseeing one of the more than 300 incorporations that take place daily in Delaware. It takes a few minutes, no questions asked, to incorporate a company, and the state office stays open until midnight Monday through Thursday. More than 50 per cent of all US publicly traded companies and 63 per cent of the Fortune 500 are incorporated in Delaware.

Source: Galimberti and Woods (2015)

As suggested earlier, Figures 7.6 (*Harrodsburg*) and 7.10 (*Liz*) illustrate the contemporaneousness of 'wealth here poverty there' – a jarring juxtaposition of the distributive and capabilitarian extremes of life in England in the late 1990s and early 2000s. Figure 7.10 is a portrait of Liz Billingham, pictured in Richard Billingham's 1997 *Ray's a Laugh*. This is an image of wealtherty written on the body. The photobook captures moments in the lives of Richard's mum and dad on a council estate in Birmingham in the 1990s. Billingham's 'squalid realism' narrates his 'parents' dreary, drunken existence in the Black Country' (Adams 2016). His mum, aged 47, is already manifesting the health issues that Tyler (2020) shows claim poorer women ahead of their richer counterparts: she dies nine years after this picture is taken of a blood clot, aged just 56. Liz and Ray, her husband, are trapped in a high rise, with no work and no resources to move (Adams 2016). The images in the collection from which this single image is taken play with and contest the idea of disgust that I introduced in Chapter 5, which is roused and provoked 'in the service of [the] prevailing social and political

Figure 7.10: Still from Richard Billingham's *Ray's a Laugh* (2014) showing Richard's mother Liz

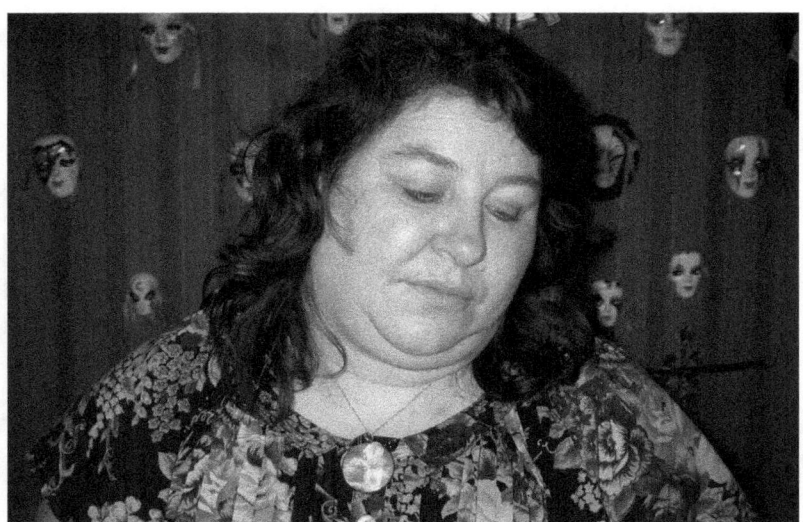

Source: Billingham (2014)

classificatory [and dividing] practices' (Tyler 2013, p 25). It sets the outer boundary of what is acceptable. It shores up the distinction between the abject and the other, contrasting sharply with the rich women in Wallace's images : clean, matt, hairless, sculpted. It is a visual rendering of several of the themes I have explored in this book: regional health inequality, restricted mobility and lack of security. Figure 7.6, for example, is an image from Dougie Wallace's (2012) *Harrodsburg* project, which explicitly engaged with '*the consequences* of the rising economic and political power of the "one per cent"' (Wallace n.d.). Wallace describes *Harrodsburg* as 'an up-close wealth safari exploring the wildlife that inhabits the super-rich residential and retail district of Knightsbridge and Chelsea'. The image evokes the particular urban nature and practices of contemporary elites, who 'depend on, mobilise in, and accumulate in cities where their presence is stamped indelibly in metropolitan centres' and where in their elective territorial exile, they form a new 'ghetto class' (Savage 2021, p 239).

Figure 7.8 is a satellite image of British Petroleum (privatised 1977–1987) from Lewis Bush's *Eleven Privatised Public Assets*. It is part of an 11-image series of privatised national assets. The image tells us about the wealth of a nation and the shift of public capital into private hands. It the photographic partner to the graph from the World Inequality Lab (see Figure 7.11), which is itself a visual assertion of duration.

Bush's work (2019) tells us about wealth-making processes rather than the bodies that reify those processes. The image is temporally complex: we

Figure 7.11: Reproduction of a graph from the World Inequality Report (2018) showing the slide of capital from public into private hands

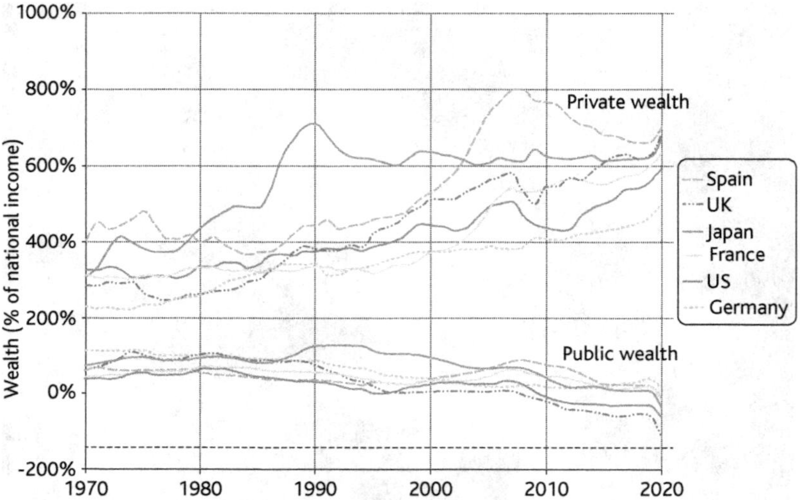

Interpretation: In the UK, public wealth dropped from 60% of national income to -106% between 1970 and 2020. Public wealth is the sum of all financial and non-financial assets, net of debts, held by governments.
Source: WIL (2018a)

know the site photographed was once in public hands, but that now it isn't. What did the workers earn? Had previous generations worked there too? What were the secondary service industries that sustained it (cleaning, education, catering or sex)? We might think about the people who used to work there and whether anyone still does, or about the role the building as workplace held in the imaginary of the community which produced its workers. We might think about the reasons for its sale; we might get angry that we never realised that we owned it or that it was sold. We might think about what the money raised was spent on. It is an image that asks questions which consciously seek to destabilise. I am including it in the critical toolbox of genealogy. It is a visualisation of wealtherty. The photograph is an invocation of the weight of the past; it is about the slide of capital from public to private hands – an instantiation in our now of older repertoires of territorial 'enclosure and engrossment', of expropriation and of extraction. Engrossment is the poorer cousin of 'enclosure' in the social imaginary, but it was the necessary second part of the process of expropriation, and is particularly important when we think about the operation of the same process today. Enclosure encloses – it expropriates from multiple smaller landowners. Engrossment, as the name suggests, aggregates these smallholdings into a larger unit under single ownership, and then charges the smaller landowners for access, in a very similar manner to the way that privatised national assets do. Visual theorist John Berger observed in *Ways of Seeing* (1980) that 'time does not unfold in images' in the same way that it does in films – all the action is on the one plane, the single canvas. But if we assume that the image has both temporal and spatial dimensions (in the way that Tōhaku's image does; see Figure 1.2), then we can read history back into it. We might see in some of the images in Bush's collection, for example, assets originally funded using fiscal revenue extracted from then colonial nations in the 1800s (Bhambra 2021a), originally held on behalf of the nation (albeit narrowly conceived) and now sequestered by nameless wealthy investors.

Figure 7.9 is taken from Galimberti and Woods' *The Heavens Annual Report* and 'aims to show what tax havens look like and what they mean' (Galimberti and Woods 2015, p 8). Moving beyond the palm-fringed beach visual epithet, the images engage instead with the processes and spaces of capital creation and protection – in all their banality and often bleakness. These are the grey spaces of wealtherty – the 'unpromising places' in '*what we tend to feel is without history*' (Foucault 1984, p 76, emphasis added). The image is an innocuous inside shot of a State Building in Delaware. Other images in *The Heavens* series engage with the same theme of the mundane, technocratic mechanisms of wealtherty – a man accessing one of hundreds of post office boxes in the Cayman Islands, which we learn hosts 'twice as many companies ... as citizens'. There are disquieting parallels with the cellular compartments in that image, and a later image of a 'cage home' in Hong Kong: the first a form of cellular discipline for money, the second for bodies. The images engage with the theme of the very different types of movement attaching to different groups within neoliberal economies that I outlined in Chapter 4 (Braidotti 2011; Hall and Savage 2016). Several of the images reveal the impact of wealtherty on women's bodies: young mother Kandra, who undertakes a 'low-paying job[s] in the service sector' in Grand Cayman; C.C., a sex worker, crack dealer and heroin addict residing in a motel room with her mum, providing services of a different kind; and an image that looks like one more wealthy woman in a domestic interior. But we read that this woman is both the Chairperson of the Financial Services Business Development Committee in the British Virgin Islands and its First Lady. The image and caption together aim to articulate 'the nonobservable' nature of her capabilities (Burchardt and Hick 2017) – her deployment of the restricted capability of political influence to further her own ends, which at the same time impoverishes the domestic population in the BVI. The image is of Savage's 'return of empire' in one of the cites of its original incarnations. These images together show the two sides of the coin of wealtherty and refuse neat separation into images of poverty and images of wealth – each is both.

In this chapter I have looked at the pastel discipline of the Jobcentre Plus offices and I have considered opposing ways of occupying and moving through spaces that belong to the rich. The very different approaches to the government of mobility evident in the contrast between the Jobcentre Plus buildings, and 'rich' London with its zoned spaces and poor doors showed how ways of knowing, governing and being explored in Part I of this book are made (built) to endure. They are sustained and nourished through contemporary ways of designing space to segregate, exclude and offend, or to protect, hide and appreciate. I then found in five images of wealth, poverty and inequality a way to articulate wealtherty, to see Braidotti's 'both sides of the same coin' in a single image. I made the case that it was possible to read the images in a way that 'put *Ma* in', in Murakami's words – that is, in way in which we could understand in the images, and the long processes of capital accumulation and their effects, not just the (present) objects that reify it in our eyes (Veyne 1997, pp 149–150).

The final chapter of Part III of this book draws even closer to the embodied experience of *wealtherty*. While Chapter 5 introduced some repertories of the self and considered how these endure and are renewed, Chapter 8 looks at how repertoires of the self are navigated in contemporary policy communications – how wealtherty is sustained and renewed through unequal participation in communicative acts and knowledge making.

8

Shaping selves: wealth and identity

This final chapter in Part III looks at the operation of what I am calling *wealthed privilege* in some of the communicative practices relating to the government of richer and poorer people using Fricker's articulation of *epistemic injustice* (Fricker 2007). My aim is to reveal how unequal relations between richer and poorer people are encoded in the way we communicate. Epistemic injustice involves 'all forms of unfair treatment that relate to issues of knowledge, understanding, and participation in communicative practices' (Kidd et al 2017, p 1) and results from prejudice specifically against someone's status as a knowing subject (Fricker 2007, p 1).

Part II of this book (Chapters 3, 4 and 5) introduced several moments in which some knowers were enabled and others were ignored. Together, these were suggestive of a systemic activation of wealth in communication practice.

Some of the often-polarised ideas about the poor and the rich that I have discussed in previous chapters underpin enduring negative or positive identity prejudices. Over time, these identity prejudices lead to disproportionate assessments of epistemic credibility at both ends of the scale: credibility *deficit* for those subject to negative identity prejudice; and credibility *excess* for those subject to positive identity prejudice. I will be exploring the effects of *credibility excesses and deficits* in the communication in two fora: one in which the state engages with the very wealthy and one in which it engages with poorer people. This chapter builds on and adds new dimensions to my work in Kerr (2023). I think about what it means when some voices are allowed to be silent and others are made to speak, and what the implications for social justice are when these *patterns of silence* (Medina 2013, p 91) allow the values of some groups to be privileged over the values of others. I will also consider how these epistemic relations are sustained over time. I'm interested in why and how some people's knowledge is (consistently) valued more than others, and why some people seem to be restricted in the epistemic roles they can inhabit (in the same way that their repertoires of self were described as restricted in Chapter 5). If, as Robeyns suggests, political power and wealth are imbricated to an extent that currently inhibits just social relations (Robeyns 2017b), then attending to how these imbrications are reproduced through communicative acts between the state and the rich, and the state and the poor will furnish insights into how the state of *wealtherty* is being sustained. I will make this case in part by contrasting epistemic dynamics in HMRC's Wealth External Forum (the WEF) (which is the primary focus of this chapter) with epistemic dynamics in the Work & Pensions Committee Inquiry into Universal Credit and Childcare, and Universal Credit and Survival Sex.

In Kerr (2023) I argued that while wealth has:

> typically been subsumed into the category of economic class as a dimension of elite group/upper class membership, new sociological scholarship has foregrounded the specificities of wealth: that it accrues over time, and therefore that its contemporary patterns of distribution carry with them and renew, historical power relations (for example, of patriarchy (Federici 2000), empire (Bhambra 2021b) and class (Savage 2021). (Kerr 2023, p 3)

This idea of 'renewal' ramifies in the renewal of historical distributions of epistemic resources too, as Medina (2011) makes the case for and as Simpson acknowledges: 'Because past states of systems remain present … *structural disparities often have as their corollaries epistemic disparities*, unfair distribution of epistemic resources' (Simpson 2017, p 255, emphasis added). As such, here I make a case for wealth as a legitimate and discrete (albeit profoundly intersectional) variable whose effects we can trace in the characteristics of knowledge-making practices. As I established in Chapter 2, the sites have a threshold related to wealth: In 2018, Universal Credit could only be claimed only be people with less than £16,000 in savings, while the WEF is a provision for those with over £20 million.

What is the relevance of epistemic inequality to other forms of inequality? Fricker notes that the frustration of epistemic contribution will tend to indicate 'wider structures of inequality, inasmuch as unequal epistemic participation is *one of the key modes in which unequal relationships and statuses of other kinds tend to express themselves*' (Fricker 2015, p 7, emphasis added). She makes a case for fair epistemic participation as an 11th capability (an addition to Nussbaum's ten) on the basis that it is of 'special egalitarian concern' (Fricker 2016, p 12). This is because it plays a fundamental role in the conversion of other capabilities into functionings (that is, it allows you to convert the right or possibility of doing something into the act of doing it should you so wish). In this way, *fair* epistemic contribution 'unlocks' other capabilities and therefore makes the achievement of full human flourishing more likely. Its absence makes this flourishing less likely. A concern with epistemic justice, then, is not peripheral to wider concerns with relational and distributive forms of justice, or more broadly a concern with justice in the world; it is central to it. This chapter looks at communication on the basis that in it we can see the operation of power at the point at which it becomes capillary (Foucault 1982, p 27).

The chapter is divided into two sections. In the first section I put in place key ideas in the epistemic justice literature. I introduce two facets of epistemic injustice – testimonial and hermeneutical – and I look at how these produce deficits and excesses of credibility. I then explore these deficits and excesses in their systemic form as 'tracker' prejudices and privileges (that is, prejudices and privileges that follow an individual through different domains of her life). Building on the exploration of forms of self given in Chapter 5, I move towards identifying the epistemic roles opened up or closed down in response to a negative or positive credibility assessment, which, as I suggest above, is related to wealth ownership. I end with a longer engagement with the idea of epistemic 'reputability' and make the case that degrees of epistemic reputability have been instrumental historically in terms of shaping policy and identities for richer and poorer people, and they continue to be so. I link high epistemic reputability to the unlocking of privileged epistemic roles (advisor, inquirer or co-creator) and privileged capabilities (privacy) which have the potential to cause harm to others. The second section applies these ideas to communications in the WPC Inquiry into Universal Credit and Childcare (WPC 2018a and b), the WPC Inquiry into Universal Credit and Survival Sex (WPC 2019a and b), and the WEF (HMRC 2023).

Epistemic injustice

Epistemic injustice results from prejudice against someone's status as a knowing subject (Fricker 2007, p 1). This prejudice might manifest in forms of unfair treatment, including 'exclusion and silencing, invisibility and inaudibility (or distorted presence or representation); having one's meanings or contributions systematically distorted, misheard, or misrepresented; having diminished status or standing in communicative practices; unfair differentials in authority and/or epistemic agency; being unfairly distrusted; being co-opted or marginalised' (Kidd et al 2017, p 1; see also Dotson 2012). These prejudices motivate differential credibility judgements leading to forms of credibility excess or credibility deficit. Then, in a process of concatenation, credibility deficits and excesses translate into forms of *relational* inequality within policy-making institutions, where some people are afforded the opportunity to contribute in meaningful and influential ways, while others are not. This unlocks forms of political privilege that can shape legislation and, ultimately, influence distributive inequality. Inequities in epistemic participation can help to 'maintain and enforce unjust power relations' by creating 'asymmetrical authority' – groups of knowers considered insubordinate or 'less than competent' (Pohlhaus 2017, p 17), and forms of knowledge that are derided as 'naïve, hierarchically inferior, below the required level of erudition or scientificity' (cited in Foucault 2003, p 7). At the same time, it also reifies other forms of knowledge and other types of knower.

Fricker (2007) identified two types of epistemic injustice: testimonial and hermeneutical. In essence, the 'testimonial' in testimonial injustice is about being a giver of information of one sort of another, while the 'hermeneutical' in hermeneutical injustice refers to the resources available for interpreting and making sense of experience. Testimonial injustice happens 'when prejudice causes a hearer to give a deflated level of credibility to a speaker's word' (Fricker 2007, p 1). This was evident in the testimony I referred to in Chapter 2: "You must manage your money better" I felt like screaming WHAT MONEY? HOW DO YOU MANAGE WHEN YOU HAVENT GOT ANY!" Subjects 'stigmatized by negative identity prejudices may not be regarded as … reliable conveyers of information, and therefore they will not receive proper recognition in testimonial exchanges and will be unfairly treated' (Medina 2011, p 16). Hermeneutical injustice occurs when 'a gap in collective interpretive resources puts someone at an unfair disadvantage when it comes to making sense of their social experiences and communicating them' (Fricker 2007, p 1). The example Fricker uses is suffering sexual harassment in a culture that still lacks that critical concept. In this case, there is no available 'interpretive framework through which to understand your suffering' (Fricker 2007, p 1). I am concerned in this chapter with both types and, primarily, when they operate in a systemic form. *Systemic* testimonial injustice describes the process whereby a negative identity prejudice of the type described earlier 'tracks' a subject '*through different dimensions of social activity* – economic, educational, professional, sexual, legal, political, religious' (Wanderer 2017, p 31, emphasis added), producing a *consistent* undervaluing of epistemic credibility. Fricker calls these 'tracker prejudices' (Fricker 2007, p 27). But a positive identity prejudice can also 'track' a subject through these different dimensions of social activity, resulting in a form of privilege that similarly follows an individual across different domains of life (Medina 2011, p 24). These tracker privileges can mean that some voices consistently gain credibility *beyond their competence* through these different domains. These epistemic privileges are 'produced by – and are at the same time productive within – a complex system of social relationships and practices in which unfair disparities among groups are maintained' (Medina 2011, p 24).

Epistemic injustice is understood by Medina as 'a temporally extended phenomena (having developmental and historical trajectories) and socially extended phenomena (being rooted in patterns of social relations)' (Medina 2011, p 15). On the basis of this observation, he asks that we look at what happens before and after specific communicative acts in the present, but also that we consider what has happened before (historically) and elsewhere (contextually/spatially). In this book I have shown that attribution of negative value to the poor accretes over time and across multiple domains (visual, spatial, discursive and legislative). I have looked at, for example, the modifications in attitudes towards the poor from the 16th century to the

18th century, and the effects of these on philanthropy and in legislation. These accretive negative prejudices bear traces of past relations of domination that are not necessarily audible in the content of individual communicative acts, but nonetheless bring with them and unfold the weight of past unequal relationships. This negative identity prejudice shapes the identities that people can embody and restricts repertoires of the self (recall the distinction between the administrative and intermediated self in Chapter 5). It is at the heart of attempts to manage behaviour at the level of population (Universal Credit and the NPL). I have also shown that attributions of *positive* value to the rich accrete over time and are renewed across multiple domains, shaping norms around privacy and underpinning the lenient approach to noncompliance described in Chapter 4, opening up restricted 'capacities' of wealth (Beckert 2023) and, relatedly, restricted privileges (privacy), for example. The relationship to processes of stigmatising here should be clear. In the doubly productive action of stigmatising, stigma renders certain populations abject in order to shore up the stability and legitimacy of the 'unmarked' groups: the process of producing the abject population simultaneously affirms the 'unmarked' population (Skeggs 2005). In contexts of relational inequality, the 'unmarked' individual or group produces the epistemic 'outgroup' while at the same time affirming their own, higher, epistemic status. Tracker prejudices and privileges can *both* be understood as specifically epistemic types of outcomes 'stigmacraft' (Tyler 2020, p 196).

It is relatively easy to see how epistemic injustice happens as a result of credibility deficit. The literature exploring contexts in which relational inequalities are in play (for example, doctor/patient consultations [Kidd and Carel 2017]) shows how these relational inequalities delimit the epistemic contributions of, in this case, the patient. This is also evident in some of the testimonies I have introduced in this book – for example, the women in Andover or Ms J. In each instance, negative identity prejudice reduced the level of epistemic contribution expected and/or granted. The witnesses were variously unable to contest harsh treatment and fearful of reporting it (Andover), were unheard when they did try and report their experiences (Ms J), or were 'relegated' to low-status forms of communication such as 'source of information', which I look at in more detail shortly. But what happens when positive identity prejudice leads to someone being judged credible beyond her actual competency? In this case, she has received a credibility judgement that is not 'proportionate to epistemic deserts and credentials' (Medina 2011, p 20). This is of interest to me because many of the dynamics I've presented in this book seek to understand more about processes of privilege making in ways of knowing, governing and being. On the one hand, there are populations who aren't recognised as knowers or who only have parts of their (epistemic) selves recognised in particular contexts. On the other hand, there are populations who are recognised as knowers in all contexts and who have their full epistemic selves recognised. They are afforded credibility beyond their competence and against the grain of the empirical evidence on behaviours of 'people like them'. The long histories of these differential attributions of credibility described by Medina can make us forget that they 'aren't as necessary as all that'. We become blind to the fact that people's position in knowledge hierarchies, as in social ones, is typically not merit-based. Position in a hierarchy is often built on estimations of credibility that are, in Medina's terms, disproportionate to their competence, and are bolstered and legitimised by the credibility of 'people like them' in the past and in other contexts.

In this chapter I will seek to show how the fact of owning a certain amount of wealth confers *epistemic* credibility excess: an excess of capital in one domain (financial) is taken as a proxy for capital in another. This link between wealth, knowledge and power has a long history: in 1818, election to the select vestries under the new Select Vestries Act (a select vestry was a body set up to manage the poor during the population boom) was based on a property scale: those occupying land worth less than £50 could cast a single vote, while those occupying land worth over £50 could cast an additional vote for each £25 of value up to a maximum of six votes, with the predictable effect that major landowners had six times more power than smaller ones (Brundage 2002). Wealth was a proxy for (epistemic) status. The richer you were, the more influence you had in the management of the poor. Money secured plural votes, amplifying the voter's opinions and allowing them to hold more sway.

In policy-making contexts, the nature of certain policy mechanisms themselves can make a 'fair hearing' problematic: formats are often transactional, such as in an inquiry seeking information from witnesses. This in and of itself presupposes a certain hierarchy of roles. But within spaces in which the rules of communication are predefined and specific to particular tasks (like a panel taking evidence), there remain choices to be made which can further constrain speakers' roles or, conversely, can extend or enable them. *Not* being asked to contribute, *not* being listened to or believed, or having your voice misrepresented delegitimises some forms of knowledge and some knowers. My contention is that the communicative practices in the WPCs produce and entrench a dynamic between a dominant 'unitary' discourse – 'the true', and Other knowledges that are variously marginalised and devalued – specifically a ground-level, 'less-than-scientific' bodily form of knowledge or 'what people know' (Foucault 2003, p 7). I suggest that this knowledge is rendered abject by the policy-making processes. Fair epistemic contribution requires that speakers are heard without prejudice. Yet, as I will show in this chapter, in the field of social and fiscal policy, some speakers – those governed by policies which have a wealth threshold of £16,000 in savings – are met with barriers to being heard and believed, while others, who are subject to policies and wider forms of government with a wealth threshold of £20 million plus, are pre-emptively believed because of the operation of wealth-motivated credibility excess, as described previously.

Epistemic roles

This second section seeks to decode communications in the WPCs and the WEF using the conceptual and analytical tools briefly described earlier. Here I aim to identify what excesses and deficits of credibility *in policy-making contexts* allow a person to do and be, what epistemic roles are opened up or closed down in response to a negative or positive credibility assessment, and how this works differently in contexts in which richer or poorer people are speaking. What relationships are presupposed by these roles? I will look first at the distinction between the *inquirer* and the *source of information* (building on Kerr 2023). I described in Chapter 5 the long history in policy making of the poor being seen as sources of information, through various forms of enforced (administrative) narratives of the self (Steedman 2000). This involved poorer people being asked to speak only in restricted circumstances in response to sets of legally required questions. I observed that this is repeated in the ways in which poorer people's 'conversations' with the state in Universal Credit contexts continued to be thus constrained, albeit now through digital means (the work journal, the Claimant Commitment and the digital decision maker). This tradition of *narratives of the self* has helped to produce an assumption that certain groups of people answer questions and others ask them; that certain groups of people have to account for themselves in minutiae, and others listen to and judge them, and of course do not have to disclose in the intimate intrusive way describes earlier. This is the distinction between *sources of information* and epistemic roles which are perceived to be sophisticated (or of higher status in a hierarchy of credibility), such as *inquirers* (Fricker 2007, p 133). These distinctions imply a relative quality and authority of speakers: 'the epistemic agency of an informant qua informant is limited and subordinated to that of the inquirer's' (Medina 2013, p 93). The women at the WPC oral evidence sessions gave evidence about the experience of being sources of information (the epistemic corollary to 'administrative self' I introduced in Chapter 5) in a context in which they were once again positioned as sources of information. They were not invited to analyse or to contribute interpretive resources; they were being used by the panel as a means of securing information about the impact of a particular policy. When the women's testimony had concluded, Panel Chair Frank Field said: "You've been hugely helpful in shaping what we're going to say and what reforms we're going to ask for ... Thank you for your journeys. And thank you for being such...wonderful witnesses each of you. Thank you very much" (WPC 2018a, 11:12:12–55), effectively deferring the higher-status epistemic work of developing recommendations to another time and space. It serves to reduce the contribution of those with firsthand experience of the policy they are scrutinising to simply providing a description of their 'journey'. Acting as a source of information is a limited epistemic role; inquirer is part of a set of more sophisticated, higher-status epistemic roles. The incomplete epistemic inclusion of the voices of people living in poverty in policy making creates a complex web of silence by: (i) failing to seek representation because of a perceived lack of credibility (the so-called pre-emptive credibility deficit); or (ii) by calling into being only the 'testifying' epistemic subject at the exclusion of the inquiring one (Kerr 2023).

Epistemic trust and reputability

I now want to think about these roles and their implications in building epistemic trust. Trust is a key variable that distinguishes the state's approach to government of richer and poorer people. In the 1834 legislation discussed in Chapter 3, the poor were conceived of as dependent, suspect, untrustworthy, likely to cheat if given the opportunity to do so and responsive to threats of punishment. The rich – despite their actual behaviours (noncompliance and avoidance) – were trusted and afforded privacy. In Chapter 4 I presented legislation as *a materialisation of* the ways of knowing described in Chapter 3. Here I want to also look at the epistemic effect of these ways of thinking and governing.

Surveillance and scrutiny, the overwhelming demands for accountability that form part of the disposition of scrutiny, contrast starkly with the ingrained forms of 'strategic ignorance' that characterise the state's approach to the government of wealth and the wealthy (Figure 1.1 and Table 3.1). Each is predicated on degrees of trust or lack of trust. In Medina's words, trust is temporally and socially extensive, having 'developmental and historical trajectories' and 'being rooted in patterns of social relations' (Medina 2011, p 15). It accrues over time and through social relations, and it coheres into levels of reputability. High epistemic reputability unlocks privileged epistemic roles (advisor, inquirer and co-creator) and privileged capabilities (political influence), which, through shaping legislative agendas or through reproducing negative prejudices, have the potential to 'cause harm to others'. Workhouse inmates routinely wrote to the PLC to bemoan the fact that their testimony was mistrusted; Pitt conceded to voluntary disclosure despite knowing that compliance would be low because of persistent tax evasion and that self-declarations were often deliberately false. Undeserved epistemic reputability continues to characterise communication between the state and the rich; conversely, underserved epistemic irreputability continues to characterise communication between the rich and the poor: poor people are distrusted at a systematic level. Alston (2018) describes the ways in which

Universal Credit in effect pre-emptively criminalises them. Rich people, as I will show shortly, are deemed trustworthy even in the process of seeking to circumvent the letter or spirit of the law. In order to bring this into focus, I'm first going to include an example of epistemic irreputability and then an example of epistemic reputability. The contrast is illustrative. Gaynor Rowles, who has been quoted elsewhere in this book, bemoans what she feels is the implication in her dealings with Universal Credit that she is lying about her childcare costs in order, we assume, to get more money than she is entitled to:

Gaynor Rowles:	You have to fork out the monthly cost first. In my situation, my children have just changed nursery. When they change nursery, you have to pay a week up front. With twins, that is two weeks plus a week each, so that is four weeks. It is £188 per week. Where do I find that money? Something needs to be done. Like I said, we will give the evidence that our children are in nursery. They have had evidence from the nursery itself. All of us have said that, haven't we?
Chair:	They have their ages?
Gaynor Rowles:	Yes, they have their ages, so why do we have to keep telling them? They are in nursery. We are not lying that they are in nursery. (WPC 2018a HC336, p 25)

This sense of frustration is echoed in the testimony of Ms J cited in Chapter 2, as she dealt with a system that simply wouldn't believe she had no money. The sense in both contexts is that 'reputability' (having a good reputation and being trusted) is hampered by negative identity prejudice. This is the converse of the dynamic in HMRC's WEF (HMRC 2023). The WEF (see Chapter 2) was formed in 2009 'to discuss, develop and promote co-operative compliance strategies for dealing with the tax affairs of this customer group ... and their representatives for the benefit of the operation of the tax system' (HMRC 2023). WEF's activities embody the principles of the 2009 OECD Report *Engaging with High Net Worth Individuals on Tax Compliance*, key among which is the idea of 'co-operative compliance' for HNWIs (OECD 2009, p 12). The adoption of these principles is cited in the WEF minutes (HMRC 2023, September 2014, p 5). Cooperative compliance is an approach to managing the tax affairs of the wealthy and of corporations that 'rel[ies] on the co-operation of the taxpayer to *volunteer* relevant information. It aims to influence his or her behaviour to reduce the prevalence of aggressive tax planning (ATP) arrangements' (OECD 2009, p 67, emphasis added). The OECD (2009) recommended specialist units to deal with the affairs of HNWIs – the WEF is such a unit. Other features recommended by the OECD (2009) and functioning within the WEF include: dedicated contact points (so-called customer relationship managers); advanced ruling on tax matters to 'provide a higher level of certainty'; and the involvement 'where appropriate' of 'the advisers of HNWIs in the development of legislation that specifically affects their clients'. Epistemic relations in the WEF, between the chair and other representatives of the HMRC, and with individual participants demonstrate quite how contrastive the balance of epistemic power is between the state and the members of the WEF, and the state and the people who claim Universal Credit.

Tuana notes that 'certain social identities can be made to indicate a lack of credibility' and that 'it is not simply facts, events, practices or technologies that are rendered not known, but individuals and groups who are rendered "not knowers"' (cited in Dotson 2012, p 243). This can result in 'an audience failing to identify a speaker as a knower'. Dotson calls this 'testimonial quieting' (Doston 2012, p 242). The converse of this from a credibility excess perspective would be what I call *testimonial amplifying*: when an audience identifies a speaker as a knower *unrelated to any proportionate assessment of his credibility*; that is, the audience or interlocuter assumes a level of sophistication based on the status, role or perceived (relative) social position – people *like this* are/were trustworthy. Similarly, *testimonial smothering* is a form of epistemic self-regulation in which a speaker truncates her 'own testimony in order to ensure that the testimony contains only content for which one's audience demonstrates testimonial competence' (Dotson 2012, p 244). This is exemplified in testimony that women in the WPC Inquiry into Universal Credit and Survival Sex when the women tried to explain to the panel the realities of having to sell or exchange sex to survive:

T: It is awful. What happens if one day we don't want to and we don't feel like it or lady things happen? Because that is another thing, like when it is your time of the month and stuff, we do not want to work.
M: You have to use a sponge.
T: Yes, you have to use sponges. You probably don't even know what they are.
M: You probably don't want to know. (WPC 2019a, p 13)

Although it is something done by the speaker, Dotson defines this as a type of '*coerced silencing*' (Dotson 2012, emphasis added). The converse of this might be what I refer to as *elective self-silencing*. In the first case, the speaker reduces the importance of what she says by parsing it to reflect the perceived testimonial (in)competence of the hearer. In the latter case, a speaker can simply elect not to speak at all, if it is in his interests to do so, and instead can nominate a 'proxy' (as recommended by OECD [2009]), or can parse information based on the limits of what he wants to be known.

I am now going to explore how reputability is established or sustained in the WEF. In the WEF, epistemic reputability is reproduced through forms of communication which assume trustworthiness. A recalibration of the balance between 'sources of information' and 'inquirer' (and other high-status epistemic roles, which I will discuss shortly) takes place when the state wants to hear about the experiences of the super-rich and their experiences of specific policies or sets of policies. The raison d'être of the WEF was described in its inaugural meeting as:

> to start the process of explaining the HNWU [High Net Worth Unit] to customers and their representatives. This has included writing 'welcome letters' as a way of starting an enhanced relationship with High-Net-Worth customers and their representatives, giving them details of a named contact within the unit and providing the opportunity to discuss concerns or open issues. (HMRC 2023, March 2010, p 2)

The first thing that becomes obvious in the WEF minutes is that in terms of its purpose and its operation, it is above all a listening function. Epistemic injustice literature places considerable emphasis on the virtue of listening in attaining epistemic justice (at an individual and an institutional level), and the frustration of not being listened to recurs in the testimony of the women at the 2018 Survival Sex Inquiry Committee, just as it did in the Andover Inquiry in 1846. Frustration in relation to not being listened to is endemic and enduring. Through the 'named contact', HMRC provides a qualitatively different services to one customer group through establishing a principle of one-to-one listening. Testimony is not thwarted, 'smothered' or 'quieted'; it is to be heard and then acted upon. The information provided to the WEF from the mediators of the rich will shape the legislation or soften its impact through the deferral of sanctions with 'educational approaches' to addressing issues, as I will show shortly. These named Customer Relationship Managers will provide continuity, again, something that the women at the WPC Inquiry bemoaned the absence of in their dealings with the state (Kerr 2023). HMRC will use its resultant enhanced understanding of their customers to 'be responsive to agent/customer needs. This should ensure that questions are resolved quickly and any enquiries are proportionate, to avoid adding unnecessarily to their compliance burden' (HMRC 2023, March 2010, p 3).

In October 2022, WEF members raised the issue of: 'Inconsistency – if a case gets passed on to another person, the knowledge seems to get lost resulting in having to go over the case.' They asked whether there could be a 'smoother handover or call to agree the open points in the case?' (HMRC 2023, October 2022, p 3). In response, HMRC reported that it would 'mitigate this from happening in the future by implementing a new handover process' (HMRC 2023, October 2022, p 3). The intermediaries (the legal representatives of the wealthy in the WEF) have been pre-emptively afforded full social uptake through the listening and understanding undertaken by the Customer Relationship Managers. They have been able to communicate their wishes and have gained solicitous uptake. The rich in this context are the *intermediated selves* I introduced in Chapter 5: they have been spoken for on behalf of agents, not because of a risk of poor social uptake, but simply because they did not need to speak up directly in order to achieve their ends. The second thing that becomes apparent in the communications in the WEF is the overwhelming sense of trust and goodwill – even during conversations that are about the risk of fraud. Reputability is a given. The November 2022 minutes include an explanation of the tax gap as 'the difference between the amount of tax that should be paid and what is actually paid *possibly arising by some taxpayers making simple errors and others not taking enough care when submitting tax returns*' (HMRC 2023, November 2022, p 2, emphasis added).

They suggest that such 'errors' might be a result of the inherently 'complex tax affairs amongst wealthy customers' and they present their 'cooperative approach' as a means of helping to lower the tax gap (HMRC 2023, November 2022, p 2). One member asked: 'What is the meaning of compliance yield?' HMRC responded that 'the compliance yield is additional tax receipts arising from HMRC intervention (including upstream nudges and prompts)' (HMRC 2023, p 3). Errors instead of fraud; 'nudges and prompts' in lieu of sanctions. This approach extends to seeking to help the very wealthy avoid legal dispute. The HMRC repeatedly expresses its commitment to creating an enabling approach to upstream dispute resolution. This is in a context in which it identifies various HNWIs as 'high risk' (that is, at high risk of not paying the taxes they should pay): its enthusiastic over-application of trust is disproportionate to the compliance behaviours of its customers, the tax gap being £1.5 billion in 2021 (HRMC 2023, November 2021, p 2). The language embodies the operation of the *centaur dispositions* I introduced in Chapter 2 towards tax citizens based on how much they are worth: 'The Dispute Resolution team prefer to discuss cases with the relevant parties through meetings rather than purely via correspondence ... [Their aim is to avoid the need for litigation] where this would be unproductive" (HRMC 2023, June 2012, p 4).

The Universal Credit system flagged some claimants as 'higher risk' and this made them subject to more intense scrutiny and investigation, often without them being aware of this fact (Alston 2018). This stands in sharp contrast to the approach of the state to its rich citizens. HNW customers are classified as higher or lower risk to HMRC, where risk refers to risk to the tax base from noncompliance, but the response is not scrutiny and investigation (Taxwatch UK 2021). HMRC representatives in the WEF are at pains to emphasise their commitment to *not* accusing people of deliberate wrongdoing. These comments infer a prelitigation informal realm of 'sorting things out' to avoid sanction or prosecution:

> [I]f a customer was classified as high risk that did not necessarily mean they would be under enquiry, it was more a decision based around complexity of their affairs, behaviour surrounding tax obligations and amount of tax at risk to HMRC. HNWU's [High Net Worth Unit's] approach remains to engage with our customers first where possible and to address risk in a voluntary collaborative way where possible. (HMRC 2023, September 2014)

> This year a number of cases have been identified where customers may have failed to declare a CG [capital gain]. The aim is to send letters to those customers identified and to ask them to consider either amendment or disclosure … Research has shown that *customers don't always realise they must consider CG* and that there may be a gain to declare … The primary aim to is to raise awareness and *not to accuse customers of deliberate wrongdoing*. (HMRC 2023, 14 October 2020, p 4, emphasis added)

> JHK (HMRC) asked if there were 'any ways HMRC could help customer who have *inadvertently overlooked* a property disposal to get things right'. (HMRC 2023, 14 October 2020, emphasis added)

The rich as governors

Tax sociologist Kevin Farnsworth observes that: 'Such is the power imbalance between government and corporations that governments have to negotiate with, implore, and even embarrass corporations to comply with tax laws' (Farnsworth 2023, p 225). The same could be said to apply to the individual wealthy customers represented in the WEF. It is an illustration of what I suggest is an inversing of the relationships of government. Who conducts whose conduct? The state has assented to becoming a *source of information* to the mediators' *inquirer* and, in doing so, has assumed the epistemically lower status role. This upside-down relationship is manifest in regular processes of 'co-development' or 'co-creation'. In the first meeting of the WEF, members suggested to the HMRC that a policy drafter attended the meeting, in essence to take ideas directly from them as to the shape of future fiscal law (HMRC 2023, 4 March 2010, p 2); In a discussion on progress in the HNWU, the HMRC representative asked 'what else the

Unit should be doing to develop' (HMRC 2023, September 2010, p 3). In the September 2012 meetings, the HMRC Chair asked the forum if they had any observations on the HNWU that they would like him to discuss with OECD colleagues at a telephone conference in which he would be participating during October. They agreed to get back to him. Excessive credibility – credibility beyond the competence of the speaker – allows a person to inhabit high-status (that is, high-complexity) epistemic roles. It might result in being in a position to command that your voice be heard by certain people or to demand to hear from them. These acts of co-creation establish the members of the WEF as empowered inquirers.

The rich as advisors

There are some 'enunciative modalities' (Fairclough 1992, p 43) (the negotiating implied in 'co-creation', for example) that, in the context of engaging with the state, are the sole domain of the elite. Another elite 'enunciative modality' is advising. Advising assumes a higher level of credibility on the person giving the advice than on the person receiving it, in context. For example, on the subject of a tax policy issue related to the number of days resident in the UK and the effects of COVID-19 on the ability to travel freely (a loophole which was being exploited for tax purposes and which was not being transparently reported by wealthy customers), HMRC noted that: 'As this is a complex area, [we] have opted for *an educational approach* to support taxpayers and their agents by concentrating our efforts on raising awareness on the issue' (HMNRC 2023, October 2022, pp 4–5, emphasis added). In the discussion that followed: '*Agents advised* that HMRC needs to remember to consider the difficulties people faced during this period of uncertainty ... HMRC *must keep this in mind* when giving advice and should continue to do so going forward' (HMRC 2023, October 2022, p 6, emphasis added).

It is hard to imagine a Universal Credit claimant 'advising' the state tax authorities in this way by, for example, recommending the continuation of the £20 uplift which had temporarily mitigated the hardships of COVID-19 by emphasising the 'difficulties people faced during this period of uncertainty'. It is equally hard to imagine the state listening and taking this on board. The PAC castigated the HNWU in 2017 for its lack of transparency and accountability (PAC 2017). It also drew attention to the fact that, unlike other customer groups, calls to the HMRC from HNWIs were not routinely recorded: 'The lack of transparency leaves the Department open to the perception that, in its dealings with taxpayers, there is one rule for the rich and another for everyone else' (PAC 2017, p 5). HMRC suggested to the PAC that the term 'customer relationship manager' belied what was in reality a very high level of compliance attention that HNWIs were subject to and which constituted, in effect, 'much closer scrutiny than most other groups, except for organised crime and large businesses' (PAC 2017, p 9). This is of course at odds with the *effects* of this accommodating strategy, which the PAC noted had led to the HNWU collecting £1 billion less in taxes per annum than had been the case before its inception, as was mentioned in Chapter 4.

Reproducing the intermediated self

In Chapter 5 I introduced the idea of the *intermediated self*. This was based on the relationships revealed in the WEF meetings. In the WEF, firsthand experience is narrated secondhand via intermediaries: the rich are represented by agents and professional bodies. Agents and professional bodies navigate and negotiate the limits of what their clients will accept in terms of compliance. The role of the intermediary mitigates against the rich themselves having to speak. What are the implications for the rich of *not* being subject to producing narratives of the self in the way that poor people are required – mandated – to? Self-exclusion can be self-serving on several levels. It implies that your 'lived experience' is not relevant to the policy matter at hand. In the context of rich voice in social policy, while the *harmed* of the social policy are invited to narrate their 'journeys', the perpetrators, both in terms of those who produce the policy and those who operate within the logic it sustains (in the context of Universal Credit, this might be the bosses of companies using zero-hours contract, private landlords creating insecure housing conditions or CEOs of multinationals profit shifting and lowering state resilience), are not considered to have 'lived experience' of the problem of *poverty* and are therefore not called upon to speak. This results in the predomination of symptom/victim voice over cause/perpetrator voice in these settings, which tilts our epistemic frame determinedly to one side.

In the context of fiscal policy, the rich don't speak because they don't need to in order to achieve their ends. The poor don't speak because wealth and the wealthy are not considered to be within their domain of experience/ expertise or relevant to their lives (of course, the data in Chapters 1 and 2 suggest otherwise). These dynamics can tell us important things about prevailing values in relation to *wealtherty* and about the prevailing epistemic facets of governmental dispositions of scrutiny and ignorance that I have argued are at the heart of 'the state we are in'. It is interesting to think about the role of the intermediary in the longer history of the 'code of capital' (Pistor 2019) and the progressive complexification of that code (Cartwright 2009). The complexity of the code is deliberately engineered. So-called 'loopholes' are, of course, simply features. They are *provisions*. It is the intermediaries' job in part to ensure that these provisions remain. The WEF is one of the means through which they achieve this. For the same to be the case with Universal Credit, this would involve all individuals having access to a dedicated legal advisor whose role would be to help them overclaim and to maximise the amount of benefits they received through forms of aggressive benefits planning (ABP).

The implications of us not hearing directly from the wealthy either in conversations within the state that relate to the management of their wealth (the WEF), or in contexts where practices of wealth making have implications at the other end of the wealth spectrum (Universal Credit), are problematic for many reasons. I want to conclude this chapter and this part of the book by exploring the idea of what it means to know *well*, and how forms of epistemic self-exile detract from knowing well. Pohlhaus posits that the 'fundamentally intertwined' nature of our epistemic lives means that 'one cannot simply ignore other knowers and know well' (Pohlhaus 2017, p 16). When policy-making practices repress some voices and amplify others, it makes it more difficult for us to produce social knowledge that reflects the full range of social voices; instead, we get 'patterns of silence' (Medina 2011, p 91). This is reflected not just in the repression of supposed 'abject' forms of knowledge ('You probably don't want to know...'), but in the 'stunting' of the epistemic contribution of some knowers – their reduction to sources of information. Similarly, when these same institutions simply don't call for some voices to speak (for example, rich people as harm causers in social policy inquiries), this too detracts from the completeness of social knowledge; this 'full range' should include poorer and richer voices, of course. Medina (2013) builds on this work to highlight that being politically privileged (holding political power) often goes hand in hand with being hermeneutically marginalised ('ill-equipped to make sense of certain things') (Medina 2013, p 109) because of a failure to listen, and a gap between the life experiences of, in my case, richer and poorer people. This is a result of forms of agnogenesis, some of which I discussed in Chapter 6: some forms of ignorance are outcomes of choices not to know inconvenient things and not to hear from inconvenient voices. As I have shown, owning the privilege of directing and participating in the means of knowledge production confers relational advantage: those in politically central but hermeneutically disadvantaged positions can maintain this advantage by *orchestrating* particular 'patterns of silence' (Medina 2011, p 91). In his conversations on music with the conductor Seiji Ozawa, the novelist Murakami explores the idea of *Ma* in music. The two discuss at length various different pauses conjured by different conductors in recordings of a single piece of music. The pause is imagined almost as the temporary withholding of sound, with the texture of specific pauses being held to define the sounds that then follow. What the musicians *do not do* is interesting and is *defining* in terms of the meaning and effects of the notes that they eventually play. The withholding is interesting in and of itself, but the way in which it affects the texture of the sounds that follow, and between which it is used, is also relevant. In sustaining the problematic of *wealtherty*, the right to withhold voice, and the art of withholding it, is a tool of composition. It radically recalibrates power relationships so that the person holding the baton is no longer the state, but (those who own) capital. Medina makes the case that there is no such thing as a *general* silence, just silence*s* resulting from 'particular ways of particular people in relation to particular others' (what he calls *polyphonic contextualism*) (Medina 2013, p 91). The contrastive inclusion of poor voices and rich voices in policy making creates a complex web of silences. On the one hand, there is the failure to seek representation because of perceived lack of credibility (the so-called pre-emptive credibility deficit), which results in the calling into being of the 'testifying' epistemic subject at the exclusion of the inquiring (hermeneutical) one which we observed in the inquiry into childcare (WPC 2018a). On the other hand, in assenting to the self-exile of the rich from some communicative processes of government and in ceding authority to 'advisors' from the wealth sector, the idea that the rich are somehow excused from processes of government by virtue of their wealth or can orchestrate their own involvement is reinforced. There is an unspoken and enduring assumption that multiple other forms of (political, cultural and epistemic) capital and credibility can simply be read off this wealth.

I noted earlier that Medina theorises epistemic injustice as 'temporally extended' with 'developmental and historical trajectories'. As part of the development of this idea, he describes the formation of 'social blindness' which takes place at multiple sites and across different historical periods. It is produced by 'an oppressive social imaginary' which establishes unjust patterns of credibility excesses and deficits' (Medina 2017, p 15). In the context of this book, this oppressive social imaginary, seen in its development in Chapters 3, 4, and 5, then ramifies into a false public narrative of poverty and the poor, and the false public narrative about wealth and the rich. This constitutes a form of *wealthed ignorance and privilege* and is, as I have tried to show here, produced and reproduced through communicative practices in policy making. The epistemic dynamics described in this chapter enable the operation of a set of 'restricted' capabilities (political influence) for the rich. These have obvious implications for relational injustices such that the epistemic dynamics given in Table 8.1 help to produce the relational inequalities given in Table 8.2.

I would like to conclude by returning to Bishop Jones, whose report I quoted in Chapter 6, in which he said that 'a false public narrative is an injustice in and of itself'. His conclusions in terms of what might constitute reparation for such a false public narrative centred around the practice of listening. He said, after taking the time to listen to and to hear the testimony of families, that 'we might be a better nation for having listened to them" (Jones 2017, p 3). In the context of *wealtherty*, this listening needs to take

Table 8.1: Epistemic dynamics

Wealthy	Epistemic dynamic	Poor
Marginal	Hermeneutical positionality	Privileged
Privileged	Political positionality	Marginal
Inquirer	Epistemic identity	Source of information
Absent	First-hand experience	Abject
Ignorance and secrecy	Wealtherty governmentality	Scrutiny and disclosure

Table 8.2: Relational inequalities

Wealthy	Relational inequality	Poor
Permissive	Behavioural conditionality	Ubiquitous
Contributor	Fiscal identity	Claimant
'Risky'	Noncompliance	Illegal
Voluntary	Disclosure	Mandatory and comprehensive

place at both ends of the wealth spectrum. Counterintuitively, as I suggested in Kerr (2023), we need to hear more from the rich: we need to demand that they are heard. And we need to hear *better* from poorer people: we need to demand they are not (pre-emptively) silenced. We might be a better nation for it.

PART IV

In conclusion

9

Ways out

This book has described moments of the emergence of the state of *wealtherty*. I situated wealtherty as part of a wider scholarly and practitioner convergence around the recognition of the past in our now, and the need to look up towards the rich and back towards the past. I made the case that wealth has a defining influence not just through manifestly unfair distributions, but in the ways in which ownership of extreme wealth has the capacity to be converted into political capital. I looked at how the influence of wealth on our politics and social practices shapes knowledge making and governing, and shapes what we see and the spaces in which we see it, as well as how we talk and are listened to. It shapes who we can be. I illustrated how these distorted relations are written on the surface, on bodies, in buildings, in communications, at the point at which power 'becomes capillary' (Foucault 1982, p 27). I presented wealtherty as a new description of the state we are in and a state that we urgently need to find ways out of, and I suggested that decentring poverty and starting to reconceptualise our 'social problem' as one of the negative effects of extreme wealth was a matter of urgency. I used wealtherty as a heuristic for thinking contemporaneously about the rich and the poor in the same conceptual and legislative frame.

Chapters 1 and 2 began the process of undertaking a genealogy by asking: 'What have we become?' I made the case that the shift is legitimate because the things of wealth have changed, the pulling away of those at the top is accelerating, and the condition of those at the bottom is deteriorating. In Part II (Chapters 3, 4 and 5), I moved on to ask: 'How have we become what we are?' I 'reserialised' the past as parallel governmental dispositions of scrutiny and ignorance, and I thought about what that meant across three axes of government: knowing; governing; and being (after Dean 2010). My aim was to recuperate the past (or to recuperate a different past and the past, differently) and to shine a light on the renewals and ratcheting of historical forces in our now (punitivism for the poor; facilitation for the rich). In Chapter 3, I looked at how the categories of the poor, poverty, the rich and wealth were calculated and 'computered' in the past and in contemporary discourse, and I asked what other forms of knowledge we need to include, with reference to the Capabilities Approach, if we are to understand and act on the relationship between distributive and categorial inequality. Chapter 4 shifted its focus to the mechanisms of government – legislative, symbolic and political – for richer and poorer people, and considered how ownership (or otherwise) of wealth shaped these. I focused on hunger, movement and work. In Chapter 5, I pulled together ideas from the previous chapters to focus on how identities are formed for individuals, groups and institutions, what these identities are and what they do. I contrasted forms of being for poorer people (the administrative self) with forms of being for the very wealthy (the intermediated self). Across Chapters 3, 4 and 5 I traced the welfare punitivism which ratcheted in the 2010s back to moments of its emergence in the 1790s and earlier, and I traced the accommodation for the rich as secretive tax subjects back to previous moments of fiscal reform, and to the durability of norms embedded in tax law 'canons'. I linked political and public assent for these contrasting approaches to the operation of the governmental dispositions of scrutiny and ignorance, which I argued are applied to differently wealthed populations. I also linked punitivism to the operation of, on the one hand, *stigmacraft* (Tyler 2020), which renders the poor abject and peripheral, and, on the other hand, to ignorance, opacity and deliberately engineered secrecy which conspire to keep the wealthy and wealth out of sight (and therefore uncalculable).

In Part II, I looked at practices which sustain wealtherty now. In Chapter 6 I started with network-level practices of knowledge and ignorance production, using the operation of the CSJ as an illustration of Robyens' (2019) 'bleed' between financial and political power, of the exploitation of 'privileged capabilities' of media and political influence. I reimagined the CSJ as a fiscal welfare vehicle whose objectives were to enhance the means of corporations and rich individuals, and I drew attention to the effects on democracy of politicised 'evidence making'. In Chapter 7 I looked at the visual and spatial field of wealtherty in an analysis of the design of disciplinary spaces of welfare (Jobcentre Plus offices), exclusive spaces for the rich in cities, and then a series of critical photographic images which I interpreted as embodying a shift to focusing on visualising the processes of wealth accumulation as a means of trying to reattach a 'moral sign' (Ruskin 2010 [1862]) to extreme wealth. Finally, in Chapter 8 I looked at the operation of *wealthed privilege* through unequal participation in knowledge-production processes, using Fricker's (2007) concept of *epistemic injustice* and Medina's work on *credibility excess* (2011). Parts II and III of the book allowed me to explore the dispositions of scrutiny and ignorance across the domains of knowing, governing and being at two moments of social and policy change.

Together, the chapters in Part II made the case that the *enduring* operation of wealtherty has contributed to an intolerable present by naturalising materially and ethically distinct ways of governing and producing polarised ways of being for the rich and the poor. The manifest injustices embodied in these distinct ways of governing have contributed to deep social unhappiness and unrest: an epidemic of deaths of despair on the one hand (Case and Deaton 2020), and an accelerating 'pulling away' at the top on the other hand. This has led to social frustration and agitation, with the players on the field now so far apart they no longer feel like they are playing the same game, leading to social disengagement (Savage 2021). After decades of the ratcheting of the meritocratic principle in public policy (May 2017), humiliated 'losers' and hubristic 'winners' battle for ownership of political and public space amid flare-ups of anger and violence (Sandel 2020). I presented now as a situation that is 'historically urgent' – a 'moment of danger' (Savage 2021, p x).

In undertaking this reversal (that is, in centring wealth and not poverty), my genealogy of wealtherty aimed to challenge some of the long-baked assumptions that underpin contemporary policy-making institutions in order to catch them in the process of their being made: that the poor are the sole legitimate central focus of social policy; that the rich are somehow not part of the 'social' that social policy concerns itself with; that poor people should and can be legitimately treated harshly in order to get them to behave in the 'right' way, but that bad choices and anti-social behaviours of the rich are not the concern of the state; that (any form of) work for poor people is always and unproblematically the best route out of poverty and inherently good (delivering health and other benefits), but that rich people are not expected to work or to show they are working in order to receive their significant fiscal and corporate welfare benefits; that poor people need to be made to suffer hardship in order to 'check' that they need or indeed deserve relief from the state but that 'fiscal', 'corporate' and 'occupational' welfare will be delivered automatically and not under the guise of a 'benefit' at all; that a state of meritocracy is something to strive towards for poorer people (work hard and rise in line with your talents – if you do not rise, it is because you did not try hard enough) or something which already exists for wealthier people (you are rich and must therefore have worked hard and deserve your wealth/status/privilege). These assumptions structure how we think not only of the problem and its legitimacy, but also of who we think is responsible and what should or could be done about it. They contribute to us continuing to look at the wrong thing. Rethinking inequality through the concept of wealtherty aimed to make space for new questions, like: 'Why and how is private wealth still at the edges of (or even outside) the scope of social policy?'; 'How and why is wealth accumulation primarily seen legislatively as a fiscal issue not a social one?'; and 'If "persistent poverty" is an accepted policy term, can we articulate the problem of persistent wealth in a way that can gain public and political salience?'

Meanwhile, I observed that in this urgent context, much scholarship, anti-poverty activity, campaigning and policy making is still looking down, distracted with conversations about poverty 'fragments' (period poverty, fuel poverty or food poverty) (Crossley et al 2020) or campaigning over amounts that shouldn't make a difference (the £20 Universal Credit uplift). To be very clear, I am not in any way suggesting that these amounts do not matter to people; part of the passion I bring to my academic work is born out of knowing that they do. I am saying that we have been reduced to arguing over crumbs when there are slices of cake in play. In a rich nation, £20 should not be the difference between eating or not eating. At the same time, I described how low levels of public and political understanding of wealth and taxation (Rowlingson 2023; Kerr and Vaughan 2024a and b) act as a brake on informed debate, which makes the case for any form of redistribution such as wealth tax unlikely to gain salience. The resultant impasse represents a comprehensive failure of public discourse. The magnitude of the problem requires a new approach. From social scientists specifically, it demands a 'better social science' (Bhambra 2021b, p 76). I will return to this shortly. I want to acknowledge here the limitations of the state and the limitations of policy in effecting change. As Savage (2021) asks, in a world in which 'nation states are losing their coherence as units of power and government', what is the capacity of policy to make a difference? Acknowledging this, I also want to make a strong case for policy as a tool that we have that, in the area of wealth inequality, is symbolically as much as economically important. It signals priorities and commitments ('Don't tell me what you value, show me your budget, and I'll tell *you* what you value' (Joe Biden Jr., cited in Taxwatch UK 2021). It is also the case that in recent years, the only sustained fall in poverty has been an effect of policy when between 1997 and 2010, child poverty fell in response to the Labour government's child poverty strategy: poverty levels are (or can be) policy responsive (Bennett 2023, p 11). So, while not putting all my faith in policy change as the pathway towards social and economic equalisation, the argument in this book does ultimately move towards the state playing the major role in changing how we govern processes of wealth creation, accumulation and distribution. And it suggests that the pathway to policy taking up this role is currently impeded by how we conceive of and talk about wealth and wealth inequality. The authors of the World Inequality Lab report made it clear that 'profound policy changes are needed for things to fall back in place. The policy solutions often exist, and when they don't, we often know how to find them. *Our [focus is on] how to get the plumbing right, so that policy can do its job*' (WIL 2022, p 3, emphasis added). My primary focus with sketching out the concept of wealtherty has been on getting the *conceptual* plumbing right. I have argued that extreme wealth needs to be more comprehensively articulated as a social bad and acted on/against accordingly.

The wealtherty manifesto revisited

I now return to the manifesto that I sketched out in Chapter 1. My hope is that some of what you have read in the intervening chapters might persuade you of the legitimacy of the need for a new frame and specifically the need to find a way of compellingly centring wealth in problematisations of the state we are in. I present this manifesto as a set of ideas to think with. I'm assuming that if you've got this far, you have an interest in social justice and change, and that one or more of the ideas given here might resonate with you. They build very explicitly on other people's work, which I cite as I go along, and they build on the ideas developed in the book about what the problem is (and what it needs to be represented to be). This aim is to help to create an environment in which we can more effectively hold 'capital to account' (Savage 2021, p 319), a space in which it is 'once more possible to think' (Foucault 1970, p 342). They are articulated as a set of positive and negative imperatives which try to match the urgent, dangerous scale of the problem.

1. Stop talking about poverty

At the 2019 Davos meeting, the historian Rutger Bregman gained notoriety when he called out wealthy attendees for avoiding the elephant in the room: tax. He asked them to stop talking about philanthropy and to start talking about 'tax, tax, tax' (cited in Farrer 2019). Here I am saying stop talking about poverty and start talking about *wealtherty* instead. Talking about poverty focuses attention on the symptoms of the problem, while helping to legitimate the sidelining of wealth from political debate and action. Given what we now know (see Chapters 1 and 2) about the scale of injustice and the social and environmental effects of hyperconcentrated wealth, this is no longer legitimate. At the 2022 British Sociological Association Conference, Torsten Bell, the Resolution Foundation's CEO, lamented the lag between knowledge making and its uptake and use in policy. He noted that since the 1980s, wealth has soared, but the amount of revenue we gain from wealth hasn't. Tax policy has simply failed to keep up with the changing nature of and growth of wealth. While there are ready-made solutions (for example, the 2020 Wealth Tax Commission proposal for a one-off wealth tax [Advani et al 2020]), salience is prevented by lack of political will or urgency. This is in part as a result of (qualified but consistent) public support *for* wealth inequality and the wealthy (see Kerr and Vaughan [2024b] for discussion of the literature in this regard). As long as we have not made extreme private wealth per se a social problem through a conceptual reversal like the one proposed through wealtherty, solutions like that of the Wealth Tax Commission (Advani et al 2020) will struggle to gain traction: they simply don't match the prevailing understanding of the problem and are misaligned with (qualified) public *support* for inequality. We need to renounce the 'self-evidence' of poverty as the driver for social policy (adapted from Ball and Collet-Sabé 2021, p 9). This will give us the ability to think what the current system does not allow us to think. It will reveal that the system shored up by centring poverty is inadequate in terms of dealing with the scale and urgency of contemporary demands for justice in the world, and therefore needs upending.

The long-term centring of poverty has sustained a cycle of stating and restating, producing and reproducing increasingly granular analyses of poverty as a (or the) problem. Academic papers, monographs and conference presentations have piled high, alongside think tank reports and calls to action from charities to 'solve the problem' of poverty, which in 2024 is severe and deepening (JRF 2024). But what if poverty is *not* the problem we need to solve? What if it is not solvable if we fail to address the pulling away of the very wealthy and if we fail to place restraints on the conversion of economic into political capital? Dr James Cockayne, erstwhile Director of the UN Centre for Policy Research, observed apropos of the consistently high global estimates for the numbers of people living in conditions of modern slavery that if a system is *consistently* producing 40.3 million of something (the 2018 global estimate of the number of people living in conditions of modern slavery), it is a design feature, not a bug. Poverty is a design feature of capitalism and needs designing out of the system rather than treating as a seemingly endlessly puzzling recursion. In a context of great wealth, deep poverty is a political choice – it is remade. Of course, a choice is *between* things and, as Robeyns makes clear in her work, political choices that enable extreme wealth are also choices against sufficiently addressing poverty. Alston made this point during his 2018 visit to the UK. He noted that since 2010, this political choice had been between sparing the poor and funding tax cuts for the wealthy, and the decision had not gone in favour of the poor. Poverty is *an* outcome of the operation of wealtherty. We might need to abandon *tout court* the ways in which we have articulated and understood our social problem and look at things from the other way round.

This book has made the case that the problem is the state of wealtherty – with these four facets: concentrated and escalating accumulation of private wealth; policy divisions; capture of political institutions; and the capture of knowledge-making processes. I explored these facets as things that have been made and that are nurtured in the present – ergo, things that can be unmade and refused in the present. We coded wealtherty into existence; we can uncode it. If inequality is made in fiscal policy, fiscal policy can be the locus of its unmaking (Rowlingson 2023). At the same 2019 Davos meeting referenced earlier and attended by Rutger Bregman, the CEO of Dell Computing laughed when asked whether, as the 39th richest person in the world, he should pay more tax. He pointed to his charitable foundation and dismissed the US Democrats' idea of a top marginal tax rate of 70 per cent: 'Name a country where that's worked. Ever.' An economist pointed out that it had in fact been in place during America's most prosperous years between the 1930s and the 1970s (Cohen 2019). But the shared laughter in the room was evidence enough that the politically influential Davos audience did not consider increased tax revenues from the wealthy an appropriate topic of discussion at the leading global summit on poverty reduction as late as 2019. Since then, *Patriotic Millionaires* (an 'establishment voice with a radical message' advocating an end to extreme wealth [Patriotic Millionaires n.d.]) and the *Good Ancestor Movement* (an advisory firm dedicated to supporting individuals and organisations with radical wealth redistribution through 'reparative and regenerative redistribution' which advances 'a more equitable society and ecological resilience' [Good Ancestor Movement n.d.]) have listed as companies (in 2022 and 2020, respectively), as part of a growing transnational movement of wealth holders advocating for an end to their extreme privilege. Philanthropic organisations are spending down (for example, Lankelly Chase) in recognition of having their feet in the mud of colonialism, or are strategically rethinking how to deploy resources to 'redistribute wealth and build economic power' (JRF).[1] There is also a new coalition-building approach in the air among charities and foundations (for example, JRF and its closer ties with the Trussell Trust) in terms of working together to shift towards a focus on structural drivers and radical change in the trusts and foundations space. What should the next pivot be from these organisations? And are the academic disciplines introduced in Chapter 1 keeping pace with this shift in focus? Or are we still looking down and being resolutely presentist in our approach? What could – must – we do differently?

2. Make extreme wealth into a social problem

We don't only need to stop talking about poverty; we need to actively make extreme wealth into a social problem. In Chapter 1 I made a clear distinction between ordinary wealth and excess private wealth, and I used Robeyns' definition of surplus wealth to point to the level and kind of wealth that I sought to problematise in this book. In Chapters 1 and 2 I looked at some of the effects of this wealth. We need to be able to problematise it in a way that doesn't trigger resistance. Talking about wealth inequality or vilifying the super-rich when there is strong but qualified public support for it/them might not be the rallying cry we want it to be (NEON 2018; Hebden 2020a).

Rulers are moving away from taxing wealth. In the decade since Piketty (2014), the number of OECD states that have a wealth tax has steadily decreased. Perret (2020) shows that most of the 12 OECD countries that levied individual net wealth taxes in 1990 had repealed these taxes in the 1990s and 2000s. By 2020, 'Norway, Spain and Switzerland were the only OECD countries that still levied individual net wealth taxes' (Perret 2020, p 5). We need to address why it isn't possible for parties on the left or right to levy a wealth tax in the current political and ideational climate (see Fastenrath et al [2022] for a recent study of why parties on the left are not putting wealth tax on the agenda). The case I have tried to foreground in this book is that our perceptions of wealth inequality are not in line with the reality of its harmful social effects (see, *inter alia*, Hills 2017). The debunking of the idea of *benign inequality* (Desmond and Wilmers 2019) needs to be matched by the development of the idea of metastatic surplus wealth, whose accumulation, distribution and operation as power corrupts the body politic and is terminal for democracy and the planet.

Shadow Chancellor Rachel Reeves' August 2023 commitment to *not* initiating a wealth tax ignores an important facet of wealth that this book tries to foreground – that is, that notwithstanding the concentrations that a wealth tax could have helped to rebalance, wealth *itself* needs to be governed differently and radically. This is because it has a social as well as an economic life. So, where a wealth tax deals with existing accumulations, it can leave the processes (and the codes – legal, social and cultural) which enabled them untroubled, and allow esteemed economists like Reeves to suggests that the *active government of wealth* is somehow peripheral to conversations about wider social prosperity: that wider social prosperity can be achieved without it. This constitutes a failure to engage on the important social and semiotic function of taxation. Taxes 'formalize our obligations to each other. They define the inequalities we accept and those that we collectively seek to redress' (Martin et al 2009, p 1). Martin et al go on to argue that taxation is crucial in the development of the 'imagined community' of the nation to the extent that it 'enmeshes us in the web of generalized reciprocity' (2009, p 3). This means that the implications of someone not contributing – of actively cheating – extend way beyond the fiscal. They rupture this web of generalised reciprocity. This aspect of taxation is what Reeves failed to recognise in her dismissal of the need for a wealth tax: if not for fiscal expediency, then for means of social cohesion and sustainability, and social justice, a wealth tax might be necessary.

What is the case for making extreme wealth into a contextual bad – into a social problem for which solutions need to extend way beyond the fiscal realm? First, wealth is made, sustained and transferred through the operation of legal code (Pistor 2019). The 'things' of wealth change over time. However, the principles that shape the legal code that creates *value* from these assets (priority, durability, universality and convertibility) *endure* (Pistor 2019, p 3, emphasis added). It is the operation of these principles that ushers wealth from one generation to the next and in so doing maintains the disequilibrium between those who have and those who don't. This is what I was seeking to draw out with the idea of contrastive dispositions of government. These dispositions endure, even as they sustain different political formations or rationalise different policy mechanisms over time: Universal Credit is not a repeat of the workhouse system (several academics took issue with Alston's comments in 2018 on points of historiographical detail [King 2019]), but elements of the knowing, doing and being that characterised the NPL are recognisable in our now-time. If we fail to engage at the level of what I have called 'dispositions', then we will likely continue to encounter new policies embodying these same dispositions. We now know more about wealth-making processes, about the things of wealth and about the trends of distribution over time. We know more about the inequities in our now that are echoes of moments of 'original accumulation' (the sequestration of women's labour described by Federici [2000)], and the racial exploitation of labour that was foundational to the transition to industrial capitalism [Virdee 2018; Bhambra 2021a]). It feels legitimate to make the case that private wealth is *intrinsically* morally concerning, and its *processes of accumulation*, not just its distributions, require political engagement: if historical analysis shows most large accumulations to be the fruit of past violence and exploitation of one kind or another (forms of enclosure), (how) can even ordinary wealth be ethically held?[2] Even if we are not persuaded that all wealth is intrinsically compromised because of these processes of historical enclosure, we might agree with Robeyns (2017; 2019) that it is at the very least a nonintrinsic or 'situational' bad: that hoarding '*surplus* wealth' in contexts of urgent unmet need (poverty) or demands for collective action (environmental emergency) that could be remedied by more financial resource is evidentially a social – and planetary – problem. We need to move beyond evoking the abstract 'wealth' and urgently complicate public discourse with distinctions between ordinary and extreme, with hopeful articulations of common and collective wealth (Federici 2019), and a richer engagement with the socially valued 'phenomenological' effects of wealth that enable a life lived with human dignity (which I will return to under point 7).

3. Describe the 'encompassing welfare universe': we are all in it together!

A 'universe' is a useful metaphorical way of describing a landscape and all its constituent parts – everything that makes it work and everything in it. We need to describe our *welfare* universe in this encompassing way to better reflect the reality that welfare has fiscal and social forms. Not doing so and maintaining the fragmented approach to our understanding (spend over here, revenue raising over there; social welfare here, fiscal welfare there) is sustaining a distorted public understanding of the state's role in processes of pre-distribution and redistribution, and is contributing to the 'us and them' narrative that I described in Chapter 5. It is shored up in academic scholarship too, with fiscal welfare still the poor cousin at major social policy conferences and in social policy journal content, despite, as Sinfield says, the working of fiscal welfare through tax reliefs being 'as, or even more, important in their impact on living standards, shaping behaviour and the wider development of societal welfare as direct benefits and services in public spending programmes' (Sinfield 2023, p 61). In the current welfare universe, much is obscured, and this obscuring means that it is not democratically possible to make informed decisions about who gets what, about what is just, about who is a (net) claimant and about who is a (net) contributor.

We currently don't conceive of the welfare universe as encompassing for many reasons: low economic and fiscal literacy among the public and politicians (Davis 2020); the separation of policy areas such that processes of taxation are somehow set apart from other policy areas and not subject to the same levels of scrutiny; and, relatedly, that HMRC and HMT are distinct ministries, existing in different locations, and both are spending money to effect policy goals, not all of which is visible. The fiercely protected separation means that spend through tax relief in one policy area is not linked to spend (through forms of public service provision) *in the same policy area*. In short, this means that we are still only describing part of the welfare universe, and the bits we aren't describing are those bits which it benefits the wealthy for us not to know about. Thinking *wealtherty* defaults to these being on the same canvas. Any domain, any field where the rich and the poor are symbolically, discursively, legislatively, culturally, politically, economically and epistemically set apart should be reconceived as the *same* field, the *same* domain and the same universe, in which expectations of, for example, *disclosure* are applied evenly and methodically, and in which privileges – like privacy – are named, their value and function described and understood, and the trade-offs with democracy laid out clearly.

Can we describe a new welfare universe or the welfare universe anew – an encompassing welfare universe? What would we need to take account of? What would we consider to be 'facienda' (that is, the business of government)? How would we distribute government tasks? Would we choose the ministerial divisions we have today or would we, for example, have a Minister and Ministry of Taxation, as suggested by Murphy (cited in Sinfield 2023, p 59)? What would need to happen to more appropriately connect issues (tax relief and spend) not just to bring *perceptions* better into line with the reality of what is going on, but also to bring *descriptions* into line with the reality of what is going on (Stantcheva 2021)? This might be more radical than we can imagine: as Surrey asked in 1973, could 'the upside-down benefits of tax reliefs ... possibly be introduced if their real nature were spelt out?' (cited in Sinfield 2023, p 54).

The social and the fiscal are 'separated out' for political purposes, and, as I have argued in this book, this demarcation impedes just social relations and disproportionately benefits the rich. It is a demarcation that is in part achieved through continuous affirmation in governmental practices at the 'surface' level: how we think; what techniques we use; how and what we see; and how identities are made – the focus of Parts II and III of this book. As such, I am drawing a link between these practices and the enduring ontological stability of these discrete policy areas. But in being actively produced and reproduced, the division is also therefore eminently revocable. Let's describe the encompassing welfare universe we live in. Let's refuse the separation of fiscal and social policy, and embrace sociofiscal thinking through a description of the 'encompassing welfare universe'. *Sociofiscal* policy and the 'encompassing welfare universe' is a conceptual, hopeful and practical statement of 'Us'.

4. Describe the pathways to wealtherty

In Chapter 6, I described asserted five interconnected pathways to poverty asserted by the CSJ (2007): family breakdown; educational failure; worklessness; addiction; and problem debt and housing. What would comparable 'pathways to wealtherty' look like? A focus on educational privilege as a pathway to wealtherty might address the monopolising of professions through buying private education (Sutton Trust 2019). Housing as a pathway to wealtherty might focus on the use of property as an investment asset, which serves to drive up prices in a way that contributes to displacement, housing insecurity and homelessness. the worklessness of the super-rich and their fiscal welfare dependency as pathways to wealtherty would seek to tackle the problem of persistent wealth through 'coaching' those addicted to fiscal welfare benefits to become more fiscally independent.

If the overarching aim of these new policy approaches is to effect behavioural change, what might it look like? What behaviours might it be aiming to change and what might the sanctions be? A solution to education as a pathway to wealtherty might be Peter Wilby's proposal to disrupt the monopolisation of higher education (and subsequently professional life) by 'offering places to the top one or two pupils from every school, regardless of grades' to the top one or two institutions (and so on down a list) (cited in Monbiot 2010); a solution to fiscal welfare dependency among the very wealthy might include punitive sanctions for failure to comply, including full cessation of fiscal welfare for three years (no tax reliefs, capital gains tax extracted 'at source' from bank accounts and multiple passport holding revoked). Can we imagine rich people having to turn up at a tax office at a certain time in order to sign on to continue to receive their fiscal welfare? Or having restrictions placed on the number of children they have that the state would support with such fiscal welfare? What would a troubl*ing* families programme comprise, one that offered a solution to the dangers of the intergenerational transfer of dynastic wealth that I discussed in Chapter 5? If we targeted resources on the 100,000 most troubling families on a global scale at the other end of the spectrum, what would we need to do? What behaviours would we need to change? What depathologising effects would we expect to see and with what effects on our social fabric? Entertaining though it is to engage in these reversals, their jarring nature tells us quite how naturalised their opposites have become. Why *do* we tolerate anti-social behaviours from the rich for which we readily criminalise the poor? Why *do* we call theft 'avoidance' when the rich perpetrate it? Why do we call errors 'fraud' when committed by the poor in accessing welfare, and frauds 'errors' when committed by the rich in doing the same?

Articulating the pathways to wealtherty would also require recognising the current status quo as an outcome of interventions in support of wealth, poverty and inequality. For example, the railing against the cost of the poor and the high levels of out-relief in the late 18th century was an effect of the perception by those *paying* relief (wealthier people) that this relief was a costly *intervention*, while at the same time failing to recognise as interventions the legislation that kept their large accumulations of wealth in place. This is an enduring response from privileged groups when they are unaware or unwilling to recognise the advantages they benefit from (and particularly unwilling to recognise these advantages and their outcomes as *unfair*). The persistent failure to recognise privilege is key to wealtherty – it shores up 'us and them' narratives because it belies the fact that that status quo is an effect of multiple temporally and social extensive interventions, and that 'benefit' accrues to both sides. These narratives are then used politically to create outgroups to scrutinise (and punish) and in-groups to ignore (and enable). Let's denaturalise what has become naturalised and articulate the pathways to wealtherty. Once we understand how we got here, we can start plotting pathways out.

5. Change the focus of research funding: it needs to look up and back

'Science responds to funding opportunities, which means that ignorance can be maintained or created in certain areas simply by defunding' (Proctor 2008, p 20). Conversely, this also means that priority areas (Grand Challenges; Global Challenges; Priority Areas; and Sustainable Development Goals) can be established. In both cases, keeping the spotlight on certain areas through funding them casts others into the shade: as was stated in Chapter 1, UK Research and Innovation (UKRI) have spent more than £752 million on projects on poverty, compared to nearly £24.5 million on projects on economic inequality, and under £3 million on projects specifically focusing on wealth-inequality since 2006. Research, and the knowledge or ignorance it perpetuates, is funding-driven: the resultant knowledge is funding-driven and the resultant ignorance is funding-driven. Let's better understand how the funding landscape is producing uneven geographies of knowledge and ignorance in relation to our social problem. Is it helping to centre the wrong problem? At what point does this spending profile constitute an enabling mechanism for *strategic* ignorance in the area of wealth inequality and its effects? New areas need legitimising as a focus for sociofiscal research, and some of them, by necessity, will need to move away from economic restatements of social problems and to the conceptual work necessary to shift the agenda. For example, in all cases where the poor are called into being in policy – as claimants, inmates, or customers (see Chapter 5) – we should ask 'Where are the rich?' and 'What are their relational positions *within the same policy area?*' started this, but as yet, there are few studies looking at the relative position of the rich and the poor at key moments in the development of social policy. A related imperative here is to fund more historical work to open up new ways of understanding what is happening today. This work has taken off since I started writing this book: on epistemological justice; on duration; on the need for new engagement on the political sociology of time; and new, hopeful work on *commoning* (Federici 2019) and on understanding the phenomenological experiences of wealth inequality (Hecht et al 2022). What else might we need to know if we are going to better problematise wealtherty – if we are going to 'get the plumbing in place' for legislative change? The sense of urgency in the literature is remarkable and timely. Whatever the new focus of this work needs to be, the funding balance between work on economic and wealth inequality and poverty needs to be reversed. Our research base and functionality needs to match the nature, scale and urgency of our social problem. We need to look up and back on the basis that we might find solutions for contemporary problems there.

6. Hear from the harm causers and not just the harmed

Although the loud voices of the economic elite/politically influential dominate the policy-making agenda, they can at the same time choose to be silent when it serves their social and fiscal interests (see Tables 8.1 and 8.2). We need to be able to turn up the volume where it is currently quiet and dial it down where it dominates. This means hearing more from the harm causers in social policy discourse and more about the harmed in fiscal policy discourse. 'Getting the plumbing right' for policy or agenda change might require explicitly epistemic means of redress.

There is manifestly a material link between how wealthy a person is, how often and how loud they are able to make their contribution (directly or through an intermediary), and the effect of that 'voice' on the eventual policy outcome (in terms of agenda and design). This is revealed in Harrington's (2016a) ethnography of the wealth management sector and in work by Gilens on affluence and influence. In the US, Gilens (2012) found that higher-income respondents' views are more strongly related to government policy. Further, he showed that the strength of the relationship between preferences and policy outcomes increases with each step up the income ladder and at an increasing rate (Gilens 2012, p 81). In short, wealth buys political influence. Are there ways, at the level of knowledge making and communication, in which this can be challenged, so that the balance between voices which typically aren't influential and voices whose influence dominates is more equitable?

First, when we hear from the harmed, we need to hear from them differently. Policy-making processes that involve testimony and collective knowledge production need to more actively enable *fair* epistemic participation. This would require full 'reversibility and reciprocity ... built on ... equality in communicative participation' (Medina 2013, p 93). As part of this, we would need to understand – from those with firsthand experience *at each end of the spectrum* – which parts of their experience are currently 'missing' and find ways to include them. After all, we *all* have lived experience of wealtherty. In Kerr (2023) I reviewed what this might look like: a *reverse select committee*, for example, with the witnesses taking the place of the panel and vice versa, establishing the terms of reference, selecting the witnesses, defining the questions, taking answers away, and developing recommendations and responses, with those responsible for precarious contracts giving evidence. It might involve sex-worker witnesses telling the panel what they don't want to know about the material ramifications of being forced to have sex to meet basic needs. This would rebalance the testimony – which is currently focused on symptoms – towards accounts of structural factors. Second, this 'hearing differently' might also extend to challenging systemic trust (from the state towards the rich) and mistrust (from the state towards the poor) when this trust is disproportionate to behaviour of the speaker and is based on enduring identity prejudices (positive or negative). Disproportionate trust or mistrust is endemic in policy making and is unfair at both ends of the wealth spectrum. Disproportionate trust between the state and the rich enables evasion, avoidance and noncompliance. Disproportionate mistrust between the state and the poor, built into technologies of surveillance and the overwhelming demands for documentation, causes individual harm (the women's testimonies at the WPC inquiry discussed in Chapter 8 are testament to this) and is socially corrosive. Let's develop our understanding of how wealth affects how we hear, who we hear from and whose voice dominates. Then let's reorchestrate communications between richer and poorer people and the state to develop more equitable patterns of silence.

7. Measure what needs to be measured, not just what can be counted

If numbers are an imperfect way of knowing about people to the extent that they risk 'disappearing' them, how might we know in a way that makes (more of) them visible? In other words, how can we measure the social effects of wealth in the world and on individuals? How can we make the particular problem of wealth, poverty and enduring inequality *visible*? Piketty makes a clear link between identifying and committing to 'verifiable social and environmental indicators [that make it possible to publicly state the extent to which different classes of income and wealth contribute to public and climate burdens] and active citizens engaged in social mobilisation' (Piketty 2021, p 244). We need to know in order to act. Citizens can only engage in social mobilisation if they are equipped with knowledge. But we need to know in a way that enables a richer critical engagement with the actual barriers to social, fiscal and environmental justice (Piketty 2021, p 243), and some of these barriers, as discussed in this book (epistemic injustice and enduring governmental dispositions of scrutiny and ignorance) are difficult to imagine or verify as indicators within the traditional parameters of social science. I am not suggesting that this is resolvable within the current paradigms. In exploring inequality and advantage in the CA, Burchardt and Hick conclude that economic resources 'are likely to remain a crucial metric for understanding distributional inequality for the foreseeable future' (Burchardt and Hick 2017, p 15). However, they argue that a deeper understanding of some 'beings and doings' enabled by wealth (tax avoidance or evasion, for example) comes from retaining income and wealth as measures of economic inequality, but also supplementing them with measures of achievements and power in other dimensions (Burchardt and Hick 2017, p 15). It is these 'measures of achievements and power in other dimensions' that are key to making visible the operation of wealtherty. Crucially, how can we know more of people who are intent on not being seen? And what ways of knowing might shed light on the intersection of distributive and categorical inequality and privilege? What are useful indicators and proxies? Piketty queries the dominance of certain indicators as measuring progress (for example, average income); he argues that because the economic is always already social and political we need more nuanced, multidimensional indicators (Piketty 2021, p 22). If progress away from wealtherty includes parity in the treatment of richer and poorer people in the mechanisms of government, what might appropriate indicators of progress be? Parity of scrutiny? Of disclosure? Of rights to financial privacy? Courtesy and respect? If we look at indicators politically, what else might need to be measured in order to shift the discourse? Could the transparency in think tank funding be a proxy indicator for degrees of wealtherty, or quality of epistemic participation, measured on a scale of degrees of reversibility and reciprocity (Medina 2011)?

8. Reframe, rename, do better social science: let's talk wealtherty

Rowlingson made the case that 'in general we need much more public education about the nature of the tax system and the level of inequality (which the public consistently underestimate)' (Rowlingson 2023, p 175). The problem is that this will not have traction within the current 'regime of truth' because we simultaneously need to deproblematise other deep-grained issues – we need to 'unmake' before we can make (Bhambra 2021c). More public education about tax feels a little bit like 'pulling an incredulous public towards a graph' – it is unlikely to change their minds (Hunt 2011). If we want to arrive at a place where the public supports taxing wealth and applies political pressure for change, we need to do more than educate people about tax; we need to change how we talk about groups of people and their interrelations, and recognise what we do in not doing so.

In 2014, the NAO's request to HMT for more information about tax reliefs provoked opposition from the Treasury and the Chancellor of the Exchequer, George Osbourne, who was reported to be 'incandescent': 'The Treasury's view is that the design and impact of a relief are questions of policy and therefore outside of the NAO's remit' (NAO 2014, cited in Sinfield 2023, p 48). However, the act of calling fiscal benefits 'relief' rather than 'expenditure' has served to keep it outside of normal expectations relating to transparency and accountability. We will look back on this with astonishment. We simply do not have the information we need to make judgements – either moral or economic –about the efficiency or ethics of our tax or welfare systems. What we do know is that it is unfair, secretive and tilted in extremis towards those who already have plenty. Talking about it differently could not be more urgent.

For sociologists *who are interested in justice in the world* and see their work as somehow working to achieve it, this means recalibrating the focus of research. It means starting with DiPrete and Fox-Williams' question: 'What is the relevance of [my] inequality research … for inequality reduction [in the world]?' (DiPrete and Fox Williams 2021). Who do we think our work helps? Who *does* our work help? If it doesn't help anyone, then why are we doing it? If it helps to sustain a problematisation that ultimately leaves the harm causers untroubled, then should we continue? What might this 'better research' look like in the context of wealtherty? An urgent first task is to bring the rich and their wealth, and the disposition of ignorance which enables them or it, into the ideational, conceptual and political frame more explicitly: we urgently need to make extreme wealth into a social and political problem. This is the purpose of the concept of wealtherty. Our work might start with a refusal to participate in enabling discourse that has run its course, and a reframing and renaming of the problem. If we clear new ground for *thinking*, we can make new knowledge 'for cutting' (Foucault 1984, pp 97–98).

Notes

Chapter 1

[1] In line with the approach in Hecht and Summers (2021, p 733), I use the labels 'rich' and 'poor' heuristically, while recognising that these are reductive categorisations that people might not identify with and which occlude important intersectional distinctions. Recent work on the complex relationships between financial and other forms of capital (see, for example, Glucksberg [2018] on gendered elites) highlights the fact that *at both ends of the wealth spectrum*, the effect of the possession or otherwise of wealth in terms of its ability to translate into other forms of capital is mediated by other characteristics, such as sex, race and class. This is the subject of an existing, rich body of scholarly work (Federici 2000; Mies 2014; Tyler 2015, 2020; Skeggs 2019; Bhambra 2021; Koram 2022; Bessière and Gollac 2023;, among others).

[2] My approach was as follows: using the UKRI API, I downloaded all projects and saved the data to a local MongoDb database. I tagged projects which contained one or more of the following tags – 'poverty', 'wealth inequality' and 'economic inequality' – and searched for the tag in the project Title, Abstract and Technical Abstract. I tagged projects (with one or more tags). I then enumerated the projects. Using the UKRI API, I downloaded the project's funds and stored the total fund amount against the project. I enumerated the projects that were award funds (see previous step). For each tag assigned to the project, I added the award to the sum for the given tag. If a project had more than one tag, the award amount would be added to multiple tags. The headline statements are correct (£xxx million was spent on research into [tag]), but the total spent across the three tags will be greater than the total spend in reality. In other words, using this approach, the award could be across one or more themes (tags).

[3] Searches carried out Monday 8 May 2023.

[4] Data exported from Charity Commission website on 12 September 2023. Amounts reflect the last submitted accounts for 5,781 charities based in England and Wales alone.

[5] This has been updated from Kerr (2021) and Kerr (2023), and I hope it will continue to evolve as my engagement with new works does. I will be working to refine this definition and to test it with other academic colleagues over the next few years, starting with a more explicit focus on the 'field of visibility' of wealtherty, which I explore briefly in Chapter 7 and which forms the focus of a research fellowship with LSE's International Inequalities Institute from September 2023.

[6] Dean (1994), Tamboukou (1999) and Garland (2014) are useful on the genealogy as method, and Dean (1991) and Tyler (2020) are useful examples of genealogy in practice.

[7] 'Look at the white interstices between them (the branches) with as much scrupulousness as if they were little estates which you had to survey, and draw maps of ...' (Ruskin 1991, p 30).

Chapter 2

[1] In Kerr (2023), I argued that while wealth has 'typically been subsumed into the category of economic class as a dimension of elite group/upper class membership, new sociological scholarship has foregrounded the specificities of wealth: that it accrues over time, and therefore that its contemporary patterns of distribution carry with them and renew, historical power relations (e.g. of patriarchy ... empire ... and class)' (Kerr 2023, p 3). Like any categorical distinction, it is never independent of others (sex, race and class).

[2] Hills et al 2013; D'Arcy and Gardiner 2017; Bangham and Leslie 2019; Advani et al 2020b; Advani and Tarrant 2022; ONS 2022a; WIR 2022; Dorling 2014 and 2023. The

wider bibliography has other great work in all of these key areas. I am not assuming that all readers will be familiar with wealth distribution data, but if you are, then you could skip this chapter.

3   ONS WAS is survey-based. WIL uses national accounts/tax data and has been able to include information on more asset types than the ONS survey data. Tax data are a lot better than survey data at capturing those at the top of the income distribution. This means that ONS data tend to represent the lower end of calculations of wealth inequality. My thanks to Mina Mahmoudzadeh from the LSE International Inequalities Institute for explaining the relative merits to me.

4   This book was written before the budget of 6 March 2024, when the Conservatives abolished non-dom status.

Chapter 3

1   As with many other areas of poor law scholarship, this is a contested claim and one that is pivotal in the differences in opinion between 'continuity' and 'revolution in government' schools of thought. Harling proposes a compromise in presenting the New Poor Law Unions as 'units in a modified administrative structure in which the centre held a modicum of authority where previously it had held absolutely none' (Harling 1992, p 32).

Chapter 4

1   The book is a record of what people were written up for. It does not reflect actual behaviours in the house. It is clear that recordkeeping was incomplete and that some masters were more or less likely to write people up than others. It is also clear that not all infractions were written up. Its time period is later than my analysis elsewhere in this book, starting in 1852 (and therefore in the 'mature' period of the NPL), but this is useful in some ways, as it describes a period during which a hardening of social attitudes to outdoor relief was taking place and by which time there was a sense of routine practice. The book is unusually complete for a workhouse punishment book and is considered a good example of this kind of source. I transcribed and then coded the original source based on offence type, punishment type and duration of punishment. I then analysed the coded data to look at trends relating to patterns of offending and punishment for men and women. Although most offences had multiple components and were coded to reflect this complexity (for example, physical and verbal assaults), I have not used the multilevel coding for this analysis. My interest here is trying to deduce the ecology of punishment, understand a hierarchy of seriousness of offences, and whether or not the system operated differently for male and female inmates, in terms of the type of offence that attracted sanctions, the type of punishment and the severity of punishment. A transcription of the book is available from the author on request.

2   Although new work by Advani et al (2022) (also discussed in Savage 2023) on the importance of the working rich as constituents within the non-dom population is revealing more of the activity and effects of the working rich.

Chapter 6

1   The CSJ provides a list of funders and supporters, but no information relating to individual donations. In its 2022 annual accounts, for example (see https://find-and-update.comp any-information.service.gov.uk/company/05137036/filing-history), it individuates three grants from trusts and foundations (p 8), but there is no further detail about the rest of its income. In the 2021–2022 report, a QR code was included with a link to this list of companies, with no information about amounts or focus of donations; see https://www.centreforsocialjustice.org.uk/support-the-csj

Notes

2. Publicly available data are inconsistent. These tables comprise data from at least two sources, but will not be fully accurate: the data is a lower limit of their involvement and each individual may possibly have had other remunerated roles and may have been involved with the CSJ at other times. For example, although Brien seems not to have been involved in 2012, this seems unlikely given this overall trajectory.
3. Whofundsyou.org (retired in 2019 and subsequently taken over by Opendemocracy.net) gave the CSJ an E in 2018 for transparency, which was later upgraded to a D for its failure to acknowledge all its funders and was then downgraded to an E again after 2021. Data recovered from https://en.wikipedia.org/wiki/Centre_for_Social_Justice#Funding in October 2021 and from https://www.opendemocracy.net/en/who-funds-you/pen in September 2023.
4. Available from They Work for You website: https://www.theyworkforyou.com/mp/10180/iain_duncan_smith/chingford_and_woodford_green/votes

Chapter 9

1. https://lankellychase.org.uk/news/lankelly-chase-to-wholly-redistribute-its-assessts-over-the-next-five-years/; https://www.jrf.org.uk/blog/reimagining-investment-transfer-wealth-and-power
2. A point made by Martin Sandbu, a European economics commentator for the *Financial Times*, at a launch event for Robeyns' 2024 book (LSE 2024, 39:55 to 40:05). He notes that a lot of wealth is tainted, and people get tainted money and are not rich. A concern with the taintedness of wealth, then, would apply to both ordinary and extreme wealth. His point was that the right answer in that situation is not necessarily to limit wealth, but to restitute wrongfully acquired money.

Bibliography

Adam, S., Besley, T., Blundell, R., Bond, S., Chote, R., Gammie, R., Johnson, P., Myles, G. and Poterba, J. (eds) (2010) *Dimensions of Tax Design: The Mirrlees Review*, Oxford: Oxford University Press.

Adams, T. (2016) 'Richard Billingham: "I just hated growing up in that tower block"', *The Guardian* [online], 13 March, Available from: https://www.theguardian.com/artanddesign/2016/mar/13/richard-billingham-tower-block-white-dee-rays-a-laugh-liz [Accessed 4 May 2017].

Advani, A. and Sturrock. D. (2024) 'Too little too late: why we need to rethink inheritance tax', *LSE* [online], Available from: https://blogs.lse.ac.uk/inequalities/2024/02/14/too-little-too-late-inheritance-tax/ [Accessed 29 February 2024].

'Advani, A. and Summers, A. (2022) 'Measuring and taxing top incomes and wealth', Warwick Economics Research Papers, No. 1403, Available from: https://wrap.warwick.ac.uk/164526/1/WRAP-twerp-1403-Advani-2022.pdf [Accessed 28 May 2024].

Advani, A. and Tarrant, H. (2022) 'Official statistics underrepresent wealth inequality in Britain', *LSE Politics and Policy* [online], 7 January, Available from: https://blogs.lse.ac.uk/politicsandpolicy/official-statistics-underestimate-wealth-inequality/ [Accessed 3 June 2023].

Advani, A., Bangham, G. and Leslie, J. (2021) 'The UK's wealth distribution and characteristics of high wealth households', *Fiscal Studies: The Journal of Applied Public Economics*, 42 (3–4), 397–430.

Advani, A., Chamberlain, E. and Summers, A. (2020) 'A wealth tax for the UK: executive summary', *Wealth Tax Commission* [online], Available from: https://www.wealthandpolicy.com/wp/WealthTaxFinalReport.html

Advani, A., Burgherr, D., Savage, M. and Summers, A. (2022) 'The UK's global economic elite: a sociological analysis using tax data' *LSE* [online] Working Paper 79, Available from: http://eprints.lse.ac.uk/114607/1/The_UKs_Global_Economic_Elite_Advani_Burgherr_Savage_Summers.pdf [Accessed 19 July 2023].

Allegretti, A. (2021a) 'David Cameron urged to address reports he made $10m from Greensill', *The Guardian* [online], 10 August, Available from: https://www.theguardian.com/politics/2021/aug/10/david-cameron-urged-to-address-reports-he-made-10m-from-greensill [Accessed 10 August 2021].

Allegretti, A. (2021b) 'MP Owen Paterson faces suspension for breaking lobbying rules', *The Guardian* [online], 26 October, Available from: https://www.theguardian.com/politics/2021/oct/26/owen-paterson-faces-suspension-breaking-lobbying-rules [Accessed 19 November 2021].

Bibliography

Alston, P. (2018) 'Statement on visit to the United Kingdom, by Professor Philip Alston, United Nations Special Rapporteur on extreme poverty and human rights', *UN Human Rights Office of the High Commissioner* [online], 16 November, Available from: https://www.ohchr.org/en/statements/2018/11/statement-visit-united-kingdom-professor-philip-alston-united-nations [Accessed 13 November 2018].

Alt, J., Preston, I. and Sibieta, L. (2010) 'The political economy of tax policy' in S. Adam, T. Besley, R. Blundell, S. Bond, R. Chote, M. Gammie, P. Johnson, G. Myles and J. Porterba (eds) *Dimensions of Tax Design: The Mirrlees Review*, Oxford: Oxford University Press, pp 1204–1277.

Amsalem, E. and Zoizner, A. (2022) 'Real, but limited: a meta-analytic assessment of framing effects in the political domain', *British Journal of Political Science*, 52: 221–237.

Anstead, N. (2018) 'The idea of austerity in British politics 2003–2013', *Political Studies*, 66(2): 287–305.

Atkinson, A.B. (2015) *Inequality: What Can Be Done?*, Cambridge, MA: Harvard University Press.

Atkinson, R. (2021) *Alpha City: How the Super-Rich Captured London*, London: Verso.

Aydelotte, F. (1913) *Elizabethan Rogues and Vagabonds and Their Representation in Contemporary Literature*, Oxford: Oxford University Press.

Bacchi, C. (2013) 'Introducing "what's the problem represented to be?" approach' in *Engaging with Carol Bacchi*, Adelaide: Adelaide University Press, pp 21–24.

Bailey, P.L. and Ball, S.J. (2016) 'The Coalition government, the general election and the policy ratchet in education: a reflection on the "ghosts" of policy past, present and yet to come' in H. Bochel and M. Powell (eds) *The Coalition Government and Social Policy*, Bristol: Policy Press, pp 127–152.

Baker, A. and Murphy, R. (2020) 'Modern monetary theory and the changing role of tax in society', *Social Policy and Society*, 19: 454–469.

Ball, J. (2013) 'Iain Duncan Smith rapped by watchdog for misusing benefits cap statistics', *The Guardian* [online], 9 May, Available from: www.theguardian.com/politics/2013/may/09/iain-duncan-smith-benefits-cap-statistics [Accessed 30 September 2019].

Ball, S.J. (2012) 'The reluctant state and the beginning of the end of state education', *Journal of Educational Administration and History*, 44(2): 89–103.

Ball, S.J. (2015) 'What is policy? 21 years later: reflections on the possibilities of policy research', *Discourse: Studies in the Cultural Politics of Education*, 36(3), 306–313, Available from: http://dx.doi.org/10.1080/01596306.2015.1015279 [Accessed 20 May 2024].

Ball, S.J. (2020) 'Following policy: networks, network ethnography and education policy mobilities', in S.J. Ball *Globalisation and Education*, Abingdon: Routledge, pp 126–143.

Ball, S.J. and Collet-Sabé, J. (2021) 'Against school: an epistemological critique', *Discourse: Studies in the Cultural Politics of Education*, 43(6): 985–999.

Ball, S.J. and Exley, S. (2010) 'Making policy with "good ideas": the "intellectuals" of New Labour', *Journal of Education Policy*, 25(2): 151–169.

Ball, S.J., Macguire, M. and Braun, A. (2012) *How Schools Do Policy: Policy Enactments in Secondary Schools*, Abingdon: Routledge.

Bangham, G. and Leslie, J. (2019) 'Who owns all the pie? The size and distribution of Britain's £14.6 trillion of wealth', *Resolution Foundation* [online], Available from: https://www.resolutionfoundation.org/publications/who-owns-all-the-pie/ [Accessed 30 January 2020].

Barnes, M. and Ross, A. (2021) 'The problem with troubled families: rethinking the analysis behind the 120,000 troubled families statistic', *Social Policy and Society*, 1–19.

Barr, N.A. (1980) 'The taxation of married women's incomes', *British Tax Review*, 478–490.

Bayly, C.A. (2000) 'Ireland, India and the Empire: 1780–1914', *Transactions of the Royal Historical Society*, 10: 377–397.

BBC News (2013) 'Economy: there is no alternative (TINA) is back' [online], 7 March 2013, Available from: https://www.bbc.co.uk/news/uk-politics-21703018 [Accessed 30 January 2020].

BBC News (2016) 'Profile: Iain Duncan Smith' [online], 18 March 2016, Available from: https://www.bbc.co.uk/news/uk-politics-35848899 [Accessed 30 January 2020].

BBC News (2019) 'Hungry children "eating from school bins" in Morecombe' [online], 10 January, Available from: https://www.bbc.co.uk/news/uk-england-lancashire-46827360 [Accessed 30 January 2020].

BBC News (2020) 'Why ear wax syringing is no longer free – minister' [online], 25 September, Available from: https://www.bbc.co.uk/news/uk-politics-54296737 [Accessed 30 January 2021].

BBC News (2021) 'What is lobbying? A brief guide' [online], 5 November, Available from: https://www.bbc.co.uk/news/uk-politics-56733456 [Accessed 30 January 2022].

Beaverstock, J., Hall, S. and Wainwright, T. (2010) 'Scoping the private wealth management of the high net worth and mass affluent markets in the UK's financial services industry', *University of Nottingham* [online], Available from: https://www.nottingham.ac.uk/business/who-we-are/centres-and-institutes/gcbfi/documents/researchreports/paper71.pdf [Accessed 12 December 2019].

Beckert, J. (2022) 'Durable wealth: institutions, mechanisms, and practices of wealth perpetuation', *Annual Review of Sociology*, 48: 233–255.

Beckert, J. (2023) 'Varieties of wealth: toward a comparative sociology of wealth inequality', *Socio-economic Review* 00, 0: 1–25, https://doi.org/10.1093/ser/mwad068

Bibliography

Beckett, J.V. (1985) 'Land tax or excise: the levying of taxation in seventeenth- and eighteenth-century England', *English Historical Review*, 100(395): 285–308.

Bennett, F. (2021) 'How government sees couples on Universal Credit: a critical gender perspective', *Journal of Poverty and Social Justice*, 29(1): 3–20.

Bennett, F. (2023) 'Framing of poverty in the UK' *JRF* [online] June, Available from: https://www.jrf.org.uk/report/framing-poverty-uk [Accessed 1 September 2023].

Berger, J. (2008) *Ways of Seeing*, London: Penguin UK.

Bernardo, A.B.I. (2021) 'Meritocracy beliefs and intolerance towards wealth inequality among higher subjective social status Filipinos', *Revista de Psicologia Social*, 36: 397–423. https://doi.org/10.1080/02134748.2021.1940705

Bessière, C. and Gollac, S. (2023) *The Gender of Capital: How Families Perpetuate Wealth Inequality*, Cambridge, MA: Harvard University Press.

Bhambra, G.K. (2016) 'Comparative historical sociology and the state: problems of method', *Cultural Sociology*, 10(3): 335–351.

Bhambra, G.K. (2021a) 'Relations of extraction, relations of redistribution: empire, nation, and the construction of the British welfare state', *British Journal of Sociology*, 73(1): 4–15.

Bhambra, G.K. (2021b) 'Webs of reciprocity: colonial taxation and the need for reparations', *British Journal of Sociology*, 73: 73–77.

Bhambra, G.K. (2021c) 'Decolonising critical theory? Epistemological justice, progress, reparations', *Critical Times*, 4(1): 73–89.

Bhambra, G.K. and Holmswood, J. (2018) 'Colonialism, postcolonialism and the liberal welfare state', *New Political Economy*, 23(5): 574–587.

Billingham, R. (2014) *Ray's a Laugh*, Zurich: Scalo, Available at: https://www.saatchigallery.com/artist/richard_billingham [Accessed 1 May 2024].

Blanchard, J. (2016) 'David Cameron's Cabinet of millionaires face mounting pressure to publish their tax returns', *The Mirror* [online], 10 April, Available from: https://www.mirror.co.uk/news/uk-news/david-camerons-cabinet-millionaires-face-7726539 [Accessed 3 February 2018].

Bland, S.M. (2018) 'The case of Ablyazov: lack of political will', *IndraStra Global*, 4(3): 1–8.

Blencowe, C. (2013) 'Participatory knowledge matters for democracy' in T. Noorani, C. Blencowe and J. Brigstocke (eds) *Problems of Participation: Reflections on Authority, Democracy, and the Struggle for Common Life*, Lewes: Authority Research Network (ARN) Press, pp 37–50.

Blencowe, C., Brigstocke, J. and Dawney, L. (2013) 'Authority and experience', *Journal of Political Power*, 6(1): 1–7.

Bochel, H. and Berthier, A. (2020) 'A place at the table? Parliamentary committees, witnesses and the scrutiny of government actions and legislation', *Social Policy and Society*, 19(1): 1–17.

Bonvin, J.-M. and Laruffa, F. (2022) 'Towards a capability-oriented eco-social policy: elements of a normative framework', *Social Policy and Society*, 21(3): 484–495.

Booth, R. (2018) 'Take action rather than criticise, UN poverty expert tells Rudd', *The Guardian* [online], 20 November, Available from: https://www.theguardian.com/society/2018/nov/20/un-poverty-expert-philip-alston-amber-rudd [Accessed 25 November 2018].

Booth, R. (2019) 'UN report compares Tory welfare policies to creation of workhouses', *The Guardian* [online] 22 May, Available from: https://www.theguardian.com/politics/2019/may/22/un-report-compares-tory-welfare-reforms-to-creation-of-workhouses [Accessed 30 May 2019].

Booth, R., Watt, H. and Pegg, D. (2016) 'David Cameron admits he profited from father's Panama offshore trust', *The Guardian* [online] 7 April, Available from: https://www.theguardian.com/news/2016/apr/07/david-cameron-admits-he-profited-fathers-offshore-fund-panama-papers [Accessed 7 April 2016].

Bourquin, P., Cribb, J., Waters, T. and Xu, X. (2019) 'Why has in-work poverty risen in Britain?' *Institute for Fiscal Studies* [online], Available from: https://ifs.org.uk/sites/default/files/output_url_files/WP201912.pdf [Accessed 4 October 2020].

Bourquin, P., Joyce, R. and Sturrock, D. (2021) 'Inheritances and inequality over the life cycle: what will they mean for younger generations?', *Institute for Fiscal Studies* [online], Available from: https://ifs.org.uk/publications/inheritances-and-inequality-over-life-cycle-what-will-they-mean-younger-generations [Accessed 5 July 2022].

Bourquin, P., Brewer, M. and Wernham, T. (2022) 'Trends in income and wealth inequalities', *Institute for Fiscal Studies (IFS) Deaton Review of Inequalities* [online], Available from: https://ifs.org.uk/inequality/wp-content/uploads/2022/10/Trends-in-income-and-wealth-inequalities-IFS-Deaton-Review-of-Inequality-final.pdf [Accessed 13 December 2022].

Bradley, S. (2020) '"It's not fair": natural justice and the New Poor Law', *In Their Own Write* [blog], 31 October, Available from: https://intheirownwriteblog.wordpress.com/category/natural-justice/ [Accessed 2 April 2021].

Braidotti, R. (2011) *Nomadic Subjects: Embodiment and Sexual Differences in Contemporary Feminist Theory*, 2nd edition, New York: Columbia University Press.

Bramall, R. (2013) *The Cultural Politics of Austerity: Past and Present in Austere Times.* London: Palgrave Macmillan.

Bramall, R. (2016) 'Tax justice in austerity: logics, residues and attachments', *New Formations: A Journal of Culture/Theory/Politics*, 87: 29–46.

British Parliamentary Papers (1970)

Brenner, N., Peck, J. and Theodore, N. (2010) 'Variegated neoliberalization: geographies, modalities, pathways', *Global Networks* 10 (2): 1–41.

Brown, R. (2017) *The Inequality Crisis: The Facts and What We Can Do about It*, Bristol: Policy Press.

Bruckmüller, S., Reese, G. and Martiny, S.E. (2017) 'Is higher inequality less legitimate? Depends on how you frame it!', *British Journal of Social Psychology*, 56(4): 766–781.

Brundage, A. (1972) 'The landed interest and the New Poor Law: a reappraisal of the revolution in government', *English Historical Review*, 87: 27–48.

Brundage, A. (2002) *The English Poor Laws 1700–1930*, Basingstoke: Palgrave.

Bullough, O. (2018) *Moneyland: Why Thieves and Crooks Now Rule the World and How to Take It Back*, London: Profile Books.

Bullough, O. (2022) *Butler to the World: The Book the Oligarchs Don't Want You to Read*, London: Profile Books.

Burchardt, T. and Hick, R. (2017) 'Inequality, advantage and the capability approach', *Journal of Human Development and Capabilities*, 19(1): 38–52.

Burt, R.S. (2007) *Brokerage and Closure: An Introduction to Social Capital*, Oxford: OUP.

Bush, L. (2019) *Eleven Privatised Public Assets*, London: Lewis Bush.

Butler, I. and Drakeford, M. (2003) *Social Policy, Social Welfare and Scandal*, Basingstoke: Palgrave Macmillan.

Byrne, L. (2024) *The Inequality of Wealth. Why It Matters and How to Fix It*, London: Apollo for Bloomsbury Publishing.

Campbell, J.L. (1998) 'Institutional analysis and the role of ideas in political economy', *Theory and Society*, 27(3): 377–409.

Carter, N. and King, S. (2021) '"I think we ought not to acknowledge them [paupers] as that encourages them to write": the administrative state, power and the Victorian pauper', *Social History*, 46(2): 117–144.

Carter, P. and Motlagh, D. (2023) 'The New Poor Law and an early example of information management', *The National Archive* [online], 4 July, Available from: https://blog.nationalarchives.gov.uk/the-new-poor-law/ [Accessed 19 July 2023].

Carter, P., James, J and King, S. (2019) 'Punishing paupers? Control, discipline and mental health in the Southwell workhouse (1836–71)', *Rural History*, 30: 161–180.

Cartwright, B.G. (2009) 'Whither the SEC now?', *Virginia Law Review*, 95(4): 1085–1104.

Case, A. and Deaton, A. (2020) *Deaths of Despair and the Future of Capitalism*, Princeton: Princeton University Press.

Cash, P.J., Hartlev, C.G. and Durazo, C.B. (2017) 'Behavioural design: a process for integrating behaviour change and design', *Design Studies*, 48: 96–128.

Chancel, L. (2020) *Unsustainable Inequalities: Social Justice and the Environment*. Cambridge, MA: Belknap Press.

Cheetham, M., Moffatt, S. and Addison, M. (2018) '"It's hitting people that can least afford it the hardest": the impact of the roll out of Universal Credit in two North East England localities: a qualitative study', Available from: https://www.gateshead.gov.uk/media/10665/The-impact-of-the-roll-out-of-Universal-Credit-in-two-North-East-England-localities-a-qualitative-study-November-2018/pdf/Universal_Credit_Report_2018pdf.pdf?m=636778831081630000 [Accessed 19 August 2019].

Chick, M. (2020) 'Taxing wealth: a historical perspective, background paper 121', *Wealth Tax Commission* [online], Available from: www.ukwealth.tax [Accessed 9 December 2020].

Christensen, M-B., Hallum, C., Maitland, A., Parrinello, Q. and Putaturo, C. (2023) 'Survival of the richest', *Oxfam* [online], Available from: https://www.oxfam.org/en/research/survival-richest [Accessed 5 September 2023].

Clark, E., Gronwald, V., Guerrero Fernandez, V. and Ramirez Casillas, E. (2020) 'The political economy of the abolition of wealth taxes in the OECD, background paper 123', *Wealth Tax Commission* [online], Available from: https://www.wealthandpolicy.com/wp/BP123_PoliticalEconomy.pdf [Accessed 9 December 2020].

Clarke, J and Newman, J. (2010) 'Summoning spectres: crises and their construction', *Journal of Education Policy*, 25(6): 709–715.

Clarke, J. and Newman, J. (2012) 'The alchemy of austerity', *Critical Social Policy*, 32(3): 299–319.

Cobham, A. (2020) *The Uncounted*, Cambridge: Polity Press.

Cohen, N. (2019) 'Forget philanthropy: the rich should be paying proper taxes', *The Guardian* [online], 2 February, Available from: https://theguardian.com/commentisfree/2019/feb/02/forget-philanthropy-super-rich-should-be-paying-proper-taxes March 2019 [Accessed 8 February 2019].

Collins, V. (2012) 'How Iain Duncan Smith came to Easterhouse and left with a new vision for the Tory party', *The Herald* [online], 23 March, Available from: https://www.heraldscotland.com/news/12131837.how-iain-duncan-smith-came-to-easterhouse-and-left-with-a-new-vision-for-the-tory-party/ [Accessed 1 December 2020].

Committee on Standards in Public Life (1995) 'The seven principles of public life', Available from: https://www.gov.uk/government/publications/the-7-principles-of-public-life [Accessed 19 November 2023].

Cousins, K. (2018) 'The failure of the first income tax: a tale of commercial tax evaders?', *Journal of Legal History*, 39(2): 157–186.

Crerar, P. (2023) 'Rachel Reeves rules out wealth tax if Labour wins next election', *The Guardian* [online], 27 August, Available from: https://www.theguardian.com/politics/2023/aug/27/rachel-reeves-rules-out-wealth-tax-if-labour-wins-next-election [Accessed 28 August 2023].

Croissant, J. (2014) 'Agnotology: ignorance and absence or towards a sociology of things that aren't there', *Social Epistemology*, 28(1): 4–25.

Crossley, S., Garthwaite, K. and Patrick, R. (2020) 'The fragmentation of poverty in the UK: what's the problem? A working paper', Available from: https://www.whatstheproblem.org.uk/a-working-paper [Accessed 30 March 2021].

CSJ (Centre for Social Justice) (2006) 'Breakdown Britain: interim report on the state of the nation', *Centre for Social Justice* [online], Available from: https://www.centreforsocialjustice.org.uk/wp-content/uploads/2018/03/Breakdown-BritainCSJ.pdf [Accessed 13 October 2016].

CSJ (2007) 'Breakthrough Britain: ending the costs of social breakdown, vol. 2, economic dependency and worklessness', *Centre for Social Justice* [online], Available from: https://www.centreforsocialjustice.org.uk/wp-content/uploads/2018/03/BBChairmansOverview.pdf [Accessed 13 October 2016].

CSJ (2009) 'Dynamic benefits: towards welfare that works – a policy Report from the Economic Dependency Working Group', *Centre for Social Justice* [online], Available from: https://www.centreforsocialjustice.org.uk/wp-content/uploads/2018/03/CSJ-dynamic-benefits.pdf [Accessed 23 November 2019].

CSJ (2011) 'History and family: setting the records straight. A rebuttal to the British Academy pamphlet *Happy Families?*', *Centre for Social Justice* [online], Available from: https://www.centreforsocialjustice.org.uk/library/history-and-family-setting-the-records-straight-a-rebuttal-to-the-british-academy-pamphlet-happy-families [Accessed 3 November 2019].

CSJ (2016) 'Annual report', Available from: https://www.centreforsocialjustice.org.uk/library/annual-report-2016-17 [Accessed 27 May 2024].

CSJ (2020) 'Annual report', Available from: https://www.centreforsocialjustice.org.uk/library/annual-report-2019-2020 [Accessed 27 May 2024].

CSJ (2022) 'Annual report', Available from: https://www.centreforsocialjustice.org.uk/wp-content/uploads/2022/12/CSJ-Annual-Report_21-22.pdf [Accessed 27 May 2024].

Cullinane, C. and Montacute, R. (2018) 'Pay as you go? Internship pay, quality and access in the graduate job market', The Sutton Trust. Available from: https://www.youthemployment.org.uk/dev/wp-content/uploads/2018/11/Pay-As-You-Go-1.pdf [Accessed 27 May 2024].

Cummins, N. (2019) 'Hidden wealth, working paper 39', *LSE International Inequalities Institute* [online], Available from: http://eprints.lse.ac.uk/102830/1/Cummins_hidden_wealth_wp39.pdf [Accessed 7 March 2020].

Cummins, N. (2022) 'Some English dynasties hiding 35% of inherited wealth according to historical research' *LSE* [online], Available from: https://www.lse.ac.uk/News/Latest-news-from-LSE/2022/h-August-22/English-dynasties-hiding-35-per-cent-of-inherited-wealth [Accessed 9 September 2022].

Cummins, N. and Ó Gráda, C. (2022) 'Two centuries of wealth gap persists for the Irish in England', *LSE* [online], Available from: https://www.lse.ac.uk/News/Latest-news-from-LSE/2022/g-July-22/Irish-Wealth-Gap [Accessed 1 September 2023].

D'Arcy, C. and Gardiner, L. (2017) 'The generation of wealth: asset accumulation across and within cohorts', *Resolution Foundation* [online], Available from: http://www.resolutionfoundation.org/publications/the-generation-of-wealth-asset-accumulation-across-and-within-cohorts/ [Accessed 3 August 2017].

Dang, M. (2019) 'Epistemology of survival: a working paper', Available from: https://www.minh-dang.com/publications [Accessed 7 September 2019].

Daniel, M. (2019) 'Local government workers can't afford to live in the towns they serve', *Unison* [online], 16 June, Available from: https://www.unison.org.uk/news/2019/06/localgo-housing/ [Accessed 7 September 2019].

Davis, A., Hecht, K., Burchardt, T., Gough, I., Hirsch, D., Rowlingson, K. and Summers, K. (2020) 'Living on different incomes in London: can public consensus identify a "riches line"?', *Trust for London* [online], Available from: https://sticerd.lse.ac.uk/dps/case/cr/casereport127.pdf [Accessed 2 March 2020].

de Benedictus, S., Allen, K. and Jensen, T. (2017) 'Portraying poverty: the economics and ethics of factual welfare television', *Cultural Sociology*, 11(3): 337–358.

Dean, H. and Melrose, M. (1998) *Poverty, Riches and Citizenship*, Basingstoke: Macmillan.

Dean, M. (1991) *The Constitution of Poverty: Towards a Genealogy of Liberal Governance*, London: Routledge.

Dean, M. (1994) *Critical and Effective Histories: Foucault's Method and Historical Sociology*, London: Routledge.

Dean, M. (2010) *Governmentality. Power and Rule in Modern Society*, London: Sage.

Deneault, A. (2018) *Legalising Theft: A Short Guide to tax Havens*, Nova Scotia: Fernwood Publishing.

Desmond, M. (2023) *Poverty, by America*, London: Penguin.

Desmond, M. and Wilmers, N. (2019) 'Do the poor pay more for housing? Exploitation, profit, and risk in rental markets', *American Journal of Sociology*, 124(4): 1090–1124.

Dibb, G., Jung, C., Parkes, H. and Nanda, S (2021) 'Prosperity and justice after the pandemic', *IPPR* [online], Available from: https://www.ippr.org/articles/prosperity-and-justice-after-the-pandemic [Accessed 28 May 2024].

DiPrete, T.A. and Fox-Williams, B.N. (2021) 'The relevance of inequality research in sociology for inequality reduction', *Socius: Sociological Research for a Dynamic World*, 7: 1–30.

Dolan, A. (2009) 'Single mothers have created a generation of uber-chavs', *Daily Mail* [online], 10 February, Available from: https://www.dailymail.co.uk/news/article-1139886/Single-mothers-created-generation-uber-chavs-costing-taxpayer-fortune-claims-deputy-head.html [Accessed 3 June 2019].

Dorling, D. (2014) *Inequality and the 1%*, London: Verso.

Dorling, D. (2015) 'The mother of underlying causes: economic ranking and health inequality', *Social Science and Medicine*, 128: 327–330.

Dorling, D. (2023) *Shattered Nation*, London: Verso.

Dotson, K. (2012) 'Tracking epistemic violence, tracking practices of silencing', *Hypatia*, 26(2): 236–257.

Driver, F. (2004) *Power and Pauperism: The Workhouse System, 1834–1884*, Cambridge: Cambridge University Press.

DWP (Department for Work and Pensions) (2008) *No One Written off: Reforming Welfare to Reward Responsibility*, London: The Stationery Office.

DWP (2010) *21st Century Welfare* (CM 7913), London: The Stationery Office.

DWP (2011) *Fraud and Error Penalties and Sanctions: Equality Impact Assessment*, London: The Stationery Office.

DWP (2012a) *Social Justice: Transforming Lives*, London: The Stationery Office.

DWP (2012b) 'JPEG – Jobcentre Plus environment guide', *The National Archives* [online], Available from: https://webarchive.nationalarchives.gov.uk/ukgwa/20130125093007/http://www.dwp.gov.uk/jpeg/ [Accessed 23 July 2023].

DWP (2019a) *Memorandum to the Work and Pensions Select Committee: 2019 Inquiry: Universal Credit and Survival Sex (UCX 0015)*, London: The Stationery Office.

DWP (2019b) *Further Written Evidence from the Department for Work and Pensions (UCX0018) 2019 Inquiry: Universal Credit and Survival Sex*, London: The Stationery Office.

DWP (2020) 'Universal Credit Work Coach Training Materials UC55 and UC108', resources made available following FOI 2020/61299, Available from: https://www.whatdotheyknow.com/request/work_coach_new_entrant_learning#outgoing-1078782 [Accessed 19 July 2021].

DWP (2021) *Guidance: Universal Credit Sanctions Statistics: Background Information and Methodology*, London: The Stationery Office, Available from: https://www.gov.uk/government/publications/universal-credit-sanctions-statistics-background-information-and-methodology/a#table-3 [Accessed 2 February 2022].

DWP (2023) 'Fraud and error in the benefit system: financial year 2022 to 2023 estimates', *Department for Work and Pensions* [online], Available from: https://www.gov.uk/government/statistics/fraud-and-error-in-the-benefit-system-financial-year-2022-to-2023-estimates [Accessed 2 February 2024].

Dwyer, P.J. (2018) 'Punitive and ineffective: benefit sanctions within social security', *Journal of Social Security Law*, 142–157.

Dwyer, P.J. and Wright, S. (2014) 'Universal Credit, ubiquitous conditionality and its implications for social citizenship', *Journal of Poverty and Social Justice*, 22(1): 27–35.

Edmiston, D. (2018) 'The poor "sociological imagination" of the rich: explaining attitudinal divergence towards welfare, inequality and redistribution', *Social Policy and Administration*, 52(5): 983–997.

Edmiston, D. (2022) 'Plumbing the depths: the changing (socio-demographic) profile of UK poverty', *Journal of Social Policy*, 51(2): 385–411.

Eltis, W. (1997) 'Capitalism with a human face by Samuel Brittan: a review', *Economic Journal*, 107(445): 1887–1889.

Endres, A.M. (1985) 'The functions of numerical data in the writings of Graunt, Petty and Davenant', *History of Political Economy*, 17(2): 245–266.

Englander, D. (1998) *Poverty and Poor Law Reform in 19th Century Britain 1834–1914: From Chadwick to Booth*, London: Longman.

Exley, S. (2021) 'Open policy making in the UK – to whom might policy formulation be "opening up"?', *Journal of Social Policy*, 50(3): 451–469.

Fairclough, N. (1992) *Discourse and Social Change*, Cambridge: Polity Press.

Fairness Foundation (2023) 'Framing advice: our advice on framing fairness', Available from: https://fairness.org.uk/appendices/framing-advice [Accessed 15 July 2023].

Farnsworth, K. (2012) *Social versus Corporate Welfare: Competing Needs and Interests within the Welfare State*, Basingstoke: Palgrave Macmillan.

Farnsworth, K. (2013) 'Bringing corporate welfare in', *Journal of Social Policy*, 41(1): 1–22.

Farnsworth, K. (2023) 'Corporate tax and corporate welfare' in A. Lymer, M. May and A. Sinfield (eds) *Taxation and Social Policy*, Bristol: Policy Press, pp 219–237.

Farolfi, S., Harding, L. and Ophanides, S. (2018) 'EU citzenship for sale as Russian oligarch buys Cypriot passport', *The Guardian* [online]. Available from: https://www.theguardian.com/world/2018/mar/02/eu-citizenship-for-sale-as-russian-oligarch-oleg-deripaska-buys-cypriot-passport [Accessed 20 May 2024].

Farrer, M. (2019) 'Historian berates billionaires at Davos over tax avoidance', *The Guardian* [online], 30 January, Available from: https://www.theguardian.com/business/2019/jan/30/historian-berates-billionaires-at-davos-over-tax-avoidance [Accessed 17 June 2020].

Fastenrath, F., Marx, P., Truger, A. and Vitt, H. (2022) 'Why is it so difficult to tax the rich? Evidence from German policy-makers', *Journal of European Public Policy*, 29(5): 767–786.

Federici, S. (2000) *Caliban and the Witch: Women, The Body and Primitive Accumulation*, Harmondworth: Penguin.

Federici, S. (2019) *Re-enchanting the World: Feminism and the Politics of the Commons*, New York: Autonomedia.

Federici, S. (2020) *Revolution at Point Zero: Housework, Reproduction, and Feminist Struggle*, Binghamton, NY: PM Press.

Federici, S. (2021) *Patriarchy of the Wage: Notes on Marx, Gender and Feminism*. Binghamton, NY: PM Press.

Field, H. and Frost Sutton, J. (1884) *The Date-Book of Remarkable & Memorable Events Connected with Nottingham and its Neighbourhood: Part I 850–1749 [and] Part II 1750–1884*, Complete edition, Nottingham: Authentic Records.

Fize, E., Grimprel, N. and Landais, C. (2022) 'Can inheritance taxation promote equality opportunities?', *LSE Public Policy Review*, 2(4): 1–14.

Fletcher, D.R. and Wright, S. (2018) 'A hand up or a slap down? Criminalising benefit claimants in Britain via strategies of surveillance, sanctions and deterrence', *Critical Social Policy*, 38(2): 323–344.

Foucault, M. (1970) *The Order of Things*, New York: Pantheon.

Foucault, M. (1972) *The Archaeology of Knowledge*, London: Tavistock Publications.

Foucault, M. (1975) *Discipline and Punish. The Birth of the Prison*, London: Penguin.

Foucault, M. (1982). 'The subject and power', Afterword to H. Dreyfus and P. Rabinow (eds) *Michel Foucault: Beyond Structuralism and Hermeneutics*, Chicago: University of Chicago Press.

Foucault, M. (1984) 'Nietzsche, genealogy, history' in P. Rabinow (ed) *The Foucault Reader*, New York: Pantheon, pp 76–100.

Foucault, M. (1988) *Politics, Philosophy, Culture: Interviews and Other Writings 1977–1984*, New York: Routledge

Foucault, M. (1990) *The History of Sexuality: Volume I: An Introduction*, New York: Vintage Books.

Foucault, M. (2001) *Fearless Speech*, Los Angeles: Semiotext(e).

Foucault, M. (2003) *Society Must Be Defended*, New York: Pantheon.

Frankfurt, H.G. (2005) *On Bullshitting*, Princeton: Princeton University Press.

Fraser, D. (2017) *The Evolution of the British Welfare State*, London: Palgrave Macmillan.

Fricker, M. (1999) 'Epistemic oppression and epistemic privilege', *Canadian Journal of Philosophy*, 29(1): 191–210.

Fricker, M. (2007) *Epistemic Injustice: Power and the Ethics of Knowing*, Oxford: Oxford University Press.

Fricker, M. (2013) 'Epistemic justice as a condition of political freedom', *Syntheses*, 190(7): 1317–1332.

Fricker, M. (2015) 'Epistemic contribution as a central human capability' in G. Hull (ed), *The Equal Society*, Hull: Lexington Books, pp 73–90.

Fricker, M. (2016) 'Epistemic Injustice and the Preservation of Ignorance,' in M. Blauw and R. Peels (eds) *The Epistemic Dimensions of Ignorance*, Cambridge: Cambridge University Press, pp 144–159.

Fricker, M. (2017) 'Evolving Concepts of Epistemic Injustice' in I.J. Kidd, J. Medina and G. Pohlhaus Jr. (eds) *The Routledge Handbook of Epistemic Justice*, Abingdon: Routledge, pp 53–60.

Friedman, S. and Reeves, A. (2020) 'From aristocratic to ordinary: shifting modes of elite distinction', *American Sociological Review*, 85(2): 323–350.

Fukuda-Parr, S., Randolph, S. and Lawson-Remer, T. (2009) 'An index of economic and social rights fulfilment: concept and methodology', *Journal of Human Rights*, 8(3): 195–221.

Galimberti, G. and Woods, P. (2015) *The Heavens Annual Report*, Heaton Moor: Dewi Lewis Media.

García-Sánchez, E., Osborne, D., Willis, G.B., Rodríguez-Bailón, R. (2020) 'Attitudes towards redistribution and the interplay between perceptions and beliefs about inequality', *British Journal of Social Psychology*, 59: 111–136, https://doi.org/10.1111/bjso.12326

Garland, D. (2014) 'What is a "history of the present"? On Foucault's genealogies and their critical preconditions', *Punishment and Society*, 16(4): 365–384.

Garthwaite, K. (2012) 'The "scrounger" myth is causing real suffering to many in society', *LSE British Politics and Policy* [online], Available from: https://blogs.lse.ac.uk/politicsandpolicy/the-scrounger-myth-is-causing-real-suffering-to-many-in-society/ [Accessed 14 July 2020].

Genosko, G. (2005) *Marshall McLuhan: Theoretical Elaborations Vol. 2*, London: Taylor & Francis.

Gentleman, A. (2012) 'We have missed in-work poverty', *The Guardian* [online], 19 June, Available from: https://www.theguardian.com/society/2012/jun/19/christian-guy-managing-director-centre-social-justice [Accessed 3 June 2016].

Gentleman, A. (2018) '"I've been here for 50 years": the scandal of the former Commonwealth citizens threatened with deportation', *The Guardian* [online], 21 February, Available from: https://www.theguardian.com/uk-news/2018/feb/21/ive-been-here-for-50-years-the-scandal-of-the-former-commonwealth-citizens-threatened-with-deportation [Accessed 17 March 2019].

Geoghegan, P. (2024) 'Home Office accused of cover-up over "golden visas" for super-rich Russians', *The Guardian* [online], 24 February, Available from: https://www.theguardian.com/politics/2024/feb/24/home-office-accused-of-cover-up-over-golden-visas-for-super-rich-russians [Accessed 24 February 2024].

Gilens, A. (2012) *Affluence and Influence: Economic Inequality and Political Power in America*, Princeton: Princeton University Press.

Giridharadas, A. (2019) *Winners Take All*, London: Allen Lane.

Glennester, H. (2012) 'Why was a wealth tax for the UK abandoned? Lessons for the policy processes and tackling wealth inequality', *Journal of Social Policy*, 41(2): 233–249.

Glucksberg, L. (2016) 'Gendering the elites: an ethnographic approach to elite women's lives and the re-production of inequality', Working Paper 7, International Inequalities Institute, London School of Economics and Political Science, London.

Glucksberg, L. and Burrows, R. (2016) 'Family offices and the contemporary infrastructures of dynastic wealth', *Sociologica*, 10(2): 1–23.

Gokmenoglu, B. (2022) 'Temporality in the social sciences: new directions for a political sociology of time', *British Journal of Sociology*, 73: 643–653.

Good Ancestor Movement (n.d.) Available from: https://www.goodancestormovement.com/ [Accessed 28 May 2024].

Gough, I., Meadowcroft, J., Dryzek, J., Gerhards, J., Lengfeld, H., Markandya, A. and Ortiz, R. (2008) 'Climate change and social policy', *Journal of European Social Policy*, 18(4): 325–344.

Grant, H. and Kelly, A. (2016) 'UK visa policy 'increasing abuse' of foreign maids, says damning review', *The Guardian* [online], Available from: https://www.theguardian.com/global-development/2016/jan/11/uk-increasing-abuse-foreign-maids-tied-visas [Accessed 27 May 2024].

Grant, H. and Michael, C. (2019) 'Too poor to play: children in social housing blocked from communal playground', *The Guardian* [online], 25 March, Available from: https://www.theguardian.com/cities/2019/mar/25/too-poor-to-play-children-in-social-housing-blocked-from-communal-playground [Accessed 13 June 2019].

Gray, N. and Mooney, G. (2011) 'Glasgow's new urban frontier: "civilising" the population of "Glasgow East"', *City*, 15(1): 4–24.

Green., F., Henseke, G. and Vignoles, A. (2017) 'Private schooling and labour market ourcomes', *British Educational Research Journal*, 43(1): 7–28.

Greenfield, L. (2017) *Generation Wealth*, London: Phaidon Press.

Griffiths, R. (2018) 'Universal Credit, women and gender equality: a retrograde step?', *Institute of Policy Research* [blog], Available from: https://blogs.bath.ac.uk/iprblog/2018/09/19/universal-credit-women-and-gender-equality-a-retrograde-step/ [Accessed 19 July 2023].

Guardian, The (2017) 'The Panama Papers, a special investigation into the leaked documents created by Panamanian law firm Mossack Fonseca', *The Guardian* [online], Available from: https://www.theguardian.com/news/series/panama-papers [Accessed 19 October 2019].

Haggerty, K.D. and Ericson, R.V. (2000) 'The surveillant assemblage', *British Journal of Sociology*, 51(4): 605–622.

Hall, S. and Savage, M. (2016) 'Animating the urban vortex: new sociological urgencies', *International Journal of Urban and Regional Research*, 40(1): 82–95.

Halpern, D. and Sanders, M. (2016) 'Nudging by government: progress, impact, & lessons learned', *Behavioral Science & Policy*, 2(2): 53–65.

Hancock, A.M. (2004) *The Politics of Disgust: The Public Identity of the Welfare Queen*, New York: New York University Press.

Hardoon, D., Fuentes-Nieva, R. and Ayele, S. (2016) 'An economy for the 1%: how privilege and power in the economy drive extreme inequality and how this can be stopped', *Oxfam International* [online], 18 January, Available from: https://policy-practice.oxfam.org/resources/an-economy-for-the-1-how-privilege-and-power-in-the-economy-drive-extreme-inequ-592643/ [Accessed 9 May 2019].

Hardos, P. (2018) 'What exactly is an expert? On the problem of defining and recognising expertise', *Sociologica*, 50(3): 268–290.

Harling, P. (1992) 'The power of persuasion: central authority, local bureaucracy and the New Poor Law', *English Historical Review*, 107(422): 30–53.

Harrington, B. (2016a) *Capital without Borders: Wealth Managers and the One Percent*, Cambridge, MA: Harvard University Press.

Harrington, B. (2016b) 'To have and have more: wealth management and the growth of global inequality', *OECD Social and Welfare Issues* [online], Available from: http://www.oecd.org/social/wealth-management-global-inequality.htm [Accessed 23 January 2017].

Hay, D. (1975) 'Property, authority and the criminal law' in D. Hay, P. Linebaugh, J.G. Rule, E.P. Thompson and C. Winslow (eds) *Albion's Fatal Tree: Crime and Society in 18th Century England*, London: Verso, pp 17–65.

Hebden, P. and Palmer, R. (2020) *What's Wealth Got to Do with It? Attitudes on Public Spending, Wealth and Tax. A Report by Tax Justice UK*, Available from: https://www.taxjustice.uk/uploads/1/0/0/3/100363766/whats_wealth_got_to_do_with_it_.pdf [Accessed 1 May 2024].

Hebden, P., Palmer, R. and O'Hagan, E.M. (2020) *Talking Tax: How to Win Support for Taxing Wealth. A Report by Tax Justice UK*, Available from: https://www.taxjustice.uk/uploads/1/0/0/3/100363766/talking_tax_-_how_to_win_support_for_taxing_wealth.pdf [Accessed 1 May 2024].

Hecht, K. (2017) 'A relational analysis of top incomes and wealth: economic evaluation, relative (dis)advantage and the service to capital', Working Paper 11, International Inequalities Institute, LSE.

Hecht, K. and Summers, K. (2021) 'The long and short of it: the temporal significance of wealth and income', *Social Policy and Administration*, 55(4): 732–746.

Hecht, K., Savage, M. and Summers, K. (2022) 'Why isn't there more support for Progressive Taxation of Wealth? A sociological contribution to the wider debate', *LSE Public Policy Review* [online], Available from: https://ppr.lse.ac.uk/articles/10.31389/lseppr.65 [Accessed 2 September 2023].

Henriques, U. (1968) 'How cruel was the Victorian Poor Law?', *Historical Journal*, 11(2): 365–371.

Hickel, J. and Kallis, G. (2020) 'Is green growth possible?', *New Political Economy*, 259(4): 469–486.

Hickman, M.J. and Ryan, L. (2020) 'The "Irish question": marginalisations at the nexus of sociology of migration and ethnic and racial studies in Britain', *Ethnic and Racial Studies*, 43(16): 96–114.

Hills, J. (2017) *Good Times, Bad Times: The Welfare Myth of Them and Us*, Bristol: Bristol University Press.

Hills, J., Bastagli, F., Cowell, F., Glennerster, H., Karagiannaki, E. and McKnight, A. (2013) *Wealth in the UK: Distribution, Accumulation and Policy*, Oxford: Oxford University Press.

Himmelweit, S. (2023) 'Gender and taxation' in A. Lymer, M. May and A. Sinfield (eds) *Taxation and Social Policy*, Bristol: Policy Press, pp 182–201.

Hindle, S. (2004) 'The changing experience of poor relief' in *On the Parish? The Micro-politics of Poor Relief in Rural England 1550–1750*, Oxford: Oxford University Press, pp 450–456.

Hirneis, V. (2023) *Towards the Manifestos: What's the Agenda for Fixing Poverty and Tackling Inequality?* [online], Available from: https://www.inclusivegrowth.co.uk/wp-content/uploads/2023/07/towards-the-manifestos-solutions-for-tackling-poverty-and-inequality-full-report.pdf [Accessed 2 September 2023].

HM Government (2010) *The Coalition: Our Programme of Government*, London: HMSO, Available from: https://assets.publishing.service.gov.uk/media/5a74a4b3e5274a5294069025/coalition_programme_for_government.pdf [Accessed 24 May 2024].

HM Government (2011) *Opening Doors Breaking Barriers: A Strategy for Social Mobility*, London: HMSO.

HMRC (2017) *Our Strategy* (withdrawn in April 2021; archived version available from: https://assets.publishing.service.gov.uk/government/uploads/system/uploads/attachment_data/file/979243/HMRC-Strategy-ARCHIVED.pdf]) [Accessed 2 September 2023].

HMRC (2023) 'Minutes from the Wealthy External Forum', Available from: https://www.gov.uk/government/groups/high-net-worth-unit-external-stakeholder-forum#meeting-minutes [Accessed 27 May 2024].

Hoppit, J. (1996) 'Political arithmetic in eighteenth-century England', *Economic History Review*, 49(3): 518–519.

Horwell, S.W. (2019) 'Taxation in British political and economic thought, 1733–1816', Doctoral dissertation, UCL (University College London).

House of Commons (1846) *Report from the Select Committee on Andover Union Together with the Minutes of Evidence, Appendix and Index*, House of Commons Parliamentary Papers [online], 20 August, Available from: https://parlipapers.proquest.com/parlipapers/result/pqpdocumentview?accountid=9630&groupid=107925&pgId=09f77799-644c-4f3b-8e87-96fe1bc923fe [Accessed 30 May 2024].

House of Commons Library (2021) 'Tax avoidance and tax evasion', *House of Commons Library Research Briefing* [online], Available from: https://commonslibrary.parliament.uk/research-briefings/cbp-7948/ [Accessed January 2024].

House of Commons Public Administration Select Committee (2013) *Public Engagement in Policy-Making*, London: The Stationery Office.

Hoyt, C.L., Moss, A.J., Burnette, J.L., Schieffelin, A. and Goethals, A. (2018) 'Wealth inequality and activism: perceiving injustice galvanizes social change but perceptions depend on political ideologies', *European Journal of Social Psychology*, 48: 81–90, https://doi.org/10.1002/ejsp.2289

Hughes, N. and Riddell, P. (2016) 'Iain Duncan Smith: minister interview', *Institute for Government* [online], Available from: https://www.instituteforgovernment.org.uk/ministers-reflect/person/iain-duncan-smith/ [Accessed 19 March 2020].

Hunt, T. (2011) 'Reviving our sense of mission: designing a new political economy' in R. Philpot (ed) *The Purple Book*, London: Biteback, pp 61–79.

In Their Own Write (2018a) 'Universal Credit: the new, New Poor Law?', Available from: https://intheirownwriteblog.com/category/poverty/ [Accessed 20 March 2020].

In Their Own Write (2018b) 'Work at any cost? Lessons from the archives', Available from: https://intheirownwriteblog.com/category/employment-rights/ [Accessed 2 December 2020].

In Their Own Write (2019a) 'Poverty, honesty and the welfare state: a reality check', Available from: https://intheirownwriteblog.com/2019/01/23/578/ [Accessed 2 December 2020].

In Their Own Write (2019b) 'The "scandal" of in-work poverty revisited', Available from: https://intheirownwriteblog.com/category/in-work-poverty/ [Accessed 2 December 2020].

In Their Own Write (2019c) 'Paupers, politics and the power of the pen', Available from: https://intheirownwriteblog.com/category/political-lobbying/ December 2020.

In Their Own Write (2020) '"Drunk, drunk, drunken bich": the crime (and occasional merits) of anonymity', Available from: https://intheirownwriteblog.wordpress.com/2020/02/26/drunk-drunk-drunken-bich-the-merits-of-anonymity/ [Accessed 2 December 2020].

In Their Own Write (2021) 'Pictures at a workhouse (after Mussorgsky ... and Emerson, Lake and Palmer!)', Available from: https://intheirownwriteblog.wordpress.com/category/pictures/ [Accessed 2 December 2020].

Ingold, K., Fischer, M. and Cairney, P. (2017) 'Drivers for policy agreement in nascent subsystems: an application of the advocacy coalition framework to fracking policy in Switzerland and the UK', *Policy Studies Journal*, 45(3): 442–463.

Inman, P. (2021) 'UK overseas territories top list of world's leading tax havens', *The Guardian* [online], 9 March, Available from: https://www.theguardian.com/business/2021/mar/09/uk-overseas-territories-top-list-of-worlds-leading-tax-havens [Accessed 9 March 2021].

James. D. (2016) 'Elite expose', *British Journal of Photography*, 7844: 32–34.

Janbur, R. and Snell, W. (2019) 'Inequality indices as tests of fairness', *Economic Journal*, 129(621): 2216–2239.

Jaworski, A. and Thurlow, C. (2017) 'Mediatizing the "super-rich", normalizing privilege', *Social Semiotics*, 27: 276–287, https://doi.org/10.1080/10350330.2017.1301792

Jay, M. (1988) 'Scopic regimes of modernity' in H. Foster (ed), *Vision and Visuality*, Seattle, WA: Bay Press, pp 3–29.

Jeffrey-Cook, J. (2010) 'William Pitt and his taxes', *British Tax Review*, 4: 376–91.

Jencks, C. (2002) 'Does inequality matter?', *Daedalus*, 131(1): 49–65.

Jobson, C. and Athey, T. (2021) 'Half in and half against the state: the voluntary sector and the relief of poverty', Available from: https://www.whatstheproblem.org.uk/ [Accessed 14 April 2022].

Jones, J. (2017) *'The Patronising Disposition of Unaccountable Power': A Report to Ensure the Pain and Suffering of the Hillsborough Families Is Not Repeated*, House of Commons (HC511), Available from: https://assets.publishing.service.gov.uk/government/uploads/system/uploads/attachment_data/file/656130/6_3860_HO_Hillsborough_Report_2017_FINAL_updated.pdf [Accessed 19 August 2018].

Jones, O. (2011) *Chavs: The Demonisation of the Working Class*, London: Verso.

Jones, O. (2018) 'Corbyn and McDonnell tax radicals? I say they aren't radical enough', *The Guardian* [online], 15 February, Available from: https://www.theguardian.com/commentisfree/2018/feb/15/corbyn-mcdonnell-tax-radical-labour [Accessed 19 September 2019].

Jones, P., King, S. and Thompson, K. (2021) 'Clothing the New Poor Law workhouse in the nineteenth century', *Rural History*, 32(2): 127–148.

Joshi, P. (2004) 'Edwin Chadwick's self-fashioning: professionalism, masculinity and the Victorian poor', *Victorian Literature and Culture*, 32(2): 353–370.

Jowit, J. (2012) 'Iain Duncan Smith advisor being paid by thinktank lobbying his department', *The Guardian* [online], 5 November, Available from: https://www.theguardian.com/politics/2012/nov/05/iain-duncan-smith-adviser-lobbying?CMP=twt_gu [Accessed 23 May 2017].

Jowit, J. (2013) 'Strivers v shirkers: the language of the welfare debate', *The Guardian* [online], 8 January, Available from: https://www.theguardian.com/politics/2013/jan/08/strivers-shirkers-language-welfare [Accessed 14 December 2017].

Joyce, R. and Norris Keiller, A. (2018) 'Poverty and low pay in the UK: the state of play and the big challenges ahead', *Institute of Fiscal Studies* [online], Available from: https://ifs.org.uk/articles/poverty-and-low-pay-uk-state-play-and-challenges-ahead (Accessed 6 October 2019].

JRF (Joseph Rowntree Foundation) (2020a) 'Reporting poverty: a guide for media professionals', *JRF* [online], Available from: https://www.jrf.org.uk/report/reporting-poverty-guide-media-professionals [Accessed 1 December 2021].

JRF (2020b) 'Destitution in the UK 2020', *JRF* [online], Available from: https://www.jrf.org.uk/report/destitution-uk-2020 [Accessed 19 December 2020].

JRF (2023) '"Hunger on this scale isn't normally associated with a society in peacetime": JRF responds to latest food bank figures from the Trussell Trust', *JRF* [online], 26 April, Available from: https://www.jrf.org.uk/news/hunger-on-this-scale-isnt-normally-associated-with-a-society-in-peacetime

JRF (2024) 'UK poverty 2024', *JRF* [online], Available from: https://www.jrf.org.uk/uk-poverty-2024-the-essential-guide-to-understanding-poverty-in-the-uk [Accessed 1 February 2024].

Junemann, C., Ball, S.J. and Santori, D. (2015) 'Joined-up policy: network connectivity and global education policy' in K. Mundy, A Green, R. Lingard and T. Verger (eds) *Handbook of Global Policy and Policy-Making in Education*, Hoboken, NJ: Wiley-Blackwell, pp 535–553.

Karagiannaki, E. (2015) 'The impact of inheritance on the distribution of wealth: evidence from Great Britain', *LSE Research Online*, Available from: https://eprints.lse.ac.uk/62622/1/Karagiannaki_Impact%20of%20inheretance_2015.pdf [Accessed 19 June 2019].

Karagiannaki, E. (2023) 'The scale and drivers of ethnic wealth gaps across the wealth distribution in the UK: evidence from Understanding Society', LSE International Inequalities Institute, Working Paper 97, Available from: https://eprints.lse.ac.uk/119885/1/III_Working_Paper_97_Karagiannaki.pdf [Accessed 30 May 2024].

Kerr, S. (2021) 'Let's talk about wealtherty: turning the poverty conversation on its head', *Sociological Review Magazine*, https://doi.org/10.51428/tsr.bwmy9895

Kerr, S. (2023) 'Recognising and addressing wealth privilege in policymaking through an analysis of epistemic practice and agency', *Journal of Social Policy*, 1–17, doi:10.1017/S0047279423000363

Kerr, S. and Vaughan, M. (2024a) 'Changing the narrative on wealth inequality', Available from: https://www.jrf.org.uk/wealth-funding-and-investment-practice/changing-the-narrative-on-wealth-inequality [Accessed 28 May 2024].

Kerr, S. and Vaughan, M. (2024b) 'Effects of the framing of wealth inequality: a literature review', Available from: https://www.jrf.org.uk/wealth-funding-and-investment-practice/effects-of-the-framing-of-wealth-inequality-a-literature [Accessed 28 May 2024].

Khan, O. (2020) 'The colour of money: how racial inequality obstructs a fair and resilient economy', *Runnymede Trust* [online], Available from: https://www.runnymedetrust.org/publications/the-colour-of-money [Accessed 20 May 2021].

Kidd, I.J. and Carel, H. (2017) 'Epistemic injustice and illness', *Journal of Applied Philosophy*, 34(2): 172–190.

Kidd, I.J., Medina, J. and Pohlhaus Jr., G. (eds) (2017) *The Routledge Handbook of Epistemic Justice*, Abingdon: Routledge.

King, S. (2019) 'Re-imagining the workhouse for the welfare state: thoughts on the Alston Report', *In Their Own Write* [online], Available from: https://intheirownwriteblog.com/category/poverty/ [Accessed 20 February 2020].

Kingdon, J.W. (2011) *Agendas, Alternatives and Public Policies*, 2nd edn, Washington DC: Longman.

Kissack, P. (2020) 'It's vital we build strong communities and solve poverty', *JRF* [online], Available from: https://www.jrf.org.uk/blog/its-vital-ever-we-build-strong-communities-and-solve-poverty [Accessed 3 December 2020].

Kitchin, R., Gleeson, J. and Dodge, M. (2012) 'Unfolding mapping practices: a new epistemology for cartography', *Transactions of the Institute of British Geographers*, 38(3): 480–496.

Knight, B. (2017) *Rethinking Poverty*, Bristol: Policy Press.

Koller, V. and Davidson, P. (2008) 'Social exclusion as conceptual and grammatical metaphor: a cross-genre study of British policy-making', *Discourse and Society*, 19(3): 307–331.

Kopczuk, W. (2015) 'What do we know about the evolution of top wealth shares in the United States?', *Journal of Economic Perspectives*, 29(1): 47–66.

Koram, K. (2022) *Uncommon Wealth. Britain and the Aftermath of Empire*, London: Hachette.

Koreh, M. (2017) 'Political economy of social insurance: towards a fiscal-centred framework', *Social Policy and Administration*, 51(1): 114–232.

Kramm, M. and Robeyns, I. (2020) 'Limits to wealth in the history of Western philosophy', *European Journal of Philosophy*, 28: 954–969.

Kuhn, T. (2012) *The Structure of Scientific Revolutions*, 4th edition, London: University of Chicago Press.

Lackey, J. (2018) 'Group lies' in E. Michaelson and A. Stokke (eds) *Lying: Language, Knowledge and Politics*, Oxford: Oxford University Press, pp 262–284.

Lansley, S. (2012) *The Cost of Inequality: Three Decades of the Super-Rich and the Economy*, London: Gibson Square.

Lansley, S. (2022) *The Richer, The Poorer. How Britain Enriched the Few and Failed the Poor: A 200 Year History*, Bristol: Policy Press.

Levi, M. (1989) 'Introduction of the income tax in 18th century Britain' in M. Levi (ed) *Of Rule and Revenue*, Berkeley: University of California Press, pp 122–144.

Lewis, P. and Bosely, S. (2010) 'Iain Duncan Smith "distorted" research on childhood neglect and brain size', *The Guardian* [online], 9 April, Available from: https://www.theguardian.com/politics/2010/apr/09/iain-duncan-smith-childrens-brains [Accessed 5 December 2020].

Lierse, H., Sachweh, P. and Waitkus, N. (2022) 'Introduction: wealth, inequality and redistribution in capitalist societies', *Journal of Social Justice Research*, 35: 367–378.

Limberg, J. (2019) 'Tax the rich? The financial crisis, fiscal fairness and progressive income taxation', *European Political Science Review*, 11(3): 319–336.

Link, B and Phelan, J. (2014) 'Stigma power', *Social Science and Medicine*, 103: 24–32.

Lister, R. (2006) '*The Bare Life*' in S. Davidson *Bare Life* (Soundings 32), London: Lawrence and Wishart.

Lister, R. (2008) 'Recognition and voice: the challenge for social justice' in G. Craig, T. Burchardt and D. Gordon (eds) *Social Justice and Public Policy: Seeking Fairness in Diverse Societies*, Bristol: Policy Press, pp 105–122.

Littler, J. (2018) *Against Meritocracy: Culture, Power and Myths of Mobility*, Abingdon: Routledge.

Littler, J. (2019) 'Normcore plutocrats in gold elevators: reading the Trump Tower photographs', *Cultural Politics*, 15(1): 15–28.

LSE (London School of Economics and Political Science) (2018) *Tackling the Information Crisis: A Policy Framework for Media System Resilience. The Report of the LSE Commission on Truth, Trust and Technology* [online], Available from: https://www.lse.ac.uk/media-and-communications/assets/documents/research/T3-Report-Tackling-the-Information-Crisis.pdf [Accessed 2 June 2023].

LSE (2021) '"The return of inequality": a panel with Mike Savage, Gurminder Bhambra, Alpa Shah and Patrick le Gales' *YouTube* [online] 7 June, Available from: https://www.youtube.com/watch?v=ecDPf1JeyqA [Accessed 20 June 2021].

LSE (2024) 'Limtarianism: the case against extreme wealth' *YouTube* [online] 2 February, Available at: https://www.youtube.com/watch?v=I3wIS0ZK DGM&ab_channel=LSE [Accessed 28 May 2024].

Lymer, A. (2023) 'Tax and the social policy landscape' in A. Lymer, M. May and A. Sinfield (eds) *Taxation and Social Policy*, Bristol: Policy Press, pp 23–45.

Lymer, A., May, M. and Sinfield, A. (2023) 'Conclusions: taxation in a social policy context' in A. Lymer, M. May and A. Sinfield (eds) *Taxation and Social Policy*, Bristol: Policy Press, pp 267–281.

Magnus, D. (2008) 'Risk management versus the precautionary principle: agnotology as a strategy in the debate over genetically engineered organisms' in R.N. Proctor and L. Schiebinger (eds) *Agnotology: The Making and Unmaking of Ignorance*, Stanford: Stanford University Press, pp 250–265.

Marsh, D. and Smith, M. (2000) 'Understanding policy networks: towards a dialectical approach', *Political Studies*, 48(1): 4–21.

Marshall, J. (1961) 'The Nottingham reformers and their contribution to the New Poor Law', *Economic History Review*, 13(3): 382–396.

Martin, I.W., Mehrotra, A.K. and Prasad, M. (2009) 'The thunder of history: the origins and development of the new fiscal sociology' in I.W. Martin, A.K. Mehrotra and M. Prasad (eds) *The New Fiscal Sociology: Taxation in Comparative and Historical Perspective*, Cambridge: Cambridge University Press, pp 1–27.

Marx, I. and Nolan, B. (2021) 'How wealth matters for social policy', *Journal of European Social Policy*, 31(5): 489–495.

Matsumoto, K. (2020) 'Ma – the Japanese concept of space and time' [online], 24 April, Available from: https://medium.com/@kiyoshimatsumoto/ma-the-japanese-concept-of-space-and-time-3330c83ded4c [Accessed 30 April 2021].

May, C. (2010) 'John Ruskin's political economy: "there is no wealth but life"', *British Journal of Politics and International Relations*, 12(2): 189–204, https://doi.org/10.1111/j.1467-856X.2010.00406.x

May, P.J., Koski, C. and Stramp, N. (2016) 'Issue expertise in policymaking', *Journal of Public Policy*, 36(2): 195–218.

May, T. (2016) 'Britain, the great meritocracy: Prime Minister's speech' [online], 9 September, Available from: https://www.gov.uk/government/speeches/britain-the-great-meritocracy-prime-ministers-speech [Accessed 15 January 2024].

May, T. (2017) 'The shared society' [online], 9 January, Available from: https://www.gov.uk/government/speeches/the-shared-society-prime-ministers-speech-at-the-charity-commission-annual-meeting [Accessed 15 June 2018].

Mayrit, D. (2015) *You Haven't Seen Their Faces*, London: Riot Books.

McCall, L. and Kenworthy, L. (2009) 'Americans' social policy preferences in the era of rising inequality', *Perspectives on Politics*, 7(3): 459–484.

McCardle, I. (2012) 'Man can be deported despite living in UK since age of three' [online], 15 April, Available from: https://ukhumanrightsblog.com/2012/04/15/man-can-be-deported-despite-living-in-uk-since-age-of-three/ [Accessed 14 December 2017].

McGee, S. and Moore, H. (2014) 'Women's rights and their money', *The Guardian* [online], 11 August, Available from: https://www.theguardian.com/money/us-money-blog/2014/aug/11/women-rights-money-timeline-history [Accessed 4 September 2023].

McGimpsey, I. (2017) 'Late neoliberalism: delineating a policy regime', *Critical Social Policy*, 37(1): 64–84.

McGimpsey, I., Bradbury, A. and Santori, D. (2016) 'Revisions to rationality: the translation of "new knowledges" into policy under the Coalition government', *British Journal of Sociology of Education*, 38(6): 908–25.

McGoey, L. (2019) *The Unknowers: How Strategic Ignorance Rules the World*, London: Zed Books.

McGovern, P., Abramovic, S. and Bauer, M.W. (2020) 'Income inequality and the absence of a Tawney moment in the mass media', *LSE International Inequalities Institute*, Working Paper 53, Available from: https://eprints.lse.ac.uk/107535/1/LSE_III_working_paper_53.pdf [Accessed 15 April 2023].

Meadows White, J. (1834) *Remarks on the Poor Law Amendment Act, as it affects Unions or Parishes under the Government of Guardians or Select Vestries by John Meadows White, The Solicitor Employed in preparing the Act*, London: Fellows (Publishers to the Poor Law Commissioners).

Medina, J. (2011) 'The relevance of credibility excess in a proportional view of epistemic injustice: differential epistemic authority and the social imaginary', *Social Epistemology*, 25(1): 15–35.

Medina, J. (2013) 'Imposed silences and shared hermeneutical responsibilities' in J. Medina (ed), *The Epistemology of Resistance: Gender and Racial Oppression, Epistemic Injustice and the Social Imagination*, Oxford: Oxford University Press, pp 90–118.

Medina, J. (2017) 'Varieties of hermeneutical injustice' in J. Kidd, J. Medina and G. Pohlhaus Jr. (eds) *The Routledge Handbook of Epistemic Justice*, Abingdon: Routledge, pp 41–52.

Meriluoto, T. (2018) 'Turning experience into expertise: technologies of the self in Finnish participatory social policy', *Critical Policy Studies*, 12(3): 294–313.

Michaelson, E. and Stokke, A. (eds) (2018), *Lying: Language, Knowledge, Ethics and Politics*, Oxford: Oxford University Press.

Mies, M. (2014) *Patriarchy and Accumulation on a World Scale: Women in the International Division of Labour*, London: Zed Books.

Mijs, J.J.B. and Savage, M. (2020) 'Meritocracy, elitism and inequality', *Political Quarterly*, 91(2): 397–404.

Millar, J. and Bennett, F. (2017) 'Universal Credit: assumptions, contradictions and virtual reality', *Social Policy and Society*, 16(2): 169–182.

Mills, C. (2008) 'White ignorance' in R. Proctor and L. Schiebinger (eds) *Agnotology, The Making and Unmaking of Ignorance*, Stanford: Stanford University Press, pp 232–245.

Monaghan, M. and Ingold, J. (2019) 'Policy practitioners' accounts of evidence-based policy making: the case of Universal Credit', *Journal of Social Policy*, 48(2): 351–368.

Monbiot, G. (2010) 'Plan after plan fails to make Oxford access fair: there is another way', *The Guardian* [online], 24 May, Available from: https://www.theguardian.com/commentisfree/2010/may/24/oxbridge-access-fair-top-universities [Accessed 22 October 2013].

Mooney, G. (2009) 'The "broken society" election: class hatred and the politics of poverty and place in Glasgow East', *Social Policy and Society*, 8(4): 437–450.

Mooney, G. (2011) 'Stigmatising poverty? The "broken society" and reflections on anti-welfarism in the UK today', *Oxfam* [online], Available from: https://oro.open.ac.uk/29714/ [Accessed 28 July 2018].

Morgan, M.S. and Sinclair, I. (2019) *Charles Booth's London Poverty Maps*, London: Thames & Hudson.

Mukherjee, A. (2010) 'How colonial India made modern Britain', *Economic and Political Weekly*, 45(50): 73–82.

Murakami, H. (2016), *Absolutely on Music: Conversations with Seiji Ozawa*, London: Harvill Secker.

Mureithi, A. (2022) 'Revealed: UK's most secretive think tanks took £14.3m from mystery donors', *Open Democracy* [online], 20 June, Available from: https://www.opendemocracy.net/en/dark-money-investigations/think-tanks-transparency-funding-who-funds-you/ [Accessed 20 June 2023].

NAO (National Audit Office) (2014) 'Tax reliefs', Report by the comptroller and Auditor General, HC 1245 Session 2013–2014, 7 April, Available from: https://www.nao.org.uk/wp-content/uploads/2014/03/Tax-reliefs.pdf [Accessed 30 May 2024].

NAO (2016) *Benefit Sanctions HC 628 Session 2016–17*, London: The Stationery Office.

NEON (New Economy Organisers Network), NEF (New Economics Foundation), Frameworks Institute and PIRC (Public Interest Research Centre) (2018) *Framing the Economy: How to Win the Case for a Better System*, Available from: https://neweconomics.org/uploads/files/Framing-the-Economy-NEON-NEF-FrameWorks-PIRC.pdf [Accessed 20 June 2023].

Nanda, S. and Parkes, H. (2019) 'Just tax. Reforming the taxation of income from wealth and work', Institute for Public Policy Research (IPPR) Centre for Economic Justice, Available from: https://www.ippr.org/articles/just-tax [Accessed 20 May 2024].

Newman, I. (2011) 'Work as a route out of poverty: a critical evaluation of the UK welfare to work policy', *Policy Studies*, 32(2): 91–108.

Ngai, S. (2004) *Ugly Feelings*, Cambridge, MA: Harvard University Press.

Nussbaum, M. (2002) 'Capabilities and social justice', *International Studies Review*, 4(2): 123–135.

Nussbaum, M. (2011) *Creating Capabilities*, Cambridge, MA: Harvard University Press.

O'Brien, P.K. (1988) 'The political economy of British taxation, 1660–1815', *Economic History Review*, 41(1): 1–32.

O'Toole, F. (2018) 'A journalist on the frontline protecting an open society', *The Guardian* [online], 1 July, Available from: https://www.theguardian.com/commentisfree/2018/jul/01/carole-cadwalladr-orwell-prize-cambridge-analytica [Accessed 2 July 2018].

OECD (Organisation for Economic Co-operation and Development) (2009) *Engaging with High Net Worth Individuals on Tax Compliance* [online], Available from: https://read.oecd-ilibrary.org/taxation/engaging-with-high-net-worth-individuals-on-tax-compliance_9789264068872-en#page [Accessed 3 March 2021].

ONS (Office for National Statistics) (2019) 'Exploring the UK's digital divide: the scale of digital exclusion in the UK' [online], 4 March, Available from: https://www.ons.gov.uk/peoplepopulationandcommunity/householdcharacteristics/homeinternetandsocialmediausage/articles/exploringtheuksdigitaldivide/2019-03-04#introduction [Accessed 18 July 2021].

ONS (2022a) 'Wealth and assets survey: total wealth; wealth in Great Britain' [online], Available from: https://www.ons.gov.uk/peoplepopulationandcommunity/personalandhouseholdfinances/incomeandwealth/datasets/totalwealthwealthingreatbritain [Accessed 23 July 2023].

ONS (2022b) 'Regional gross disposable household income, UK: 1997–2020' [online], Available from: https://www.ons.gov.uk/economy/regionalaccounts/grossdisposablehouseholdincome/bulletins/regionalgrossdisposablehouseholdincomegdhi/1997to2020 [Accessed 23 July 2023].

Orton, M. (2006) 'Wealth, citizenship and responsibility: the views of the "better off" citizens in the UK', *Citizenship Studies*, 10(2): 192–207.

Orton, M. and Rowlingson, K. (2007) 'A problem of riches: towards a new social policy research agenda on the distribution of economic resources', *Journal of Social Policy*, 36(1): 59–77.

Orwell, G. (1933 [2001 edition]) *Down and Out in Paris and London*, London: Penguin.

Osbourne, G. (2012) 'Party conference speech 8 October 2012', *New Statesman* [online], Available from: https://www.newstatesman.com/blogs/politics/2012/10/george-osbornes-speech-conservative-conference-full-text [Accessed 14 November 2019].

PAC (Public Accounts Committee) (2017) *Collecting Tax from High Net Worth Individuals. Thirty-Sixth Report of Session 2016–17* (HC774), Available from: https://publications.parliament.uk/pa/cm201617/cmselect/cmpubacc/774/774.pdf

PAC (2016) *Tackling Tax Fraud. Thirty-Fourth Report of Session 2015–2016* (HC674), Available from: https://publications.parliament.uk/pa/cm201516/cmselect/cmpubacc/674/674.pdf

PAC (2018) *Universal Credit. Sixty-Fourth Report of Session 2017–2019* (HC1183), Available from: https://publications.parliament.uk/pa/cm201719/cmselect/cmpubacc/1183/1183.pdf

Palmer, R. (2020) 'Wealth, tax and gender', *Tax Justice UK* [online] January, Available from: https://wbg.org.uk/wp-content/uploads/2020/03/Paper-2-Wealth-tax-and-gender.pdf [Accessed 3 March 2020].

Patel, P., Swift, R. and Quilter-Pinner, H. (2023) 'Talking politics: building support for democratic freedom', *Institute of Public Policy Research (IPPR)* [online] June, Available from: https://www.ippr.org/research/publications/talking-politics-building-support-for-democratic-reform [Accessed 26 June 2023].

Patriotic Millionaires (n.d.) 'About us', Available from: https://patrioticmillionaires.uk/about-us [Accessed 28 May 2024].

Pautz, H. (2013) 'The think tanks behind "Cameronism"', *British Journal of Politics and International Relations*, 15: 362–377.

Pautz, H. and Heins, E. (2016) 'Government and "independent expertise": think tanks represent a blind spot for critical analysis', *LSE* [online], 6 January, Available from: https://blogs.lse.ac.uk/politicsandpolicy/52710-2/ [Accessed 7 August 2019].

Payne, G. (2017) 'The pessimism of earlier academic mobility analysis' in *The New Social Mobility: How Politicians Got It Wrong*, Bristol: Policy Press, pp 89–108.

Peck, J. and Theodore, N. (2010) 'Mobilizing policy: models, methods and mutations', *Geoforum*, 41: 169–174.

Peck, J. and Tickell, A. (2007) 'Conceptualizing neoliberalism, thinking Thatcherism', *Contesting Neoliberalism: Urban Frontiers*, 26(50): 1770–1187.

Pegg, D. (2017) 'The "golden visa" deal: we have in effect been selling off British citizenship to the rich', *The Guardian* [online], 4 July, Available from: https://www.theguardian.com/uk-news/2017/jul/04/golden-visa-immigration-deal-british-citizenship-home-office [Accessed 14 December 2017].

Pellicer, M. and Ranchhod, V. (2023) 'Understanding the effects of racial classification in apartheid South African', *Journal of Development Economics*, 160: 1–13.

Perret, S. (2020) 'Why did other wealth taxes fail and is this time different', *Wealth Tax Commission Evidence Paper*, 6(1–31).

Pfeffer, F.T. and Killewald, A. (2017) 'Generations of advantage: multigenerational correlations in family wealth', *Social Forces*, 96(4): 1411–1442.

Philp, M. (2014) 'Public ethics and political judgement', *Committee on Standards in Public Life* [online], Available from: https://assets.publishing.service.gov.uk/government/uploads/system/uploads/attachment_data/file/336977/2902536_CSPL_PublicPoliticalEthics_acc.pdf [Accessed 10 August 2017].

Piketty, T. (2014) *Capital in the 21st Century*, Cambridge, MA: Harvard University Press.

Piketty, T. (2021) *A Brief History of Equality*, Cambridge, MA: Belknap Press of Harvard University Press.

Piketty, T. and Zucman, G. (2013) 'Capital is back: wealth-income ratios in rich countries 1700–2010', *Quarterly Journal of Economics*, 129(3): 1255–1310.

Pistor, K. (2019) *The Code of Capital: How the Law Creates Wealth and Inequality*, Princeton: Princeton University Press.

Plunkett, J. (2023) 'Unequality: when inequality changes, our strategies must too', *JRF* [online], 31 January, Available from: https://medium.com/@jamestplunkett/unequality-when-inequality-changes-our-strategies-must-too-d4676d621b6b [Accessed 1 February 2023].

Pohlhaus Jr., G. (2014) 'Discerning the primary epistemic harm in cases of testimonial injustice', *Social Epistemology*, 28(2): 99–114.

Pohlhaus, G. (2017) 'Varieties of epistemic injustice 1', in *The Routledge Handbook of Epistemic Injustice*, Abingdon: Routledge, pp 13–26.

Pomeranz, K. (2000) *The Great Divergence: China, Europe, and the Making of the Modern World Economy*, Princeton: Princeton University Press.

Poor Law Commissioners (1847) *The General Consolidated Order Issued by the Poor Law Commissioners 24th July 1847 and the Other General Orders Applicable to the Unions to which that Order is Addressed; with a Commentary and Notes on the Several Articles*, London: Shaw & Sons.

Poynter, J.R. (1969) *Society and Pauperism: English Ideas on Poor Relief 1795–1834*, Liverpool: Kegan Paul.

Prabhakar, R. (2023) 'What are the barriers to taxing wealth? The case of a wealth tax proposal in the UK', *Journal of Social Policy*, 52: 700–717, https://doi.org/10.1017/S0047279421000891

Proctor, R.N. (2008) 'Agnotology: a missing term to describe the cultural production of ignorance (and its study)' in R. Proctor and L. Schiebinger (eds) *Agnotology: The Making and Unmaking of Ignorance*, Stanford: Stanford University Press, pp 1–33.

Proctor, R.N., and Schiebinger, L. (eds) (2008) *Agnotology: The Making and Unmaking of Ignorance*, Stanford: Stanford University Press.

Rancière, J. (2004) *The Politics of Aesthetics: The Distribution of the Sensible*, trans. by G. Rockhill, London and New York: Continuum.

Randall, A. and Newman, E. (1995) 'Protests, proletarians and paternalists: social conflict in rural Wiltshire, 1830–1850', *Rural History*, 6(2): 205–227.

Raworth, K. (2017) *Doughnut Economics: Seven Ways to Think Like a 21st-Century Economist*, Vermont: Chelsea Green Publishing.

Resolution Foundation (2010) 'Emergency budget 2010 and low earners', *Resolution Foundation* [online], 29 June, Available from: https://www.resolutionfoundation.org/app/uploads/2014/08/2010-Emergency-Budget-and-low-earners.pdf [Accessed 13 October 2019].

Resolution Foundation (2021) 'Top 1% has almost £800bn more wealth than official statistics show', *Resolution Foundation* [online], 3 January, Available from: https://www.resolutionfoundation.org/press-releases/top-1-per-cent-has-almost-800-billion-more-wealth-than-official-statistics-show/ [Accessed 3 January 2021].

Riddell, R. (2013) 'Changing policy levers under the neoliberal state: realising coalition policy on education and social mobility', *Journal of Education Policy*, 28(6): 847–863.

Riddell, R., Ahmed, N., Maitland, A., Lawson, M. and Taneja, A. (2024) 'Inequality Inc: how corporate power divides our world and the need for a new era of public action', *Oxfam International* [online], Available from: https://policy-practice.oxfam.org/resources/inequality-inc-how-corporate-power-divides-our-world-and-the-need-for-a-new-era-621583/ [Accessed 3 April 2024].

Ridge, T. and Wright, S. (2008) *Understanding Inequality, Poverty and Wealth*, Bristol: Policy Press.

Roberts, D. (1963) 'How cruel was the Victorian Poor Law?', *Historical Journal*, 6(1): 97–107.

Robeyns, I. (2017a) *Wellbeing, Freedom and Social Justice*, Open Book Publishers [online], Available from: http://library.oapen.org/handle/20.500.12657/30821 [Accessed 3 April 2024].

Robeyns, I. (2017b) 'Having too much', *Nomos*, 58: 1–44.

Robeyns, I. (2018) 'Philosophy with feet in the mud: an interview with Ingrid Robeyns', *Erasmus Journal for Philosophy and Economics*, 11(1): 80–99.

Robeyns, I. (2019) 'What, if anything, is wrong with extreme wealth?', *Journal of Human Development and Capabilities*, 20(3): 251–266.

Robeyns, I., Buskens, V., van de Rijt, A., Vergeldt, N. and van der Lippe, T. (2021) 'How rich is too rich? Measuring the riches line', *Social Indicators Research*, 154: 115–143, https://doi.org/10.1007/s11205-020-02552-z

Robeyns, I. (2024) *Limitarianism: The Case against Extreme Wealth*. London: Penguin.

Robinson, J.A. and Acemoglu, D. (2012) *Why Nations Fail: The Origins of Power, Prosperity and Poverty*, London: Profile Books.

Rose, N. (1999) *Powers of Freedom*, Cambridge: Cambridge University Press.

Rowlingson, K. (2011) 'Does income inequality cause health and social problems?', *JRF* [online], 22 September, Available from: https://www.jrf.org.uk/report/does-income-inequality-cause-health-and-social-problems [Accessed 19 October 2017].

Rowlingson, K. (2023) 'Wealth taxation: the case for reform' in A. Lymer, M. May and A. Sinfield (eds) *Taxation and Social Policy*, Bristol: Policy Press, pp 164–181.

Rowlingson, K. and Connor, S. (2011) 'The "deserving" rich? Inequality, morality and social policy', *Journal of Social Policy*, 40(3): 437–452.

Rowlingson, K. and McKay, S. (2011) 'What is wealth and who are the wealthy?' in *Wealth and the Wealthy: Exploring and Tackling Inequalities between Rich and Poor*, Bristol: Policy Press, pp 53–80.

Rowlingson, K. and Orton, M. (2007) 'A problem of riches: towards a new social policy research agenda on the distribution of economic resources', *Journal of Social Policy*, 36(1): 59–77.

Rowlingson, K., Sood, A. and Tu, T. (2020) 'Public attitudes to a wealth tax', *Fiscal Studies*, 42(3–4): 431–455.

Ruane, S. (2012) 'Bringing corporate welfare in – and pushing further at the boundaries of social policy: a reply to Farnsworth', *Journal of Social Policy*, 42(1): 23–29.

Ruskin, J. (2010 [1862]) *Unto this Last: Four Essays on the First Principles of Political Economy*, London: Pallas Athene.

Ruskin, J. (1991) *The Elements of Drawing*, London: Herbert Press.

Sandel, M.J. (2020) *The Tyranny of Merit: What's Become of the Common Good?*, London: Penguin.

Savage, M. (2015) 'Interview with Thomas Piketty', International Inequalities Institute Working Paper 1, *LSE* [online], Available from: http://www.lse.ac.uk/International-Inequalities/Assets/Documents/Working-Papers/Working-Paper-1-Mike-Savage.pdf [Accessed 20 December 2017].

Savage, M. (2018) 'Britain's low-paid face decade of wage squeeze', *The Guardian* [online], 3 June, Available from: https://www.theguardian.com/money/2018/jun/02/low-paid-face-decade-wage-squeeze [Accessed 19 June 2018].

Savage, M. (2021) *The Return of Inequality: Social Change and the Weight of the Past*, Cambridge, MA: Harvard University Press.

Savage, M. (2023) 'Why non-domiciled tax payers are a sociological – and political! – issue', *Discover Society: New Series* 3(3), https://doi.org/10.51428/dsoc.2023.03.0003

Savage, M. (2024) 'Why wealth inequality matters – and what to do about it!', *LSE* [online], Available from: https://blogs.lse.ac.uk/inequalities/2024/02/20/why-wealth-inequality-matters/ [Accessed 21 February 2024].

Savage, M., Mahmoudzadeh, M., Mann, E., Vaughan, M. and Hilhorst, S. (2024) *Why Wealth Inequality Matters*, London: LSE International Inequalities Institute.

Sayer, A. (2015) *Why We Can't Afford the Rich*, Bristol: Policy Press.

Scheurich, J.J. (1994) 'Policy archaeology: a new policy studies methodology', *Journal of Education Policy*, 9(4): 297–316.

Schwartz, B. (1974) 'Waiting, exchange, and power: the distribution of time in social systems', *American Journal of Sociology*, 79(4): 841–870.

Scott, J. (1994) *Poverty and Wealth: Citizenship, Deprivation and Privilege*, New York: Longman.

Scott Paul, A. (2017) 'Abigail Scott Paul: context is vital to anti-poverty storytelling', *Third Sector* [online], 2 August, Available from: https://www.thirdsector.co.uk/abigail-scott-paul-context-vital-anti-poverty-storytelling/communications/article/1440997 [Accessed 3 August 2017].

Seely, A. (2021) 'Tax avoidance and evasion: House of Commons Library briefing paper number 7948', *House of Commons Library* [online], 24 November, Available from: https://commonslibrary.parliament.uk/research-briefings/cbp-7948/ [Accessed 2 December 2021].

Seligman, E.R.A. (1914) *The Income Tax: A Study of the History, Theory and Practice of Income Taxation at Home and Abroad*, New York: Augustus M. Kelley Publishers.

Sen, A. (1999) *Development as Freedom*, Oxford: Oxford University Press.

Sen, S. (2017) 'From dispossession to dissection: the bare life of the English pauper in the age of the Anatomy Act and the New Poor Law', *Victorian Studies*, 59(2): 235–259.

Serafini, P. and Maguire, J. (2019) 'Questioning the superrich: representations, structures and experiences', *Cultural Politics*, 15: 1–14.

Shave, S. (2017) *Pauper Policies: Poor Law Practice in England, 1780–1850*, Manchester: Manchester University Press.

Shaxson, N. (2012) *Treasure Islands; Tax Havens and the Men Who Stole the World*, London: Vintage.

Shaxson, N. (2018) *The Finance Curse: How Global Finance Is Making Is All Poorer*, London: Vintage.

Shaxson, N., Christensen, J. and Mathiason, N. (2012a) 'Inequality: you don't know the half of it, or why inequality is worse than we thought', *Tax Justice Network* [online], 19 July, Available from: https://taxjustice.net/wp-content/uploads/2020/11/Inequality_120722_You_dont_know_the_half_of_it.pdf [Accessed 23 July 2017].

Siddons, E. (2024) 'HMRC has not charged a single company over tax evasion under landmark legislation', *The Guardian* [online], 20 January, Available from: https://www.theguardian.com/politics/2024/jan/20/hmrc-has-not-charged-a-single-company-over-tax-evasion-under-landmark-legislation [Accessed 20 January 2024].

Siddons, E. and Ungoed-Thomas, J. (2024) 'HMRC investigations of wealth tax dodgers halve in five years', *The Guardian* [online], 18 February, Available from: https://www.theguardian.com/politics/2024/feb/18/hmrc-investigations-of-wealthy-tax-dodgers-halve-in-five-years?CMP=Share_AndroidApp_Other [Accessed 29 February 2024].

Sieghart, M.A. (2010) 'Profile – Iain Duncan Smith, Work and Pensions Secretary', *BBC Sounds*, 16 October, Available from: https://www.bbc.co.uk/sounds/play/b00vc1ry

Simpson, L. (2017) 'Epistemic and political agency' in I.J. Kidd, J. Medina and G. Pohlhaus Jr. (eds) *The Routledge Handbook of Epistemic Injustice*, London: Routledge, pp 254–261.

Sinfield, A. (2023) 'Fiscal welfare and tax expenditure' in A. Lymer, M May and A. Sinfield (eds) *Taxation and Social Policy*, Bristol: Policy Press, pp 44–66.

Skeggs, B. (2005) 'The making of class and gender through visualising moral subject formation', *Sociology*, 39(5): 965–982.

Skeggs, B. (2014) 'Legitimating slow death: a brief but long history of the use, abuse and demonization of labour by the media' [online], Available from: https://values.doc.gold.ac.uk/blog/17/ [Accessed 6 November 2019].

Skeggs, B. (2019) 'The forces that shape us: the entangled vine of gender, race and class', *The Sociological Review*, 67(1): 28–35.

Skidelsky, R. and Skidelsky, E. (2013) *How Much Is Enough? Money and the Good Life*, London: Penguin.

Skilling, P. and McLay, J. (2015) 'Getting ahead through our own efforts: public attitudes towards the deservingness of the rich in New Zealand', *Journal of Social Policy*, 44(1): 147–169.

Sklair, J. (2018) 'Closeness and critique among Brazilian philanthropists: navigating a critical ethnography of wealth elites', *Focaal*, 81: 29–42, https://doi.org/10.3167/fcl.2018.810103

Sklair, J. (2023) 'The win-win discourse of impact investing: legitimising accumulation for a new generation of Brazilian wealth elites', *Canadian Journal of Development Studies*, https://doi.org/10.1080/02255189.2023.2251645

Sklair, J. and Glucksberg, L. (2021) 'Philanthrocapitalism as wealth management strategy: philanthropy, inheritance and succession planning among the global elite', *Sociological Review*, 69(2): 314–329.

Slack, P. (1980) 'Social policy and the constraints of government 1547–58' in J. Loach and R. Tittler (eds) *The Mid-Tudor Polity 1540–1560*, London: Macmillan, pp 94–115.

Slack, P. (1988) *Poverty and Policy in Tudor and Stuart England*, Harlow: Longman

Slack, P. (2004) 'Government and information in seventeenth century England', *Past and Present*, 184: 33–68.

Slater, T. (2008) '"A literal necessity to be re-placed": a rejoinder to the gentrification debate', *International Journal of Urban and Regional Research*, 32(1): 212–223.

Slater, T. (2011) 'From "criminality" to marginality: rioting against a broken state', *Human Geography*, 4(3): 106–115.

Slater, T. (2012) 'The myth of "broken Britain": welfare reform and the production of ignorance', *Antipode*, 46(4): 948–969.

Slater, T. (2018) 'The invention of the "sink estate": consequential categorisation and the UK housing crisis', *Sociological Review*, 66(4): 877–897.

Smirnova, O. (2016) 'Just who owns what in central London?', *BBC News* [online], 21 March, Available from: http://www.bbc.co.uk/news/business-35757265 [Accessed 13 February 2017].

Smith-Merry, J. (2020) 'Evidence-based policy, knowledge from experience and validity', *Evidence and Policy*, 16(2): 305–316.

Smith, M. (2021) 'Boris Johnson says rich parents can buy private tuition because they work hard', *The Mirror* [online], 9 June, Available from: https://www.mirror.co.uk/news/politics/boris-johnson-says-rich-parents-24282642 [Accessed 9 October 2022].

Smithson, M.J. (2008) 'Towards a social theory of ignorance' in R. Proctor and L. Schiebinger (eds) *Agnotology: The Making and Unmaking of Ignorance*, Stanford: Stanford University Press, pp 209–230.

Smyth, D. (2016) 'A new wave of political art?', *British Journal of Photography*, 2016 #7844: 4–20.

Spicker, P. (1984) *Stigma and Social Welfare*, London: Palgrave Macmillan.

Standing, G. (2019a) 'Sharing public wealth: why we need a Charter of the Commons', *LSE Blog* [online], Available from: https://blogs.lse.ac.uk/politicsandpolicy/charter-of-the-commons/

Standing, G. (2019b) *Plunder of the Commons: A Manifesto for Sharing Public Wealth*, London: Penguin.

Standring, A. (2018) 'Depoliticising austerity narratives of the Portuguese debt crisis 2011–2015', *Policy and Politics*, 46(1): 149–164.

Stantcheva, S. (2021) 'Understanding tax policy: how do people reason?', *The Quarterly Journal of Economics*, 136(4): 2309–2369.

Stebbings, C. (2009) 'Consent and constitutionality in 19th century English taxation', *Studies in the History of Tax Law*, 3: 305–334.

Steedman, C. (2000) 'Enforced narratives: stories of another self' in T. Cosslett, C. Lury and P. Summerfield (eds) *Feminism and Autobiography: Texts, Theories, Methods*, London: Routledge, pp 25–39.

Stewart, E., Smith-Merry, J. and Geddes, M. (2020) 'Opening up evidence-based policy: exploring citizen and service user expertise', *Evidence and Policy*, 16(2): 199–208.

Stone, D. (2004) 'Transfer agents and global networks in the "transnationalization" of policy', *Journal of European Public Policy*, 11(3): 545–566.

Stroud, P. and Leonard, C. (1999) *God's Heart for the Poor*, Eastbourne: Kingsway Publications.

Summers, A. (2022) 'Abolishing the non-dom regime would raise more than £3.2 billion each year, finds new report', *LSE News* [online], Available from: https://www.lse.ac.uk/News/Latest-news-from-LSE/2022/i-September-22/Abolishing-the-non-dom-regime-would-raise-more-than-3.2-billion-each-year-finds-new-report [Accessed 3 October 2022].

Summers, S. (2024) 'More capital gains are received in one neighbourhood in Kensington than in Liverpool, Manchester and Newcastle combined', *LSE News*, February 2024, Available from: https://www.lse.ac.uk/News/Latest-news-from-LSE/2024/b-February-2024/More-capital-gains-are-received-in-one-neighbourhood [Accessed 20 May 2024].

Summers, K., Accominotti, A., Burchardt, T., Hecht, K., Mann, E. and Mijs, J. (2022) 'Deliberating inequality: a blueprint for studying the social formation of beliefs about economic inequality', *Journal of Social Justice Research*, 35: 379–400.

The Sutton Trust and the Social Mobility Commission (2019) 'Elitist Britain 2019: the educational backgrounds of Britain's leading people', Available from: https://www.suttontrust.com/our-research/elitist-britain-2019/ [Accessed 28 May 2024].

Tamboukou, M. (1999) 'Writing genealogies: an exploration of Foucault's strategies for doing research', *Discourse: Studies in the Cultural Politics of Education*, 20(9): 201–207.

Tawney, R.H. (1964) *Equality*, London: Unwin Books.

Tawney, R.H. and Power, E. (1951) *Tudor Economic Documents*, Volume II, London: Longman, Green and Company.

Taxwatch UK (2021) 'Equality before the law? HMRC's use of criminal prosecutions for tax fraud and other revenue crimes. A comparison with benefits fraud', Available from: https://www.taxwatchuk.org/tax_crime_vs_benefits_crime/ [Accessed 24 May 2024].

Taylor-Gooby, P. (2013) 'Why do people stigmatise the poor at a time of rapidly increasing inequality, and what can be done about it?', *Political Quarterly*, 84(1): 31–42.

Thane, P. (1978) 'Women and the Poor Law in Victorian and Edwardian England', *History Workshop*, 6: 29–51.

Thane, P. (2010) *Happy Families? History and Family Policy*, London: British Academy Press.

Thane, P. (2019) *How Poverty in Modern Britain Echoes the Past*, London: British Academy Press.

The National Archives (n.d.) 'Agenda and minutes of the HNWU External Stakeholder Forum', Available from: https://webarchive.nationalarchives.gov.uk/ukgwa/20140206220801/http:/www.hmrc.gov.uk/consultations/hnwu-agenda.htm [Accessed 24 May 2024].

Thomas, C., Jung, C, Patel, P., Quilter-Pinner, H. and Statham, R. (2022) 'Health and prosperity: introducing the IPPR Commission on Health and Prosperity', Institute for Public Policy Research (IPPR), Available from: https://ippr-org.files.svdcdn.com/production/Downloads/health-and-prosperity-april22.pdf [Accessed 20 May 2024].

Thompson, K. (2024) 'City council cuts "cruel" and "short-sighted"', *BBC News* [online], 28 February, Available from: https://www.bbc.co.uk/news/articles/c06mkxn54pmo [Accessed 28 February 2024].

They Work for You (n.d.) 'Iain Duncan Smith', Available from: https://www.theyworkforyou.com/mp/10180/iain_duncan_smith/chingford_and_woodford_green [Accessed 28 February 2024]

Titmuss, R.M. (1955) 'The social division of welfare: some reflections on the search for equity' in R.M. Titmuss (ed) *Essays on 'The Welfare State'*, New Haven: Yale University Press, pp 34–55.

TNA (The National Archives) (1866) '"Allow me to support myself": a letter from a woman wanting to maintain her two children outside the workhouse', 21 November, Catalogue ref: MH12/9812, Available from: https://www.nationalarchives.gov.uk/education/resources/workhouse-voices/allow-me-to-support-myself/ [Accessed 30 May 2024].

TNA (1888) '"A sample of potatoes": a pauper letter to the local Board of Guardians for Polar Workhouse, listing a series of complaints', 23 November, Catalogue ref: MH12/7700. Available from: https://www.nationalarchives.gov.uk/education/resources/workhouse-voices/sample-of-potatoes/ [Accessed 30 May 2024].

Todd, S. (2014) *People: The Rise and Fall of the Working Class, 1910–2010*, London: Hachette.

Triantafillou, E. (2019) 'To make what is vertical horizontal: picturing social domination', *Journal of Visual Culture*, 18(3): 265–288.

Trouillot, M. (2015) *Silencing the Past: Power and the Production of History*, Boston: MA: Beacon House Books.

Trump, K.-S. (2018) 'Income inequality influences perception of legitimate income differences', *British Journal of Political Science*, 48: 929–952. https://doi.org/10.1016/j.cobeha.2019.12.001

Trussell Trust (2021) 'State of hunger: building the evidence on poverty, destitution, and food insecurity in the UK', Available from: https://www.trusselltrust.org/wp-content/uploads/sites/2/2021/06/State-of-Hunger_Exec-Summary.pdf [Accessed 27 May 2024].

Tuana, N. (2008) 'Coming to understand: orgasm and the epistemology of ignorance' in R. Proctor and L. Schiebinger (eds) *Agnotology: The Making and Unmaking of Ignorance*, Stanford: Stanford University Press, pp 108–148.

Tyler, I. (2008) 'Chav mum, chav scum', *Feminist Media Studies*, 8(1): 17–34.

Tyler, I. (2013) *Revolting Subjects*, London: Zed Books.

Tyler, I. (2015) 'Classificatory struggles: class, culture and inequality in neoliberal times', *Sociological Review*, 63: 493–511.

Tyler, I. (2018) 'Rethinking the sociology of stigma', *Sociological Review*, 66(4): 721–743.

Tyler, I. (2020) *Stigma: The Machinery of Inequality*, London: Zed Books.

UK Parliament (n.d.) 'Lobbying Parliament' [online], Available from: https://www.parliament.uk/get-involved/contact-an-mp-or-lord/lobbying-parliament/ [Accessed 1 May 2024].

Urry, J. (2014) *Offshoring*, Cambridge: Policy Press.

Valleley, P. (2020) *Philanthropy from Aristotle to Zuckerberg*, London: Bloomsbury Continuum.

Vaughan, M. and Kerr, S. (2024) 'Visual framing of wealth inequality in political communication', *International Communication Association Conference*, Communication and Global Human Rights, Gold Coast, Sydney.

Vaughan, M. and Kerr, S. (forthcoming) 'Visual framing of wealth inequality in political communication', *Journal of Visual Communication*.

Veyne, P. (1997) 'Foucault revolutionises history' in A.I. Davidson (ed) *Foucault and His Interlocutors*, Chicago: University of Chicago Press, pp 146–182.

Virdee, S. (2018) 'Racialised capitalism: an account of its contested origins and consolidation', *Sociological Review*, 67(10): 3–27.

Wacquant, L. (2008) 'Ordering insecurity: social polarization and the punitive upsurge', *Radical Philosophy Review*, 11: 9–27.

Wacquant, L. (2012a) 'Three steps to a historical anthropology of actually existing neoliberalism', *Social Anthropology*, 20(1): 66–79.

Wacquant, L. (2012b) 'A Janus-faced institution of ethnoracial closure: a sociological specification of the ghetto' in R. Hutchison and B. Haynes (eds) *The Ghetto: Contemporary Global Issues and Controversies*, Boulder, CO: Westview Press, pp 1–31.

Wacquant, L., Slater, T. and Pereira, V.B. (2014) 'Territorial stigmatization in action', *Environment and Planning A: Economy and Space*, 46(6): 1270–1280. https://doi.org/10.1068/a4606ge

Wade, S. (2019) *Foucault in California: A True Story – Wherein the Great French Philosopher Drops Acid in the Valley of Death*, Berkeley: Heyday.

Waitkus, N. and Minkus, L. (2021) 'Investigating the gender wealth gap across occupational classes', *Feminist Economics*, 27(4): 114–147.

Waitkus, N. and Wallaschek, S. (2022) 'Legitimate wealth? How wealthy business owners are portrayed in the press', *Social Justice Research*, 35: 404–435.

Walker, P. (2018) 'Amber Rudd condemns UN poverty report in combative return to frontline politics', *The Guardian* [online], 19 November, Available from: https://www.theguardian.com/politics/2018/nov/19/amber-rudd-un-poverty-report-return-frontline-politics [Accessed 2 September 2019].

Wall, T. and Osborne, H. (2018) '"Poor doors" are still creating wealth divide in new housing', *The Guardian* [online], Available from: https://www.theguardian.com/society/2018/nov/25/poor-doors-developers-segregate-rich-from-poor-london-housing-blocks [Accessed 27 May 2024].

Wallace, D. (n.d.) 'About Harrodsburg', Available from: https://www.dougie wallace.com/new-page [Accessed 27 May 2024].

Wallace, D. (2012) *Harrodsburg*, London: Dewi Lewis Publishing.

Wanderer, J. (2017) 'Varieties of testimonial injustice' in J. Kidd, J. Medina and G. Pohlhaus Jr. (eds) *The Routledge Handbook of Epistemic Justice*, Abingdon: Routledge, pp 27–40.

Warren, C. and Laslett, B. (1977) 'Privacy and secrecy: a conceptual comparison', *Journal of Social Issues*, 33(3): 43–52.

Webb, B. and Webb, S. (1927) *English Local Government: English Poor Law History. Part I. The Old Poor Law*, London: Longman, Green and Company.

Wicker, K. (2022) 'Credibility contests: the contributions of experiential knowledge to radicalisation expertise', *Journal of Critical Social Policy*, 42(3): 510–530.

WIL (World Inequality Lab) (2018a) 'World Inequality Report 2018', Available from: https://wir2018.wid.world/ [Accessed 9 November 2019].

WIL (2022) 'World Inequality Report 2022', Available from: https://wir2 022.wid.world/ [Accessed 23 July 2023].

Wilkinson, R.G. and Pickett, K. (2010), *The Spirit Level: Why More Equal Societies Almost Always Do Better*, London: Allen Lane.

Wintour, P. (2005) 'Blair does mind the wealth gap', *The Guardian* [online], 24 March, Available from: https://www.theguardian.com/politics/2005/mar/24/uk.election2005 [Accessed 7 November 2019].

Wintour, P. and Butler, P. (2013) 'Iain Duncan Smith defends use of statistics over benefits cap', *The Guardian* [online], 15 July, Available from: https://www.theguardian.com/politics/2013/jul/15/iain-duncan-smith-statistics-benefits-cap [Accessed 2 February 2018].

Wolff, J., Lamb, E. and Zur-Szspiro, E. (2015) 'A philosophical review of poverty', *JRF* [online], Available from: https://www.jrf.org.uk/report/philosophical-review-poverty [Accessed 3 September 2016].

Women's Budget Group (2019) 'Written evidence to the Economic Affairs Committee Inquiry into the Economics of Universal Credit, EUC0016', *UK Parliament* [online], Available from: https://committees.parliament.uk/work/31/the-economics-of-universal-credit/publications/written-evidence/ [Accessed 13 July 2023].

Women's Budget Group (2023) 'Why taxation is a feminist issue: a gendered analysis of wealth in Great Britain', Available from: https://wbg.org.uk/analysis/reports/why-taxation-of-wealth-is-a-feminist-issue-a-gendered-analysis-of-wealth-in-great-britain/ [Accessed 27 May 2024].

Women's Budget Group and Runnymede Trust with RECLAIM and Coventry Women's Voices (2017) 'Intersecting inequalities', Available from: https://wbg.org.uk/analysis/intersecting-inequalities/ [Accessed 27 May 2024].

WPC (Work and Pensions Committee) (2018a) 'Universal Credit Roll-out Oral Evidence Session' [online], 24 October, Available from: https://parliamentlive.tv/Event/Index/2793b17d-8815-40d6-ba05-583c29772a34, 10.37:48–11.17:58 [Accessed 22 November 2018].

WPC (2018b) 'Oral evidence: Universal Credit roll-out', HC 336, 24 October.

WPC (2018c) 'Oral evidence: Universal Credit roll-out, HC 336, Wednesday 14 November 2018', Witnesses: Sir Ian Diamond and Victoria Todd, Social Security Advisory Committee.

WPC (2019a) *Universal Credit and 'Survival Sex', Second Report of Session 2019–2020*. HC 83. Report, together with formal minutes relating to the report.

WPC (2019b) 'Universal Credit: survival sex. Oral evidence', HC 2025 Wednesday 22 May 2019.

WPC (2020) 'Appointment of the Chair of the Social Security Advisory Committee', Parliamentlive.tv [online], Available from: https://www.parliamentlive.tv/Event/Index/b3d60990-abc0-463d-9a3b-72e6efd3325a [Accessed 1 May 2024].

Wright, S. (2016) 'Conceptualising the active welfare subject: welfare reform in discourse, policy and lived experience', *Policy and Politics*, 44(2): 235–252.

Wright, S. and Dwyer, P. (2020) 'In-work Universal Credit: claimant experiences of conditionality mismatches and counterproductive benefit sanctions', *Journal of Social Policy*, 51(1): 20–38.

Wright, S. and Patrick, R. (2019) 'Welfare conditionality in lived experience: aggregating qualitative longitudinal research', *Social Policy and Sociology*, 18(4): 597–613.

Wylie, A. (2008) 'Mapping ignorance in archaeology: the advantages of historical hindsight' in R. Proctor and L. Schiebinger (eds) *Agnotology: The Making and Unmaking of Ignorance*, Stanford: Stanford University Press, pp 183–205.

Zucman, G. (2015) *The Hidden Wealth of Nations: The Scourge of Tax Havens*, Chicago: University of Chicago Press.

Archival sources

Nottinghamshire Archives Source A: The Southwell Union Punishment Book (1852–1936) (SO/PUS/3/3/1).

Nottinghamshire Archives Source B: The Minutes of the Board of Guardians: Minutes of the Southwell Union Workhouse Boards of Guardians (SO/PU/S/1/1/1-6).

Nottinghamshire Archives Source C: Southwell Union Workhouse Dietaries.

TNA (The National Archive) Source A: Letters from Paupers to the Poor Law Commission (TNA/MH12), Available from: https://intheirownwriteblog:wordpress.com/about/

Bibliography

TNA Source B: Letters between Sir Roger Bromley and the Poor Law Commissioners (from Sir Roger Bromley: MH12/9525/282; MH12/9524/79; MH12/9524/79/7; from the Commissioners: ML16 Folio 236).

TNA Source C: A drawing of the machine that produces nothing (MH12/9360/303/2)

TNA Source D: JB51 Series (Jobcentre Plus design and space planning material), Available from: https://webarchive.nationalarchives.gov.uk/ukgwa/20130125103105/http://www.dwp.gov.uk/jpeg/about%2Djpeg/ [Accessed 30 May 2024].

Index

References to figures and photographs appear in *italic* type; those in **bold** type refer to tables. References to endnotes show both the page number and the note number (231n3).

A

Ablyazov, Madiyar 27–28, 29–30, 37, 45, 92
Ablyazov, Mukhtar 27
Abramovich, Roman 28
abstraction 36, 50, **51**, 58–59, 104–105
accommodating jurisdictions 75, 96
1798 Act *see* Income Tax Bill (1798)
1834 Act *see* New Poor Law (1834)
adjustment hypothesis 18
administered/administrative self **101**, 104–105, 108, 161, 176
Advani, A. 8–9, 192n2
advising 168–169
Agamben 78, 81
agnotology 43, 114, 126, 127, 129, **130**, 145–146, 170
Alston, Philip 30, 41, 61, 86, 87, 134, 143, 162–163, 180
Anatomy Act (1832) 82
Andover Workhouse 76, 80, 95, 159, 165
antecedent strategies 137, 143
apathy *see* structural apathy
assets 13, 16, 40, 106–107
Atkinson, R. 93
Atkinson, Tony 25

B

Bacchi, C. 34, 50
Barnes, Louise 88
basic capabilities *see* capabilities
Beaverstock, J. 14
Beckert, J. 6–7, 27, 31, 33
behavioural change approaches 137–138, 139–141, 143, 185
Behavioural Insights Team (BIT) 137
being *see* states of being
Bell, Torsten 179
benefits fraud 42, 57, 91, 92, 168
benign inequality 14–15, 36–37, 147, 182
Bennett, Fran 36, 61, 73
Bentham, 41, 87, 136
Berger, John 153
Bessière, C. 36, 37, 63
Bhambra, Gurminder 10, 17, 32–33
Billingham, Liz 150, *151*
Billingham, Richard 150
BIT (Behavioural Insights Team) 137
bleed *see* capital; power

bodies
 about 23–24
 data doubles 104–105
 dependency and 98
 management of 26, 93
 paupers', donation of 82
 women's 23, 24, 88–89, 148, 153
bone crushing 76, 80, 84, 86
Booth, R. 61, 135, 146
Braidotti, R. 93, 154
Bramall, R. 129
Breakdown Britain report (CSJ) 129
Breakthrough Britain report (CSJ) 129
Bregman, Rutger 179, 180
Bridgwater scandal 76
Brien, Stephen 117, 119, 120–121, **122–123**, 193n2 (chap 6)
'Broken Britain' *see* narratives
Bromley, R.H. 64
Burchardt, T. 37, 189
Burt, R.S. 121
Bush, Lewis 148, 151, 152, 153
Byrne, L. 7

C

CA (Capabilities Approach) 24, 37–39, 50, 148, 175, 189
Cameron, David 36, 116, 137, 138
capabilities
 about 39
 fair epistemic participation as 156
 violations of 84, 87–89, 139
Capabilities Approach *see* CA (Capabilities Approach)
capability inequalities 30, 37–38
capacities of wealth 7, 27, 92, 96–97, 144, 159
capital
 bleed between forms of 6, 26, 39, 125, 176
 economic, importance of 38–39, 93–94
 inheritance and 107
 power of 171
 privatisation of 151, *152*
 real estate 93
Capital in the 21st Century (Piketty) 14, 34
capitalism 15, 180
Carter, P. 76, 82
Cash, P.J. 137
Caveat for Common Cursetors (Harman) 58

Index

censuses 51, 55, 62
Centaur State 11, 24, 40, 166
Centre for Social Justice *see* CSJ (Centre for Social Justice)
Chadwick, Edwin 54, 57, 62, 99–100, 115, 133
Changing Lives 72
charities 4, 59–60, 72–73, 124–125, 180–181, 191n4
Charity Organisation Society (COS) 73
Cheetham, M. 72
children
  hunger 80, 81, *82*
  legislation and 61–62
  wealth, passing of to 7, 106–107
  workhouses **80**
citizen juries 8
citizenship 7, 27, 28, 30, 139
claimants
  behavioural change approaches 137–138, 139–141
  experiences of 42, 72, 79, 81, 86–88, 90
  poor as, only the 75, 97, **107**, 107–108
classes
  ghetto class 151
  inequalities of, structural 11, 13, 15, 36
  middle class 100
  power relations 156
  privilege, hiding of 108
  sex and 24, 36, 191n1 (chap 1)
  sex difference within 63
  working class 55, 102
classification 24, 100, 104, 136, 147, 151
Cockayne, James 180
co-creation 167–168
collective wealth 1–2, 7–8, 33, 94, 183
colonialism 15, 16, 37, 61, 153, 181
compliance *see* cooperative compliance
composition of wealth *see* wealth
conditionality 42, 76, 77–78, 79, 86–87, **172**
conducting conduct
  government as 18, 25, 30, 34, 81–82
  spatial management as 135, 136, 143–144
  ways of 25–26
  wealthy as 167–168
Connor, S. 14, 20
consequence strategies 137, 143
The Constitution of Poverty (Dean) 45, 125
construct agnogenesis 128–129, 130, **130**
  see also agnotology
cooperative compliance 11, 61, 66–67, 163
Corden, William 89
corporate welfare 121, 124–126, 132, 177
COS (Charity Organisation Society) 73
COVID-19 pandemic 4, 106, 168
credibility 155, 157–161, 161–162, 164, 168, 171

critical history 20
  see also genealogy
CSJ (Centre for Social Justice)
  about 26, 115–116
  career map of interlockers **122–123**
  construct agnogenesis 129, 130, **130**
  corporate welfare agenda of 121, 124–125, 132–133
  DWP, blurred boundaries with 117, 120–121
  false public narrative of 113, 116–117, 127, 128, 133
  formation of 99–100, 116
  funding/donations 124, 125–126, 192n1 (chap 6)

D

data
  about 49–50, 52, 58, 192n3
  political numbers 50, 52, 54, 57, 68, 115–116
  population 54–55, 55–56
  on wealth 5, 12–13, 34, 40
  WIL, provided by 12, 14, 16, 192n3
  women, exclusion of from 36–37, 61–62
data doubles 104–105
Davis, A. 6
Dean, Mitchell 45, 125
'Decolonising critical theory?' (Bhambra) 10
deficit credibility *see* credibility
Deleuze 105
dependency
  government technique, as 57, 98
  poor, as belonging to the 52–53, 55, 56, 63
  wealthy and, the 63
Deripaska, Oleg 28
desert 14, 16
  see also meritocracy
Desmond, M. 18
destitution *see* poverty
DiPrete, T.A. 190
discipline 89
  see also punishment
disclosure
  inequality of 36, 99
  knowledge hierarchies and 68–69
  sanctioned response, as *12*, 57, 67
  wealtherty and 9, 11, 66, 67
  see also scrutiny
discursive misdirection 145–146
dispositions, government 11–12, *12*, 40, **51**
  see also ignorance; scrutiny
distraction research *see* construct agnogenesis; research
domicile *see* non-doms
donations *see* funding

Dotson, K. 164
doughnut model 16–17
Down and Out in Paris and London (Orwell) 82–83, 88
Duncan Smith, Iain 99–100, 105, 116, 118, 120, **122–123**, 144
duration 22–23, 97, 147, 151
DWP (Department for Work and Pensions)
  benefits fraud 42, 57, 91, 92
  CSJ, blurred boundaries with 117, 120–121
  experiences with 29
  National Audit Office on 42
  repayments due to 72–73
  Social Justice: Transforming Lives 102–103
  witness testimonies, response to 88
Dwyer, P.J. 76, 86, 140
dynamics *see* epistemic dynamics

E

economic capital *see* capital
economic inequality *see* wealth inequality
Eleven Privatised Public Assets (Bush) 151
Eltis, W. 119
empire 15, 33, 37, 40, 59, 153
enclosure 50, 55, 59, 60, 61, 68, 152, 183
Endres, A.M. 50
Engaging with High Net Worth Individuals on Tax Compliance (OECD) 134, 163
Englander, D. 78
engrossment/engrossing 59, 64, 68, 71, 152
environmental harm 2, 3
epistemic dynamics 171, **172**
epistemic injustice
  about 155, 157–158, 171
  credibility and 159–160, 161–162
  listening and 165, 188
  wealtherty and 26
epistemic reputability 162–164, 165–167
epistemic trust 162–167, 188
epistemological justice 9, 10, 187
An Essay on the Principle of Population (Malthus) 53, 54, 55
excess credibility *see* credibility
excessive wealth *see* extreme wealth
exclusion *see* spatial exclusion
expertise 9, 16, 17, 64–65, 99–100, 119, 169
  see also knowledge
expropriation 17, 50, 152
extraction 33, 61, 152
extreme poverty *see* pauper/pauperism; poverty
extreme wealth
  about 6–8, 15
  data on, lack of 34
  effects of 2
  frame of, legitimising 17–18

generations, transitions between 13
HNWU (High Net Worth Unit) 44, 165, 167–169
illth 8, 101, 146
inheritances 16, 106–107
see also social problem/problematisation; wealth

F

facets of wealtherty *see* wealtherty
Falciani list 91
families *see* troubled families
Farnsworth, Kevin 167
Federici, S. 10, 24, 33, 62
feudalism 3, 15
Field, Frank 118, 161
fields of visibility
  behavioural change strategies and 137, 138, 140, 141
  wealthy, for the 143–144, 146
Finance Act (1842) 62
fiscal relief 73–75, 133
Florman, Mark 116, 117, 118
food *see* punishment
formation *see* identity making; self-making
forms of wealth *see* wealth
Foucault, M. 1, 17, 18, 19, 23–24, 104
Fox Williams, B.N. 190
frames
  about 17
  agnogenesis and 113–114, 129
  media 11, 17–18
  poverty 4, 5, 16, 18, 56
  unmaking of 18–19, 178–179
  wealth-legitimising 17–18
framing 15, 17, 55, 190
fraud 89, 186
  see also benefits fraud; tax fraud
Fricker, M. 155, 156, 158, 176
funding 124, 125–126, 192n1 (chap 6)
  see also research

G

Galimberti, Gabriele 16, 147, 153
gatekeeping 9, 17, 39, 147
Geisenberger, Richard J. *150*
gender
  class differences and 63
  wealtherty and 61
  wealth gap 35–37
  see also bodies; men; sex; women
Gender Equality Impact Assessments 36
genealogy
  about 18–20, 134–135
  sources 20–23, 23–24
  writing of a 25
  see also bodies; visual culture; wealtherty
Genosko, G. 21, 22
gentlemen's clubs 143, 144

George, Lloyd 37
Gilens, A. 187
Gini coefficient 31
Glucksberg, L. 63, 107
Gokmenoglu, B. 142
golden visa *see* Tier 1 'golden' visa
Gollac, S. 36, 37, 63
Good Ancestor Movement 181
government/governing
　about 18–19
　bodies, management of 26
　dependency technique 57, 98
　dispositions of 11–12, *12*, 40, **51**
　means-enhancing techniques 74–75, 92, 96
　ways of governing **51**, **101**
　see also conducting conduct; ignorance; scrutiny; state, the; wealth tax
Grace, Jane 87, 95
'green meat' scandal 76, 80, 95, 165
guilt, presumption of 148

H

Hacking 51
Hall, S. 93
Harling, P. 192n1 (chap 3)
harm 2, 3
Harman, T. 58
Harrington, B. 40, 44, 92, 187
Harrodsburg (Wallace) 147, 150, 151
Hay, D. 59
health inequality 32, 150, 151
The Heavens Annual Report (Galimberti and Woods) 153
Hecht, K. 7, 144, 191n1 (chap 1)
Henriques, U. 70, 76, 83, 140
hermeneutical injustice 158, 170, 171
Hick, R. 37, 189
hierarchies 54, 60, 68–69, 157, 160, 161, 192n1 (chap 4)
　see also power
high-net-work individuals *see* HNWIs (high-net-worth individuals)
High Net Worth Unit *see* HNWU (High Net Worth Unit)
Hills, J. 31, 101, 102
Himmelweit, S. 35, 61
HMRC (Her Majesty's Revenue and Customs) *see* HNWU (High Net Worth Unit); RTI (Real Time Information) system; WEF (Wealthy Unit's Wealth External Forum)
HNWIs (high-net-worth individuals) 27, 90, 98, 132, 163–164, 166, 168–169
HNWU (High Net Worth Unit) 44, 165, 167–169
How the Other Half Lives (Riis) 146
hunger *see* punishment
hyperconcentration of wealth *see* wealth

I

ICIJ (International Consortium of Investigative Journalists) 14
identity making 97–98, 99, 108–109
identity prejudices 155, 158–159, 163, 188
ignorance
　about 11, 12, *12*, 128, 134
　agnotology 43, 114, 126, 127, 129, **130**
　history of disposition of 43–44, 51, **51**, 96
　means-enhancing techniques 74–75, 92, 96
　structural apathy 20, 90, 131
　trust and 162, 169
　ways of being, and **101**
　wealtherty and 9, 20, 23, 39–40
　white ignorance 10
　see also government/governing; privacy; wealthy, the
illth 8, 101, 146
images *see* visual culture
imperial state *see* state, the
Income Tax Bill (1798)
　about 24–25, 37, 62
　history of 74
　wealtherty and 43–44, **51**, 65–67
inequality
　class 11, 13, 15, 36
　health 32, 150, 151
　relational 157, 159, 171, **172**
　segregation and 26
　tolerance for 18, 88–89, 90–91, 185–186
　wealth as cause of 3–4
　see also benign inequality; capability inequalities; wealth inequality
influence *see* power
in-group *see* relational selves
inheritances 16, 106–107
injustice *see* epistemic injustice; hermeneutical injustice; testimonial injustice
innocence, presumption of 30
inquiries *see* WPC (Work and Pensions Committee)
Institute for Public Policy Research *see* IPPR (Institute for Public Policy Research)
intermediated self 97, 108–109, 166, 169, 176
International Consortium of Investigative Journalists (ICIJ) 14
IPPR (Institute for Public Policy Research) 8, 29, 126
Ireland 50–51

J

James, D. 22
Jaworski, A. 146

Jenkin, Bernard 118
Jobcentre Plus
  about 136
  deficit model used by 140
  sanctioning rates 86–87
  spatial management in 26, 135, 136–137, 138
  visibility, field of 137, 138, 140, 141
Jobcentre Plus Designers' Handbook (DWP) 137
Jobcentre Plus Environment Guide (JPEG) 137
joint taxation 36, 62
Jones, J. (Bishop) 113, 171
Joseph Rowntree Foundation *see* JRF (Joseph Rowntree Foundation)
Joshi, P. 100
Joyce, Hannah 95–96, 98
JPEG (Jobcentre Plus Environment Guide) 137
JRF (Joseph Rowntree Foundation) 31, 81, 113, 181
juries *see* citizen juries
justice *see* epistemological justice

K

Kerr, S. 146, 156, 172, 188, 191n1 (chap 2), 191n5
Kingdon, J.W. 56
knowing *see* knowledge
knowledge
  abstraction 36, 50, **51**, 58–59, 104–105
  gatekeeping of 9, 17, 39, 147, 180
  hierarchies of 54, 68–69, 157, 160
  mapping 50–51, 52, 89, 100
  political numbers 50, 52, 54, 57, 68, 115–116
  ways of coming to know **51**, 133
  see also expertise
Koram, K. 33, 37, 40
Kuhn, T. 17

L

Laslett, B. 39
legal codes 9, 13, 37, 39–40, 65, 70, 107, 182
letters *see* New Poor Law (1834); pauper/pauperism
liberalism 11
  see also neoliberalism
limitarianism 6, 125
Littler, J. 108
Lock, Catherine 83

M

Ma 20, *21*, 21–23, 97, 109, 134, 147, 154, 170
Magnus, D. 128–129, 130
Maguire, J. 145

making *see* identity making; self-making
Malthus 53–55, 56, 60, 65, 98, 116–117, 133
manifesto *see* wealtherty manifesto
mapping 50–51, 52, 89, 100
Marshall Institute *see* MI (Marshall Institute)
Martin, I.W. 182
Mayrit, D. 108, 147, 148
means-enhancing techniques 74–75, 92, 96
media *see* frames
Medina, J. 156, 158, 160, 162, 170–171, 176
men
  gentlemen's clubs 143, 144
  legislation, as target of 62–63
  wealth statistics of 32, 35–37
  workhouses, treatment of in 79, *79*, **80**, 80–81
  see also gender; women
meritocracy 4, 13, 15, 16, 177
MI (Marshall Institute) 129, 130, **130**
Mies, M. 33
milling 84, *85*, 86
Mills, C. 10
minimum wage legislation 55, 56
misdirection *see* discursive misdirection
mobility *see* punishment
Montgomerie, Tim 116, 117, 118, 120
movement *see* punishment
Ms J 27, 28–29, 30, 32, 37, 44–45, 72, 99, 159, 163
Mukherjee, A. 59
Murakami, H. 23, 154, 170
Murphy 184
Muspratt, Sarah 95, 99

N

NAO (National Audit Office) 42, 131, 190
narratives
  'Broken Britain' 114, 127
  persistence of 129
  poverty 1–2, 102–103, 146
  redemption 106
  self, of the 99, 101–102, 161–162, 169
  singular 113–114
  us and them 183, 186
  wealth 145–146
  see also CSJ (Centre for Social Justice)
The National Archives 80, 137
National Audit Office *see* NAO (National Audit Office)
National Health Service 33
National Insurance Act (1911) 61–62
nation state *see* state, the
negative space 21, 22, *22*
neoliberalism 11, 84, 105, 140–141, 153

Index

networks *see* policy networks
New Deal for Young People (2002) 76, 77
New Labour 76, 102, 116
New Poor Law (1834)
  about 24–25, 41, 42, 52, 71
  challenges with 73
  impacts of 88
  letters, paupers to PLC 41, 71–72, 76, 80, 83, 162
  political numbers 50, 52, 54, 57, 68, 115–116
  punishment and 76, 83, 84
  scrutiny and 56–57
  stigmatisation / vilification by 58–60, 98, 102
  wealtherty and 64, 67
  see also Poor Law Commission (1832)
NHS (National Health Service) 33
Nolan Principles 115, 117
nondisclosure *see* ignorance; privacy; secrecy
non-doms 37, 192n2 (chap 4), 192n4
Northumberland, Duke of 83
NPL *see* New Poor Law (1834)
Nussbaum, M. 38, 39, 50, 84, 86, 87, 139

O

Oakshott, Lord 117
oakum picking 84, 86
objectivity 54
OECD (Organisation for Economic Co-operation and Development) 134, 163, 164, 181
Office for National Statistics *see* ONS WAS (Office for National Statistics Wealth and Assets Survey)
Old Poor Law (1601–1834) 41, 52–53, 54, 55, 71
  see also New Poor Law (1834)
oligarchs *see* Russian oligarchs
ONS WAS (Office for National Statistics Wealth and Assets Survey) 12, 34, 37, 72, 90, 134, 192n3
OPL *see* Old Poor Law (1601–1834)
ordinary wealth *see* wealth
Orton, M. 14
Orwell, G. 82–83, 88
Osbourne, George 103–104, 190
outdoor relief *see* workhouses
out-group *see* relational selves
out relief *see* workhouses
Ozawa, Seiji 170

P

PAC (Public Accounts Committee) 42, 70, 91, 92, 168–169
pandemic *see* COVID-19 pandemic
panopticon principle 56, 87, 96, 137–138

parishes 41, 55–56, 57, 62, 64, 71, 83, 88
  see also workhouses
pathways *see* poverty; wealtherty; wealtherty manifesto
patriarchy 15, 33, 62, 94
Patriotic Millionaires 181
The Patronising Disposition of Unaccountable Power (Jones) 113
pauper/pauperism
  dependency and 52–53, 55, 56, 63
  letters to PLCs 41, 71–72, 76, 80, 83, 162
  self, and the 99, 104
  statistics 55
  see also poor, the; poverty; punishment; stigmatisation; vilification; workhouses
Pautz, H. 116
pensions *see* private pensions; WPC (Work and Pensions Committee)
The People: The Rise and Fall of the Working Class (Todd) 63
Piketty, T. 14, 34, 181, 188–189
Pistor, K. 13, 39, 40
Pitt, William 43, 67, 68, 89, 91, 138, 162
Pitt's Income Tax Bill *see* Income Tax Bill (1798)
PLC *see* Poor Law Commissioners
Pohlhaus, G. 170
policy networks 114–115, 125–126, 177
  see also CSJ (Centre for Social Justice); Jobcentre Plus
political numbers *see* data; knowledge
political privileges *see* privileges
poor, the
  about 8, 61, 191n1 (chap 1)
  dependency and 52–53, 55, 56, 63
  dispositions towards, government 11–12, *12*, 40, **51**
  knowing, historical ways of 52–53
  photographing 146
  segregation 26
  subpopulations of 88, 100
  tribute relationships 59–60, 68, 74
  wealthy, and the **107**, 107–108, 171, **172**
  see also narratives; pauper/pauperism; poverty; scrutiny; stigmatisation; vilification
Poor Law *see* New Poor Law (1834); Old Poor Law (1601–1834)
Poor Law Amendment Act (1834) 41, 52, 62, 64
  see also New Poor Law (1834)
Poor Law Commission (1832) 54, 56, 57, 62, 64, 76, 99, 133
  see also New Poor Law (1834)
Poor Law Commissioners 41, 71, 83, 162
Poor Law Report (1834) 78
population data 54–55, 55–56
population principle 55, 56

poverty
  about 14
  crime, as a 82–83
  essential to wealth, as 53–54, 180
  extreme (destitution) 4
  pathways to 116, 129, 185
  research funding focus on 2, 13–14
  solving, resources spent on 4
  statistics 3, 4, 30–32, 55, 104
  stop talking about 1, 179–181
  wealth and 1
  see also frames; narratives; poor, the; social problem/problematisation
power
  bleed between forms of 6, 26, 39, 125, 176
  bodies and 24
  capacity, as 27
  of material resources 11, 53
  relationships 15, 16, 98, 142, 156, 157, 164, 171, 191n1 (chap 2)
  unequal access to political 7, 9, 16, 39, 147, 180, 187–188
  see also hierarchies
Poynter, J.R. 60, 63
prejudices *see* identity prejudices; tracker prejudices
presumption of innocence/guilt 30, 148
privacy
  about 40, 138
  income tax and 43–44, 66–67
  inequality and 36, 57, 138, 139
  wealtherty and 23, 28, 39–40
  see also ignorance; means-enhancing techniques
private pensions 3, 31, 32, 35
private wealth *see* extreme wealth
privileges
  health 33
  political 97, 116, 121, 124, 162, 170, 176, 187–188
  tracker 157, 158, 159–160
  wealthed 9, 36, 39, 65, 73, 106–107, 144, 155–157, 185–186
problematic wealth *see* extreme wealth
problem/problematisation *see* social problem/problematisation
Proctor, R.N. 126, 127, 131, 133
Public Accounts Committee *see* PAC (Public Accounts Committee)
public wealth 35, *152*
punishment
  hunger as 78, 79, *79*, 80–81
  impact of 78
  movement, restriction of 81, 82–84, 92–93
  stigmatisation and 98
  work as 84, *85*, 86–88
  workhouse system 76, 104, 192n1 (chap 4)
  see also sanctions

R

race 3, 32, 35, 61
Rancière, J. 135
Raworth, K. 16–17
Ray's a Laugh (Billingham) 150, *151*
Rea, Salvatora *145*
redeemed self 105–106, 108, 141
'red herring' research *see* research
Reeves, Rachel 5, 182
reframing *see* framing
relational inequality 157, 159, 171, **172**
relational selves 101–104, 106
relief *see* fiscal relief; tax relief; workhouses
rematerialisation 21
repertoires of the self 97, 98, 104, 105, 108, 135, 155, 159
1817 Report from the Select Committee on the Poor Laws (Dean) 55
reputability *see* epistemic reputability
research
  anti-poverty 4, 5
  distraction (red herring) research 129, 130, **130**, 131, 133
  funding focus of, changing the 2, 13–14, 186–187
  statistics, funding 186
reversal 20, 104, 177, 179–180, 185–186
rich people *see* wealthy, the
Rickman 69
Ridge, T. 14
Riis, Jacob 146
Robeyns, I. 6, 11, 26, 125, 155, 180, 181, 183
Rowles, Gaynor 87, 163
Rowlingson, K. 14, 20, 189
Rowntree 61
RTI (Real Time Information) system 138
Ruane, S. 121
Ruskin, J. 8, 21, 22, 29, 84, 86, 108, 146
Russian oligarchs 27–28
'Russia Report' 27

S

sanctions
  impact of 72, 78
  misalignment of 79
  rates of 86–87
  Universal Credit 76, 77–78, 79, 81, 96, 105, 136–137, 140, 142
  wealtherty and 102, 185
  wealthy, minimal for the 90–91, 93–94, 165, 166, 167
  workhouse system 41–42, 76
Sandbu, Martin 193n2 (chap 9)
Savage, Mike 22, 23, 33, 37, 93, 97, 129, 153, 178
Sayer, A. 30
Schiebinger, L. 126, 127

Index

scientificity 54, 55, 56, 115, 133, 157
Scott, J. 14
scrutiny
  about 11, 12, *12*, 40–41, 104–105, 137–138
  history of disposition of 51, **51**, 96
  trust and 162, 166–167, 169
  ways of being, and **101**
  wealtherty and 9, 20, 23, 39–40
  see also disclosure; government/governing; poor, the
secrecy 9, 11, *12*, 39–40, 134
  see also ignorance; privacy
segregation 26
Select Vestries Act 160
self *see* administered/administrative self; intermediated self; redeemed self; relational selves; repertoires of the self
self-making 26, 97, 99, 108, 110
Sen, S. 81
Serafini, P. 145
Serwotka, Mark 117
sex
  -based inequalities 3, 35, 63, 191n1 (chap 1)
  data gaps and 36–37
  wealtherty and 24
  see also gender; survival sex
sexual assault 88–89
Shiva, Vandana 92–93
'Shooting the Rich' 146
SIC (Standard Industrial Classification) codes 126, **127**, **128**
Sieghart, M.A. 118
silencing 164–165
Simpson, L. 156
Sinfield, A. 74, 92, 103–104, 130, 184
Skeggs, B. 99, 108–109
Sklair, J. 107
Slack, P. 51
Slater, T. 127
smuggling 89–90
Smyth, D. 146
social harm 2, 3
Social Justice: Transforming Lives (DWP) 102–103
social problem/problematisation
  about 5
  extreme wealth as 1, 3–4, 5, 6, 9, 12, 175, 179–180, 181–183
  images and 20–21
  poverty as 14, 52, 53, 55, 56, 116, 131, 133
  relational selves 101–104
  research funding, focus of on 186–187
  state, of the 33
  wealth inequality, relevance of 33–34
  women, excluded from 61–62

Society for Trust and Estate Practitioners *see* STEP (Society for Trust and Estate Practitioners)
sociological scholarship 10–11, 14–17, 156, 191n1 (chap 2)
'in the soup' metaphor 56
Southwell Workhouse
  Punishment Book 76, 78, 84, 104, 192n1 (chap 4)
  treatment of workers 64, 71, 81, 84, *85*, 99
spacetime 22–23
  see also Ma
spatial exclusion 144, *145*
spatial management 26, 83–84, 135, 136–137, 138, 140, 143–144
  see also punishment
spillover (bleed) *see* capital; power
Standard Industrial Classification codes *see* SIC (Standard Industrial Classification) codes
state, the
  poor, and the 52–55, 55–58, 58–60, 60–64
  problematisation of 33
  wealthy, and the 65–67
  see also government/governing; wealth tax
states of being 14, **51**, 58, 96, 101, **101**, 104–109, 176–177
statistics
  about 49–50, 52
  see also data; men; pauper/pauperism; poverty; research; wealth; wealth inequality; women; workhouses
Steedman, C. 146
STEP (Society for Trust and Estate Practitioners) 44, 90, 121
stigma 15, 98, 139
stigmacraft 100, 132, 159, 176
stigmatisation
  epistemic injustice and 158–159
  legislation and 101, 102
  poor, progressive towards 58–60, 75
  territorial 135
  women, of 96
stigmatisers 98
stone breaking 84
Strathern 108
Stroud, Philippa 116, 117, 118, 120–121, **122–123**
structural apathy 20, 90, 131
stuff *see* wealth
subjectivation 26, 97, 110, 144
subpopulations 88, 100
super rich, the *see* extreme wealth
surplus wealth *see* extreme wealth
Surrey 130, 131, 184
surveillance 137–138, 162
  see also total surveillance

239

survival sex 28, 29, 42–43, 72, 88–89, 164
    see also WPC (Work and Pensions Committee)

T

Tamboukou, M. 25
Tawney, R.H. 3
tax, wealth *see* wealth tax
taxation
    about 182
    history of 65–66, 73–74
    joint 36, 62
    non-doms 37, 192n2 (chap 4), 192n4
    see also Income Tax Bill (1798)
tax avoidance 90–91, 92, 143, 189
tax evasion 43, 90–91, 92, 162, 189
tax fraud 27, 90, 91, 92, 166, 186
tax gap 91, 166, 179
tax relief 34, 74, 130–131, 133, 183–184, 185, 190
Taxwatch UK 91
ten basic capabilities *see* capabilities
testimonial injustice 158, 164
them *see* relational selves
there is no alternative *see* TINA (there is no alternative)
things of wealth *see* wealth
think tanks 42, 100, 115, 116, 121, 126, **127**, **128**
    see also CSJ (Centre for Social Justice)
thresholds *see* wealth thresholds
Thurland, C. 146
Tier 1 'golden' visa 27, 93
TINA (there is no alternative) 129, **130**
TIRC (Tobacco Industry Research Council) 129, 130, **130**, 131
TNA (The National Archives) 80, 137
Tobacco Industry Research Council *see* TIRC (Tobacco Industry Research Council)
Todd, S. 63
Tōhaku, Hasegawa *21*, 22, 71, 102
total surveillance 30, 70, 87, 94, 96, 134, 143
tracker prejudices 157, 158–159
tracker privileges *see* privileges
tribute relationships 59–60, 68, 74
troubled families 106–107, 110, 185–186
Trouillot, M. 20
Trump, K.-S. 18
Trussell Trust 72–73, 81
trust 162
    see also epistemic trust
Tuana, N. 131, 164
Tyler, I. 98, 132, 150
Tynemouth Workhouse 83

U

ubiquitous conditionality 42
    see also conditionality

UK Research and Innovation *see* UKRI (UK Research and Innovation)
UKRI (UK Research and Innovation) 4, 186, 191n2 (chap 1)
undeserving, the 14, 20, 21, 101, 102, 130
unequal access 7, 9, 16, 39, 147
unions 41, 64, 71, 78, **80**, 83, 84, 192n1 (chap 3)
    see also workhouses
Universal Credit
    about 26, 42
    application process 72
    challenges with 42–43, 72–73
    Claimant Commitment form 77, *77*
    epistemic reputability and 162–164
    scrutiny and **51**, 56–57, 104–105, 166
    waiting period 28–29
    wealth threshold of 28, 42, 156, 160
    work as punishment 86–88
    workhouse system, comparison to 41–42
    see also sanctions; survival sex; WPC (Work and Pensions Committee)
us *see* relational selves

V

Vasanti's story 38–39
Vaughan, M. 146
vilification 58–59, 60, 76, 83, 90, 102, 106
visibility, fields of *see* fields of visibility
visual culture 20, 21, 26
    see also Ma

W

Wacquant, Loic 11
Wallace, Dougie 151
Warren, C. 39
Waterman, Vikki 105
Ways of Seeing (Berger) 153
wealth
    about 6–9, 156, 191n1 (chap 2)
    capacities of 7, 27, 92, 96–97, 144, 159
    collective wealth 1–2, 7–8, 33, 94, 183
    distribution of 30–31
    frames of, legitimising 17–18
    hiding of 40
    hyperconcentration of 3, 9, 15–16, 147, 179
    images of 146, 147, 148
    legal codes and 9, 13, 37, 39–40, 65, 70, 107, 182
    ordinary wealth 7–8, 29, 144, 181, 183, 193n2 (chap 9)
    poverty as essential to 53–54, 180
    public 35, *152*
    research funding focus on 2, 13–14
    statistics 3, 30–32
    things of (stuff) 3, 13, 31, 182
    see also extreme wealth; privileges; wealthy, the

Index

Wealth and Assets Survey *see* ONS WAS (Office for National Statistics Wealth and Assets Survey)
wealtherty
  about 1, 19, 61, 95–96, 143, 147
  facets of 9, 11, 180
  focus to, shifting of 10–11
  history of 2, 11–12, *12*, 175–176
  movement and 92–93
  pathways to 2, 185–186
  present situation 26, 176
  see also genealogy; Ma
wealtherty manifesto 1–2, 13–14, 179–190
wealth gap 35–36, 37
wealth inequality
  effects of 36
  statistics 12–13, 30–33, 35–37
  welfare and 7
wealth tax
  benefits of 5, 15
  early attempts at 69
  resistance to 34–35, 179, 181–182
wealth thresholds 28, 42, 156, 160–161
wealthy, the
  about 8, 61, 191n1 (chap 1)
  data on, lack of 34, 40
  dispositions towards, government 11–12, *12*, 40, **51**
  fiscal relief for 73–75, 133
  images of 147
  intermediated self 97, 108–109, 166, 169, 176
  poor, and the **107**, 107–108, 171, **172**
  tribute relationships 59–60, 68, 74
  voices of 2, 187–188
  see also ignorance; privacy; wealth
Wealthy Unit's Wealth External Forum *see* WEF (Wealthy Unit's Wealth External Forum)
WEF (Wealthy Unit's Wealth External Forum)
  about 43–44, 163–164
  epistemic reputability and 165–167
  intermediated self and 169–170
  wealtherty and **51**
  wealth threshold of 156, 161
  wealthy, role of in 167–169
Welfare Reform Act (2012) 42, 101, 102, 103, 118
welfare state/universe
  dependency and 57
  describing of 1–2, 183–185
  structural apathy and 131–132
  wealth inequality and 7
  see also corporate welfare

Whitbread, Samuel 55, 56
white ignorance 10
WIL (World Inequality Lab)
  data provided by 12, 14, 16, 192n3
  reports 30–31, 34, *152*, 178
  on wealth distribution 30–31, 35, 36
Wilby, Peter 185
Williams, Hewill 88–89
Wolff, J. 24
women
  bodies of 24, 88–89, 148, 153
  exclusion of from data 61–62
  health inequalities 150
  joint taxation 36, 62
  legislation, as subject of 62–63
  out relief and 73
  wealth statistics of 32, 35–37
  workhouses, treatment of in 79, **80**, 80–81, 95–96
  see also gender; men; survival sex; WPC (Work and Pensions Committee)
Women's Budget Group 35
Wood, Nick 118
Woods, Paolo 16, 147, 153
Work and Pensions Committee *see* WPC (Work and Pensions Committee)
workhouses
  about 41, 104
  hunger as punishment 76, 78–81, *79*, **80**
  movement restriction as punishment 81, 82–84
  out relief 41, 64, 71–72, 73, 78, 186, 192n1 (chap 4)
  physical abuse in 87–88
  scrutiny and **51**
  statistics 55
  unproductive labour of 84, *85*, 86
  workhouse test 41–42, 71
  see also Andover Workhouse; Southwell Workhouse
World Inequality Lab *see* WIL (World Inequality Lab)
WPC (Work and Pensions Committee)
  Inquiry into Universal Credit Roll Out and Childcare 26, 43, 78, 87–88, 105, 155–156
  Inquiry into Universal Credit Roll Out and Survival Sex 28–29, 42–43, 72, 78, 88, 96, 155–156
Wright, S. 14, 42, 76, 86, 140

Y

You Haven't Seen Their Faces (Mayrit) 108, *148*

www.ingramcontent.com/pod-product-compliance
Lightning Source LLC
Chambersburg PA
CBHW070042040426
42333CB00041B/1952